The
EMOTIONALLY
ABUSED
and
NEGLECTED CHILD

WILEY SERIES
in
CHILD CARE AND PROTECTION

Edited by

Kevin D. Browne
School of Psychology
The University of Birmingham, UK

Margaret A. Lynch
Newcomen Centre
Guy's Hospital, London, UK

Dorota Iwaniec — The Emotionally Abused and Neglected Child: Identification, Assessment, and Intervention

Further Titles in Preparation

Ann Buchanan — Cycles of Child Maltreatment: Facts, Fallacies and Interventions

Jacqui Saradjian — Women who Sexually Abuse Children: From Research to Practice

Potential authors are invited to submit further proposals to Wendy Hudlass, Publishing Editor, John Wiley & Sons Ltd, Baffins Lane, Chichester, West Sussex PO19 1UD, UK. Alternatively, proposals can be discussed with either of the series editors and should include a short statement of the target readership, scope and features of the book proposal and short notes on two or three of the nearest books in the field.

Proposals on the following topics would be especially welcome:

Child Neglect; Children on the Street; Prostitution, Homelessness and Poverty; Child Development and Delinquency; Childhood Disadvantages and Consequences; Children's Rights; Child Health and Community Interventions; Child Labour; Children and Post Traumatic Stress Disorder; Treating Violent Families; Child Sexual Abuse; Consequences and Development of Sexuality; Children with Disabilities; Cross-cultural Perspectives on Child Care and Protection

The
EMOTIONALLY ABUSED
and
NEGLECTED CHILD

Identification, Assessment
and
Intervention

Dorota Iwaniec

JOHN WILEY & SONS

Chichester · New York · Brisbane · Toronto · Singapore

Copyright © 1995 by John Wiley & Sons Ltd,
Baffins Lane, Chichester,
West Sussex PO19 1UD, England

National   01243 779777
International (+44) 1243 77977

Reprinted January 1996

Other Wiley Editorial Offices

John Wiley & Sons, Inc., 605 Third Avenue,
New York, NY 10158-0012, USA

Jacaranda Wiley Ltd, 33 Park Road, Milton,
Queensland 4064, Australia

John Wiley & Sons (Canada) Ltd, 22 Worcester Road,
Rexdale, Ontario M9W 1L1, Canada

John Wiley & Sons (SEA) Pte Ltd, 37 Jalan Pemimpin #05-04,
Block B, Union Industrial Building, Singapore 2057

Library of Congress Cataloging-in-Publication Data

Iwaniec, Dorota.
  The emotionally abused and neglected child : identification,
assessment, and intervention / Dorota Iwaniec.
    p.   cm. — (Wiley series in child care and protection)
  Includes bibliographical references and index.
  ISBN 0-471-95579-5 (paper)
    1. Psychologically abused children—Mental health.   2. Child
psychotherapy.   I. Title.   II. Series.
RJ507/A29I93   1995
618.92'858223—dc20   95-9879
                                                         CIP

British Library Cataloguing in Publication Data

A catalogue record for this book is available from the British Library

ISBN 0-471-95579-5 (paper)

Typeset in 10/12pt Palatino by Dobbie Typesetting Ltd
Printed and bound in Great Britain by Biddles Ltd, Guildford and King's Lynn
This book is printed on acid-free paper responsibly manufactured from sustainable forestation,
for which at least two trees are planted for each one used for paper production.

*Non ignara mali miseris succurrere disco**

[Not a stranger to misfortune, I
learn to succour those who are
unhappy]

---

*Publius Vergilius Maro (70–19 BC): *Æneid*, Book 1, Line 630.

for

my husband, James,
and my sons,
Zygmunt and Andrzej,
whom I love

CONTENTS

Section I   Identification of Emotional Abuse and Neglect

Introduction—Defining Features—Emotional Neglect—Defining Emotional Abuse—Problematic Parenting—Causal Factors—Parental Characteristics—Conclusion

Introduction—Historical Introduction—Definition of Failure-to-Thrive—Socio- and Psycho-Genesis—Maternal Pathology and Growth-Failure—Mother–Child Interactions—Including Feeding—Conclusion

Introduction—Case Study—Description of Psychosocial Dwarfism—Causal Mechanisms—Manifestations of Disturbed Behaviour—Development—Social and Emotional Behaviour—Maternal Characteristics—Parent–Child Relationship and Interaction—Conclusion

Introduction—Infancy—Attachment Behaviour—Early Childhood—Middle Childhood—Conclusion

Section II   Assessment of Emotional Abuse and Neglect

Section III   Intervention and Treatment

ABOUT THE AUTHOR

Dorota Iwaniec—Department of Social Work, The Queen's University of Belfast, 7 Lennoxvale, Belfast BT9 5BY, Northern Ireland

Dorota Iwaniec is Professor and Head of the Social Work Department at The Queen's University of Belfast and also Director of the Centre for Child-Care Research attached to the University.

Prior to her academic appointment she worked for the Leicester Social Services Department as a generic and paediatric social worker, Student Unit Supervisor, and Team Leader in the Practice Teaching Resource Centre. She has been an active researcher in the child-care field and is best known for her work and publications on failure-to-thrive and behaviour management of children.

SERIES PREFACE

The **Wiley Series in Child Care and Protection**, is a new series of books primarily written for all professionals in research and practice concerned with the care, welfare and protection of children and their families.

The aim of the series is to publish books on child care and protection covering both the psychological and physical welfare of the child and to include legal and social policy aspects. The series was prompted by the need to view child protection within the wider concepts of child care and social welfare. After three decades of remarkable growth in child protection work, which has led to widespread public awareness and professional understanding of child maltreatment, it has become increasingly recognised that child protection is enhanced by the improvements in the welfare of families and the promotion of positive parenting and child care. Indeed, child care, family welfare and effective child protection are inter-linked and cannot be separated.

For example, the inability of maltreating parents to adaptively interact with their children is seen by many professionals as being representative of a general lack of interpersonal skills. Abusive and neglective parents often share a common pattern of social isolation, adverse living conditions, poor work history and few friendships with others outside the home. This isolation means that parents unable to cope are usually unwilling, or unable, to seek help by themselves from outside agencies who could provide assistance or emotional support. If such parents do interact with others they are most likely to choose those with similar problems to themselves, thereby gaining no experience of alternative parenting styles or positive coping strategies and continuing to be ineffective in promoting the optimal development of their children. Hence, child protection is multi-faceted involving many different aspects of child care and the social welfare of families.

Books in the series will be from a wide range of disciplines and each book will be encouraged to link research and practice to inform, in an easily accessible way, professionals, policy makers and the public in general. In this way it is hoped to further the knowledge and understanding of health, psychosocial and cultural factors that influence the development of the child, early interactions and the formation of relationships in and outside the family.

The book series has started most appropriately with a volume on *The Emotionally Abused and Neglected Child: Identification, Assessment and Intervention* by Professor Dorota Iwaniec, Head of the Department of Social Work at The Queen's University, Belfast. The author presents a theoretical consideration of the various presentations of emotional abuse and neglect from the perspectives of child growth, development and well being. More importantly, the author goes on to describe her own practical approaches for the assessment and treatment of families in need of help. These practical approaches are based on the author's experience of linking research knowledge to clinical work.

Kevin Browne
Margaret Lynch

INTRODUCTION

Here I disclaim all my paternal care,
Propinquity and property of blood,
And as a stranger to my heart and me
Hold thee from this for ever*

This book is the result of experience and knowledge gained over the last two decades in working with, and carrying out research on, emotionally abused and neglected children. In that time awareness of the serious consequences of the effects of emotional abuse on children has greatly increased, and with it the unpalatable facts of sexual abuse have started to come to the surface in ways unthought-of 20 years ago.

It is hoped that this publication will help all those working in the child-protection and -abuse field (including general practitioners, health visitors, nursery nurses, paediatricians, psychiatrists, psychologists, and social workers) to be able to identify, assess, and treat families where such abuse has occurred.

The book is organised in three sections. Section I describes manifestations of and the identification of various forms of emotional abuse and neglect (such as psychosocial dwarfism, non-organic failure-to-thrive, and psychological pathology with normal physical growth), parent–child bonding, behavioural and temperamental characteristics of children, a discussion dealing with parent–child interaction, and the effects of abuse and neglect on child-development. It is largely based upon an extensive review of the available literature on the subject as well as on data collected by the author over many years, and provides an historical perspective to show how concepts of (and understanding of) emotional maltreatment have evolved over the years. Therefore Section I aims to provide a synopsis of differing types of emotional abuse and neglect and to enable readers to become aware of how these often elusive problems can affect a child's growth, development, and well-being.

---

*William Shakespeare (1564–1616): *King Lear* (1605–6), Act I, Scene 1, Line 108.

Section II is essentially about diagnosis: it provides a suggested framework for assessment, some descriptions of issues to be addressed, a few useful checklists, and a sample of an assessment report. The aim of this section is to help practitioners to collect and collate evidence that would support (or otherwise) an initial identification of or hypothesis concerning emotional abuse and neglect.

Section III is largely based upon the author's personal professional and research experience. Having carried out longitudinal studies of non-organic failure-to-thrive and psychosocial dwarfism, the author has been able to assess the effectiveness of various methodologies based on different theories in dealing with children within the age group 0–12-years-old. In cases involving teenagers the issues require quite separate consideration, and are beyond the scope of this book. The aim of this section is to provide those dealing with emotional abuse and neglect with various methods and techniques for intervention and treatment that have proved, in the author's experience, to be relatively effective. Sections II and III are therefore more of a practical manual for assessment, intervention, and treatment, mostly based on the author's practice and research experience. These sections contain much less critical appraisal of the information presented, and so are based to a much lesser degree on the literature review than is the case with Section I: they attempt to demonstrate how research can inform practice, and for this reason the literary style differs from that of Section I.

There is still much controversy among researchers and practitioners regarding the phenomenon of emotional abuse of children, and there are many issues that need to be researched, evaluated, defined, and resolved. However, progress has been made, and emotional abuse has been recognised as a serious problem of child maltreatment by legislators, policy makers, and practitioners on both sides of the Atlantic. As knowledge and understanding increase, provision of resources to alleviate the problem (which until very recently was overlooked and neglected) must be allocated by decision-makers and resource-providers, but there is also a heavy responsibility to be shouldered by those in immediate proximity to families and children in need of support, help, and understanding. Professionals are becoming more aware of the significant harm done to children by rejection, emotional indifference, neglect, and psychological cruelty. It is hoped that this book will add a little to the understanding and awareness of all involved.

ACKNOWLEDGEMENTS

I record here my gratitude and appreciation to my husband, James Stevens Curl, for his unfailing support and assistance during the writing of this book.

Sterling help with the preparation of references and literature was given by Leszek Bełdowski, of the University of Leicester library, and by Séan O'Brien, of the Northern Ireland Health and Social Services Library: they have my thanks for their unfailing courtesy. I am grateful to my many former students, my friends, and my former colleagues in Leicester for their assistance, co-operation, and support without which much of the material herein would not have existed. I am especially indebted to Joan Barratt, Christa Freer, Pauline Hardiker, Martin Herbert, Sue Jacob, Liz King, Sandy McNeish, the late Rhoda Oppenheimer, Alice Sluckin, Carole Sutton, and all those who participated directly or indirectly in research and practice by my side. I also thank my colleagues at The Queen's University of Belfast for their support, especially Maura Dunn, Eileen Maguire, and Pam McIntyre, who prepared the typescript for this book.

My sons, Zygmunt and Andrzej, gave me their interest and encouragement during the preparation and writing of the book and have my gratitude.

I

IDENTIFICATION OF EMOTIONAL ABUSE AND NEGLECT

1

EMOTIONAL ABUSE AND NEGLECT

Go practise if you please
With men and women: leave a child alone
*For Christ's particular love's sake!**

INTRODUCTION

In the last few years the topic of emotional and psychological abuse has received considerable attention on both sides of the Atlantic. It would also be fair to say that no other form of child abuse has created so many difficulties for practitioners and so much confusion for researchers and theorists alike. The literature (although not all that extensive) is full of contradictions. Some difficulties lie in the absence of a unified and precise definition of what exactly constitutes emotional abuse, and in how it is possible to provide measurable evidence that would be convincing and scientifically sound. The continuing debate is still far from resolving the thorny question of definition in a general and operational sense: lack of clarity and consistency when using appropriate labels further confuses this issue.

Some writers have tried to make a distinction between psychological and emotional abuse (O'Hagan, 1993), while others have preferred to use the term *psychological maltreatment* to describe both types of abuse (Garbarino, Guttmann, & Seeley, 1986; and McGee & Wolfe, 1991). Some have separated emotional abuse from neglect (Whiting, 1976), while others, like Garbarino, Guttmann, and Seeley (1986), have felt that neglectful and abusive acts are interrelated and better considered within the broader concept of psychological maltreatment of children.

---

*Robert Browning (1812–89): *The Ring and the Book* (London: Smith, Elder, & Co., 1868–69), Book 3, Line 88.

The problem of defining psychological maltreatment is complicated further by uncertainty regarding whether the emphasis should be on abnormal parental behaviour or on the detrimental child outcomes (Kavanagh, 1982; Yates, 1982; and Rosenberg, 1987). Some researchers have focused on parental behaviour considered to be damaging (Baily & Baily, 1986); others, however, have proposed that parental behaviour is an inadequate predictor of emotional damage, and have focused on child outcomes (Aber & Zigler, 1981). These difficulties of definition are not surprising. Emotional abuse is an elusive phenomenon. It cannot be seen as a distinct mark (the result of violent physical abuse); it will not generate public interest or even outrage (as has been the case with sexual abuse); and it will not attract censure (as in documented investigations of physical neglect). There are also cultural differences in child-rearing practices that need to be taken into consideration, as well as the psychological make-up of a child and the unique individuality which might contribute to the way parents relate to, interact with, and perceive the child. In addition a better understanding is needed of how some children (although emotionally maltreated) survive relatively unscathed and often the stronger for their experiences. What are those protective factors which are helpful for the child's mental health and development?

Practitioners often find themselves in a difficult position when they identify an emotionally harmful interaction as painful and damaging to the child, but are unsure of how to measure this process in a convincing way. The absence of empirical findings and longitudinal studies into the effects of emotional abuse have not made the task easier for those who protect and those who legislate.

In spite of various difficulties there is a growing consensus among professionals that emotional maltreatment (which includes active abuse and passive neglect) might be more damaging in its impact (if severe and persistent) than other forms of maltreatment (Brassard, Germain, & Hart, 1987; Iwaniec, 1983; Garbarino, Guttmann, & Seeley, 1986; Skuse, 1988; and McGee & Wolfe, 1991, to mention but a few). It is also generally recognised that emotional abuse is at the core of physical and sexual abuse, and might have a greater effect in the long term than physical or sexual abuse.

DEFINING FEATURES

Emotional abuse and neglect refer to hostile or indifferent parental behaviour which damages a child's self-esteem, degrades a sense of achievement, diminishes a sense of belonging, and stands in the way of healthy, vigorous, and happy development. Emotional abuse is described as overtly rejecting behaviour of carers on the one hand, or as passive neglect on the other (Iwaniec, *Child-Care in Practice*, 1994).

Parents and carers who persistently criticise, shame, rebuke, threaten, ridicule, humiliate, put down, induce fear and anxiety, who are never satisfied with the child's behaviour and performance (and do so deliberately to hurt the child), are emotionally abusive and cruel. Equally, those who knowingly distance themselves from the child—by ignoring signals of distress, pleas for help, attention, comfort, reassurance, encouragement, and acceptance—are emotionally abusive and neglectful. Their behaviour towards the child can be described as overtly abusive, actively painful, and developmentally and cognitively damaging. Literature on child abuse describes such parental behaviour as an act of commission or omission (Whiting, 1976). A negatively-charged interaction between the child and the carers can induce pain, anxiety, confusion, and cognitive distortion, and therefore can be described as emotionally harmful.

EMOTIONAL NEGLECT

Such neglect refers to the passive ignoring of a child's emotional needs; to lack of attention and of stimulation; and to parental unavailability to care, to supervise, to guide, to teach, and to protect. Whiting (1976) states that 'emotional neglect occurs when meaningful adults are unable to provide necessary nurturance, stimulation, encouragement, and protection to the child at various stages of development, which inhibits his optimal functioning.' Whiting concludes that emotional neglect should be distinguished from emotional abuse. Emotional neglect more often than not originates from parental unawareness and ignorance, depressive moods, chaotic life-styles, poverty, lack of support, and lack of appropriate child-rearing models (often based on parental childhood experiences), unwittingly impairing child-development and well-being.

Parents who seldom interact with their children, who do not speak, play, or encourage new activities and opportunities to learn will inhibit a child's vigorous and happy development. Neglectful parenting may sometimes be attributed to lack of knowledge and poor judgement. Some parents might know nothing of normal developmental milestones and be unaware of children's needs for stimulation: they might not recognise the importance of emotional nurturing as a need of the child. Parental judgement might be at fault: the child might not be perceived to be ill, or abnormally thin and failing to thrive, or crying because of hunger, wetness, coldness, unhappiness, boredom, etc. Such emptiness and loneliness will create an emotional vacuum and have an adverse effect on a child's growth, contentment, and well-being.

The distinction between neglect and abuse (as defined by deliberate and non-deliberate parental action) is very important for treatment and intervention purposes. Those differences will be discussed later.

DEFINING EMOTIONAL ABUSE

Emotional abuse as a separate form of abuse (and highly damaging if on a continuum and severe) was only recognised in England and Wales by legislators in the 1980s, although in the United States it has been part of the child-abuse statutes in several states since 1977.

The British Department of Health and Social Security (DHSS) Circular *Local Authority Social Services Letter* (LASSL) (80) 20 (1980) states that children under the age of 17 years, whose behaviour and emotional development have been severely affected, and where medical and social assessments have found evidence of either persistent or severe neglect or rejection, are in need of protection. Crippling overprotection is also included in this definition. This Circular was further revised, following several public inquiries into cases where the death and serious maltreatment of children (including emotional abuse) had created public concern. *Working Together*, a Department of Health guidance (DOH 1991; 1.8), states that emotional abuse is the actual or *likely* adverse effect on the emotional development and behaviour of a child caused by persistent or severe emotional ill-treatment or rejection. The first definition (or rather statement) advocated action after the harm was done; the second paper recommended protection before adverse consequences are recognised.

The fact that very few children tend to be registered in the emotional-abuse category is due to the lack of precise and operational definitions. The globality and vagueness of criteria laid down do not inspire confidence among child-care and child-protection workers. The fact that children are so seldom identified as victims of emotional abuse should not in itself be taken to suggest that there is no significant problem (Sluckin, 1987). The very private and highly nebulous qualities of emotional abuse make it a difficult concept to define in a useful operational sense. The major deterrent in bringing cases of emotional abuse to the courts of law is the difficulty in assessing and proving that child-development, behaviour, and well-being have been adversely affected to the point of 'significant harm' by the care-givers' emotional maltreatment of the child. It has been recognised that there is a significant number of children on the Child-Protection Register for whom the main concern is a fear of emotional abuse, but, for the purposes of registration, the 'discovery' of a simple unexplained bruise may be much more convincing than making a case for emotional abuse on its own. As a consequence of professional inability to come forward with convincing answers to many puzzling questions, many children will suffer and many carers will unwittingly or wittingly damage their children's lives. But we were there before. As Kempe and Helfer (1980) said, 'countries and societies progress through distinct stages in consideration of child abuse. First the problem is denied, after which attention is focused on dramatic and distressing manifestations of physical ill-treatment before finally subtle forms of sexual and emotional abuse are recognised.'

Attempts have been made to define emotional/psychological abuse in a general and operational way. Garbarino, Guttmann, and Seeley (1986) define psychological maltreatment as 'a concerted attack by an adult on a child's development of self and social competence.' They put forward five damaging parental behaviours: rejecting, isolating, terrorising, ignoring, and corrupting. Hart, Germaine, and Brassard (1987) describe other acts of parental behaviour as emotionally and psychologically damaging: missocialising, exploiting, and denying emotional responsiveness. Behavioural definitions of these acts are, however, very difficult to construct—firstly, because most children experience some of these acts from time to time, and, secondly, because the impact of a single or seldom-occurring emotional act of abuse or of neglect will not have the severe and harmful effects of physical abuse. It is recognised that the harm of emotional maltreatment results from the cumulative effects of repeated acts of psychological maltreatment. These subtypes, although difficult to measure, provide a useful framework for practitioners' assessment purposes. Barnett, Manly, and Cicchetti (1991) describe their working definition as parental acts that thwart children's basic emotional needs (like 'psychological safety', the need for a family environment free of extensive hostility and violence, the need for a stable and available care-giver, and the need for self-esteem (i.e., the need for positive regard and the absence of excessively negative or unrealistic evaluation)). Skuse (1989), on the other hand, defines emotional abuse as habitual verbal harassment of a child by disparagement, criticism, threat, ridicule, and the inversion of love, and the substitution of rejection and withdrawal by verbal and non-verbal means. More recently O'Hagan (1993) defines emotional abuse as 'the sustained, repetitive, inappropriate emotional response to the child's expression of emotion and its accompanying expressive behaviour'.

As we can see, there are differences and similarities in definitions of psychological maltreatment. There are also problems in differentiating emotional abuse and psychological maltreatment. Yet all of them include descriptions of the same or similar parental behaviour. So far there is no agreement as to which label to use in order to describe this type of maltreatment. It could be that part of the difficulty lies in the attempts to fit such complex and varied behaviours into a medical model of the physical abuse of children. It might be necessary to re-examine this issue.

PROBLEMATIC PARENTING

The definition of problematic (disturbed) parental behaviour is particularly difficult in relation to emotional abuse and neglect, because it is largely a relative judgement, and a socially subjective one. It is usually formulated in terms of its consequences for the child—his or her well-being. The emotionally abusive parent is defined in terms of his or her neglect of all or some of the basic needs of children. The needs of children are of two kinds: the first kind is survival functions (such as the need for food, shelter, and physical care), and the second kind is psychological functions (including the child's requirements of love, security, attention, new experiences, acceptance, education, praise, recognition, and belongingness) (Iwaniec, Herbert, & Sluckin, 1988).

In order to grow healthily, happily, and vigorously, children must also acquire vast amounts of information about the world around them in a way which will help them to formulate realistic and culturally appropriate perceptions. The transmission of information from adults to children, and from one generation to another (as a socialisation process) is of great importance. Yet it is known that not all emotionally-abused children are affected permanently by the maltreating behaviour of their parents. As Lourie and Stefano (1978) point out, 'children differ, often dramatically, in their responses to parental treatment; and the existence of "stress-resistant" children suggests that harsh and even hostile environments can produce pro-social, competent children.' Some adults who were exposed to emotional abuse as children testified to their success in life as a determined desire to prove to themselves, and in particular to those who undermined them, that they can achieve and can be respected (Osborne, 1985). In an average family it is not unusual for the parents to find at least one of their children difficult to rear and to enjoy. Some children (due to their challenging behaviour and lack of responsiveness to the socialisation processes) create tensions and bring out negative (and at times hostile) feelings towards themselves (Herbert & Iwaniec, 1977a).

Goldstein, Freud, and Solnit (1979) state: 'as a prototype of a true human relationship, the psychological child–parent relationship is not wholly positive, but has its mixture of negative elements. Both partners bring to it the combination of loving and hostile feelings that characterise the emotional life of all human beings, whether mature or immature'. Winnicott (1958) stressed that parenting should not be expected to be perfect, but rather 'good-enough'—parenting should be judged in terms of being adequate for a particular child at a particular time. It would seem that he is advocating reasonable flexibility in child-rearing practices, taking into account differing needs of children along the developmental spectra. Winnicott puts forward five basic needs of children as a measure of 'good-enough' parenting:

(1) physical care and protection;
(2) affection and approval;
(3) stimulation and teaching;
(4) disciplines and controls which are consistent and appropriate to the child's age and development; and
(5) opportunity and encouragement to acquire gradual autonomy (that is for the child to take gradual control over his or her life).

Emotional abuse is defined here in terms of the neglect of all or some of these basic needs. But 'good-enough' parenting is as elusive as emotional abuse itself. What is good enough for one child in the family might not be good enough for the other. Parents are not always aware of the individual differences between their children and of the necessity to apply different child-rearing methods to meet their individual needs. Frustration can lead to anger when parents fail to be effective with their child-rearing practices in the case of one particular child (although similar practices were successful in the rearing of the previous child). Parental perceptions about a child can be seriously distorted, and can lead not only to a fraught interaction, but to hostility and rejection.

Difficulties of providing nurturance in parenting can arise from a lack of knowledge of the physical and psychological needs of children, as well as from a lack of guidance and support-systems that might help the parents achieve a more positive and less stressful experience of child-rearing. A child's difficult behaviour (which might trigger off frustration, anger, helplessness, and resentment), as well as poverty and other environmental stresses, can stand in the way and can considerably curtail adequate parenting. The quality of parenting is often a mirror of parental experiences as children. Those parents tend to provide quality of care to their children similar to that they themselves received as children. There are, of course, more serious factors which not only contribute to the passive physical and emotional neglect, but also to the safety of the child: family violence, alcoholism, drug- and solvent-abuse, and much else all play their damaging parts.

Dubanoski, Evans, and Higuchi (1978) identified five factors which in their view require attention: lack of knowledge about normal developmental processes; punitive disciplinary methods; impulsive aggression; high stress-levels; and negative attitudes towards the child. Negative attitudes are important to consider when dealing with emotional abuse.

Parenting is influenced by historical and contemporary factors. Childhood experiences of parents influence their personalities and psychological resources, which in turn determine their child-rearing attitudes, behaviour, and capacity to form supportive relationships with others. The behaviour of the parents influences the personality and behaviour of the child which in turn influences the way in which the parents respond to the child. The social environment and the availability of resources will determine not only the quality of care, but also the quality of the relationship between parents and child.

CAUSAL FACTORS

Causal factors of neglect and abuse are complex and varied, and will differ from one family to another and from one society to another. Causality of abuse and neglect is also seen and interpreted differently, according to specific theoretical orientation and perspectives. Recent studies emphasise the necessity to adopt a broad ecological perspective when examining child abuse and neglect (Belsky & Vondra, 1989; Dubowitz, 1993). Dubowitz promotes a view that the omission of meeting children's basic needs is at the core of child maltreatment, rather than deliberate and intentional parental behaviour. Child abuse and neglect should be seen as a social construct in the context of the society where it occurs and in the context of the life of the child. It operates on a continuum, ranging from a very good provision of nurturance from society, local community, and the family to very poor provision of care, attention, resources, or even neglect. If the family and societal systems are deficient in promoting sensitive and adequate nurturing, then the child is exposed to harm on a short- and long-term basis. This would imply that responsibility for the child's welfare and well-being lies not only with parents and families, but also with the communities in which they live and with society at large. Ecological perspectives are in tune with the philosophy of the current British child-care legislations. The *Children Act* (1989) strongly addresses children's needs and collaborative partnerships with parents in difficulties.

PARENTAL CHARACTERISTICS

Numerous studies have linked child abuse and neglect with certain parental and family characteristics and behaviour. Among them are: poor marital relationships, social isolation, impulsive personalities, ill-health, poverty, chaotic life-style, psychiatric problems, poor social and problem-solving skills, difficulties in social communication, neglectful and abusive backgrounds of parents, and lack of knowledge of children's age-appropriate needs, as well as alcohol-, drug-, and substance-abuse (Crittenden & Ainsworth, 1989; Zuravin, 1988; Polansky, 1992; Egeland, 1987; Johnston, 1990; and Oates, 1982).

Lack of harmony and warmth between parents and children characterises families where emotional abuse and neglect are apparent. They tend to function more as individuals than as a family unit, and seldom address and attend to the emotional needs of individual family members (Crittenden, 1988; Browne & Saqi, 1988). Many neglectful and rejective parents are unwilling to take the responsibility for the child, and whenever possible they defer both authority and responsibility to someone else. Observing these parental attributes reminds one of the cuckoo-parenting style: these birds are incapable of raising their own offspring, so they lay their eggs in other birds' nests, themselves escaping the responsibility of nurture and protection. One can say that their chicks are raised by 'foster-parents'.

Poor, and often violent, relationships between parents is a common feature. Frequent quarrels, physical spouse-abuse, cruelty, and an atmosphere of permanent anxiety and fear characterise the home environment, which in turn distresses the children (O'Hagan, 1993). Parental interaction is either violent or silent: communication between parents and children is of poor quality, and limits itself to commands and rebukes. Being exposed to frequent parental violence and abuse, the children pick up the same model of behaviour and show aggressive reactions when dealing with siblings and peers (Patterson, 1982). A prolonged exposure to violence is evident even after marital breakdown, for a decision to part does not mean that friction or violence will cease. Shepard (1992) examined the problems associated with paternal visits to children (following separation) and found serious physical and emotional abuse went on. Many of the children witnessed it, and were not adequately cared for during this period. Children and mothers were often threatened and intimidated and were frightened to leave the house.

Alcohol-abuse is closely linked with violence and serious financial problems for the family. The Savage (1993) study showed that 75% of mothers in the sample seriously misused alcohol, leaving the children to fend for themselves. These children were not provided sufficiently with food, clothing, and other necessities. The mothers' interaction with their children was almost non-existent. They were found understimulated, dirty, unkempt, and emotionally neglected. Supervision of these children was weak and they did not get personal attention and guidance. Mothers of emotionally-abused and neglected children are socially isolated and lonely, and have little support from their families even if they live in the same geographical location. They find their neighbours unhelpful, and tend to distance themselves to avoid criticisms and unpleasant remarks regarding their treatment of the children and the life-style they lead. Unsupportive and cold relationships with the extended family appear to be a continuation of early childhood. These mothers reported lack of affection and attention to them when they were children, and as time went on they kept little contact with their parents and siblings. Many of these parents left home just after leaving school to escape insults and the heavy atmosphere at home (Iwaniec, 1983; Polansky, 1992). These mothers suffer from very low self-esteem, and perceive themselves as incompetent, worthless, and unable to deal with life tasks. There is an air of helplessness, lack of purpose, motivation, and drive. Frequent bouts of depression and general apathy contribute to an inability to engage physically and emotionally with their children.

Single parents dominate among neglectful parents. Additionally, they are young, immature, and unprepared for the responsibilities with which they are faced. Lack of support, social isolation, and inadequate financial provision complicate their children's plight even further. Polansky (1992) and Oliver and Buchanan (1979) found that neglectful mothers do not put their children's interests first, and that their sense of commitment to children is almost non-existent. They show a tremendous urge to be loved and wanted, so they care for their cohabitees more than they care for their children.

Parent–child interaction in these families is marked by unresponsiveness to the children's needs and lack of attention to supervision. The parents tend to be withdrawn and detached, living from day to day with few goals and aims in their lives (Crittenden, 1988).

However, some emotionally abusive and neglectful parents have quite affluent backgrounds, good education, and good current material standards, yet they severely emotionally neglect and abuse their young. Their physical care and the attention they give to educational needs might be good, so therefore emotional maltreatment is not obvious. In these families there is an air of coldness and tension (almost a clinical atmosphere) which prohibits freedom of play, activity, and expression, as well as the development of individuality. Interaction between parents and children lacks warmth and approval. There are commands instead of requests, criticisms instead of correction and guidance, and pressures to achieve at school without considering the child's ability and expectations to behave and perform correctly (disregarding the fact that a child is a 'learner' and is bound to make mistakes). These children tend to be anxious, apprehensive, unsure of themselves, and unable to interact with family members and outsiders in a confident manner. These parents' social status tends to serve as a buffer, yet their behaviour should be subject to accountability and exposure in the same way as that of the less affluent.

Emotional abuse is often hidden in suburban areas, where there is a clear 'no entry' for the protective services. Problems might come to professional attention through hospital investigation for what appears to be a medical reason for parental concern, such as poor weight-gain, chronic constipation and soiling, recurring infections, bed-wetting, sleeping problems, and other behavioural problems. Assessment of these families often reveals negative attitudes and lack of affection towards the children. Sexual abuse frequently enters the picture as well.

Parents of these children tend to come from families where affection is not shown or is even discouraged. They do not particularly like children, but feel they should have them. They tend to feel resentful because of the disruption of their career, social life, interests, and hobbies. They feel isolated and unfulfilled. If the child happens to be difficult to rear, then the risk of being emotionally abused and neglected is much greater.

When examining emotionally-abusive parental behaviours (across all sections of society) the following may be identified, in that a child is:

(1)   not included in the family circle;
(2)   ignored, or not taken notice of;
(3)   not allowed to play an active part in family activities and decision-making;

(4)   seldom spoken to in an easy way;
(5)   persistently deprived of privileges and treats;
(6)   frequently punished for minor misbehaviour;
(7)   persistently ridiculed and criticised;
(8)   never praised;
(9)   not acknowledged or reinforced in any good behaviour or positive action;
(10) frequently shamed and put down in front of peers, siblings, and other people;
(11) not noticed or disregarded in any attempts to please care-givers;
(12) ignored and discouraged when attempting to attract attention or affection;
(13) not allowed to mix with peers;
(14) socially isolated;
(15) told that it is disliked or unloved (or both);
(16) blamed when things go wrong in the family;
(17) not in receipt of proper supervision and guidance;
(18) corrupted by the care-givers by means of drugs, prostitution, stealing, etc.;
(19) encouraged in inappropriate prejudices such as religious, racial, cultural, or other hatreds (attitudinal corruption);
(20) not allowed to get physically close to care-givers; and
(21) not permitted to show emotion.

CONCLUSION

It might be appropriate to conclude this chapter with a definition of emotional abuse as seen by the author and used throughout this book:

hostile or indifferent parental behaviour which damages a child's self-esteem, degrades a sense of achievement, diminishes a sense of belonging, prevents healthy and vigorous development, and takes away a child's well-being.

Emotional abuse is evident in all forms of child maltreatment, like physical and sexual abuse and neglect, but it occurs in its own right, and has detrimental effects on child-growth and development.

2

NON-ORGANIC FAILURE-TO-THRIVE: PHYSICAL AND EMOTIONAL NEGLECT

Use three Physicians still, First Doctor Quiet,
*Next Doctor Merryman, and Doctor Diet**

INTRODUCTION

The family is much venerated as the bedrock of a stable society. Stability within the family is rooted in the mutual attachment of parents and their children. The nature and conditions of attachment (as it is called when discussing infant love) and of bonding (as it is referred to when speaking of adult love) have received a great deal of attention in the last four decades. It was John Bowlby (in his report *Maternal Care and Mental Health*) who brought to the attention of a wider public the pioneering 1940s work of Spitz, Wolf, Goldfarb, Burlingham, and Anna Freud. In 1953 the popular version of that report was published as a Pelican original entitled *Child Care and the Growth of Love*, and the concept of 'maternal deprivation' (for better or for worse—it was, in fact, both) was launched, and with it came concepts such as anaclitic depression and hospitalism. The book cited many examples of deprived and rejected children who failed to thrive, and referred to dramatic effects following separation of an infant from its mother (without adequate substitute care), and the beneficial results of restoring it to her. These effects were exemplified by a boy who, at four months of age (the last two in an institution), weighed less than at birth and whose condition was critical:

Sir John Harington (1561–1612): *The Englishman's Doctor. Or, The Schools of Salerne* (London: John Helme & John Busby, Jun., 1607).

... his appearance was that of a pale, wrinkled old man. His breathing was so weak and superficial that it seemed as though he might stop breathing at any moment. When seen twenty-four hours after he had been at home he was cooing and smiling. Though no change had been made in his diet he started to gain promptly and by the end of the first year his weight was well within the normal range. He appeared to be in every way a normal child. (Bowlby, 1953)

It is now a cliché that a baby needs a close, confident, and caring physical and emotional contact with the parent (be it mother, mother-surrogate, or father) in order to grow well, be healthy, and vigorously develop. The absence of such continuing nurturance and physical intimacy can bring about anxiety in the child, fretting, and disruption of biological functions.

Montagu (1978), in his chapter on 'Tender Loving Care', described high mortality rates in institutions, and related an interesting anecdote. In a German hospital before World War Two, a visiting American doctor, while being shown over the wards in one of the hospitals, noticed an ancient hag-like woman who was carrying a very undernourished infant. He enquired of the director the identity of the old woman and was told that she was 'Old Anna': when the staff at the hospital had done everything medically they could do for a baby, and it still failed to thrive, they handed it over to Old Anna, who succeeded in remedying matters every time. She rocked, held, carried the baby, and talked to it, giving caring and tender attention plus the close physical contact which every baby needs. It is small wonder that babies passed to her which had been near death's door, despite all the physical treatment then available to doctors, did better with her unsophisticated but nurturant tender care. Theoretical forging of an aetiological link between deprivation of maternal care and affection and non-organic failure-to-thrive is of relatively recent origin in the literature, but the importance of a warm physical contact with, and stimulation of, the baby had been acknowledged long before the theory of maternal deprivation was known.

HISTORICAL INTRODUCTION

Infanticide has been accepted by many cultures, and has been practised in cases where children were deformed, were handicapped, or who failed to thrive. It was sometimes employed for economic reasons (as in Polynesia, where the relative smallness of the islands ensured the practice was imposed on all families without distinction), but was common in advanced ancient civilisations such as those of Egypt, Greece, and Rome to ensure destruction of weak, deformed, or unsightly children.

Among early recorded investigations of infant deprivation and failure-to-thrive were those carried out by Frederick II of Hohenstaufen (b. 1194), Holy Roman Emperor, King of Sicily and Jerusalem, and *Stupor Mundi et Immutator Mirabilis* [wonder of the world and marvellous transformer]. His Sicilian court (1215–1250) was a centre of intellectual activity and attracted the translator, mathematician, and astrologer, Michael Scot (*c.* 1175–*c.* 1232), known as the Scottish Merlin, as well as Leonardo of Pisa (whose work secured the introduction of Arabic notation into Europe and provided the bases for works on algebra and arithmetic in the following centuries). Under Frederick's aegis studies were made of the effects of deprivation in children, albeit in the realms of language acquisition: in order to establish what was the original language of mankind, newborn infants were reared by foster-mothers who suckled and bathed the children, but who were not permitted to speak to them so that they would not learn a language from the foster-mothers. No spontaneous acquisition of Hebrew, Greek, Latin, Arabic, or the languages of the parents to whom the children were born occurred, for in those silent domains the subjects of the experiment all died, although it is not recorded if infection, lack of hygiene, disease, or silence caused the mortalities.

There were sundry studies on the fringes of Renaissance enquiry, but in the seventeenth century Sir John Harington (1561–1612) published his *The Englishman's Doctor. Or, The Schools of Salerne* (1607) in which he proposed that digestion was encouraged by pleasurable emotions but inhibited by disagreeable ones. He recommended the three 'Doctors' (figuratively speaking), referred to under the chapter heading, to increase an awareness that the quality and amount of food we eat (proper diet) will be beneficial if we consume it in an atmosphere which is relaxed, calm, and happy. As he put it, 'Use three Physicians still, First Doctor Quiet, Next Doctor Merryman, and Doctor Diet'.

Those who work closely with children who fail to thrive (and their families) will find Harington's three 'Doctors' very poignant. The quotation indicates that those 'three wise men' are often absent from the lives of what are often sad, undernourished children, and of parents who may be anxious, frustrated, demoralised (unsuccessfully trying to feed the child), or neglectful and indifferent to the child's nutritional needs.

DEFINITION OF FAILURE-TO-THRIVE

So what is failure-to-thrive? It is defined as failure to grow and develop healthily, vigorously, and happily. This concept (which is mainly used in paediatrics) has become a popular term to describe infants and young children whose weight, height, and general development are significantly below expected norms. It is conceived as a variable syndrome of severe growth-retardation, delayed skeletal maturation, and problematic psychomotor development, all of which are associated frequently with specific disturbances in mother–child interaction and relationship, insecure attachment, and family dysfunctions.

The phrase 'failure-to-thrive' was used as early as 1899 in the first edition of Holt's *Diseases of Infancy and Childhood* to describe babies who failed to grow after weaning from the breast. The term has changed its meaning substantially over the intervening near-century. Until the first part of the twentieth century the condition of a wasted body was called marasmus, and was always associated with some known or unknown physical disease: it was only a few decades ago (when growth began to be studied scientifically) that failure-to-thrive was recognised as not necessarily a disease, but as a symptom which might have many possible causes. Aetiological factors are complex and varied: they include inadequate nutrition, malabsorption, chronic infection, major structural congenital abnormalities, and metabolic and endocrine defects. However, there are some infants and young children who fail to thrive in whom none of the above factors is obvious, yet who do not grow, and whose well-being gives cause for concern.

A dichotomy between causes due to organic illness and psychosocial causes due to failure of the child's environment to provide appropriate nurturing is most significant, and further complexities occur when organic and non-organic factors combine: indeed, this combination is commoner than was thought, and may be apparent when treatment of what had seemed to be a clear-cut organic condition does not produce the expected improvement. Emotional overlays and/or secondary gains are known to complicate so-called psychosomatic disorders, not least those which have a clear organic basis. The question of the nature of the problem in a non-organic group is one that has led to considerable controversy, particularly over whether the cause is nutritional (that is inadequate calorific intake due to neglect), or whether psychosocial factors operate directly, possibly via a mechanism such as disturbances of growth-hormone triggered off by severe emotional maltreatment. Recent studies shed more light and made the division between failure-to-thrive, non-organic failure-to-thrive, and psychosocial dwarfism more clear, but there are still many difficult questions to answer in order to understand this problem in a comprehensive way.

Growth retardation
- child falls below the 3rd percentile in weight and often in height

Physical description
- wasted body, thin arms and legs
- large stomach
- red, cold, and wet hands and feet
- thin, wispy, dull, and falling hair
- dark circles around the eyes

Physical symptoms
- refusal to take feeds
- vomiting
- diarrhoea
- frequent colds and infections

Developmental retardation
- motor development
- language development
- social development
- intellectual development
- emotional development
- cognitive development

Psychological description and behaviour
- sadness, withdrawal, and detachment
- expressionless face
- general lethargy
- tearful
- frequent whining
- minimal or no smiling
- diminished vocalisation
- staring blankly at people or objects
- lack of cuddliness
- unresponsiveness
- insecure attachment
- passivity

Aetiology—physical and emotional neglect, insufficient calorific intake, inadequate attention to and understanding of children's emotional and physical needs.

Figure 1: Profile of Non-Organic Failure-to-Thrive.
Source: Iwaniec, Herbert, and McNeish (1985)

A profile of Non-Organic Failure-to-Thrive (Physical and Emotional Neglect) is given in Figure 1. The profile of non-organic failure-to-thrive might differ from case to case. It will depend on the severity of the child's neglect, the child's age, and the length of the presenting problem.

The term 'failure-to-thrive' is not generally used (although often applicable) when speaking of a large population of children world-wide who suffer from malnutrition as a result of the shortage of suitable food for themselves or their breast-feeding mothers. Where there is total food deficiency resulting in the stunting of growth we still refer to it as marasmus. Suskind (1977) estimated that there were some 100 million children under five-years-of-age who were severely or moderately malnourished throughout the world—most of them in the underdeveloped countries where famine, war, and widespread poverty make food scarce. Yet we now know that in Britain and other Western countries many children suffer from malnutrition, which is often undetected because of inadequate medical and social-work attention in the early years, or failure to diagnose it in children who suffer from illnesses or present other problems.

Failure-to-thrive as a diagnosis becomes significant in a society which can presume food will be available to all its children and where knowledge of paediatric disease and normal growth and development has become sufficiently precise to define the reasons for growth-failure. The distinction between failure-to-thrive and non-organic failure-to-thrive became more apparent after the introduction of maternal deprivation theories over four decades ago: these shed new light on the failure of some children to grow and develop according to norms, despite the absence of 'disease' (Bowlby, 1965). The hypothesis of a psychological aetiology for this condition has its roots in the extensive literature on the effects of institutionalisation, hospitalisation, and emotional deprivation in infants. Lack of stability and continuity in child-care was thought to be a major factor, affecting a child's mental health and physical growth.

Non-organic failure-to-thrive over the last four decades has acquired various labels such as environmental retardation (Coleman & Provence, 1957), masked deprivation (Prugh & Harlow, 1962), environmental failure-to-thrive (Barbero & Shaheen, 1967), deprivation dwarfism (Silver & Finkelstein, 1967), psychological dwarfism (Wolff & Money, 1973), and linear growth-retardation (Skuse, 1988). These reports share a general attempt to provide psychological and social explanations for the causation of the postulated non-organic failure-to-thrive syndrome. However, there is no general agreement on the precise nature of the psychological problems which result in or contribute to the clinical manifestation of the disorder.

SOCIO- AND PSYCHO-GENESIS

The hypothesis of a psychological aetiology for the non-organic failure-to-thrive syndrome has its roots in the extensive literature on the effects of institutionalisation, hospitalism, and maternal deprivation in infants. Some of the best documentations of the failure-to-thrive syndrome were those of Spitz (1945, 1946) and Widdowson (1951). The disorder of 'hospitalism' (as Spitz termed it) occurred in institutionalised children in the first-year of life, and the major manifestations involved emotional disturbance, failure to gain weight, and developmental retardation, resulting in poor developmental test performance. A significant aetiological factor was gleaned from Spitz's study of infants cared for by their mothers whom Spitz compared with another group raised in virtual isolation from other infants and from adults. Spitz demonstrated that physical illnesses, including infections, are contracted more frequently by infants deprived of environmental stimulation and maternal care than those not so deprived. The failure-to-thrive syndrome according to Spitz is a direct result of inadequate nurturance. Indeed he actually documented long-term intellectual deficits in the survivors of the non-nurtured group. Of the deprived group 37% had succumbed (died) by two years of age, compared with none in the adequately mothered control group. Spitz stated that a condition of anaclitic depression in the deprived infants manifested itself in decreased interest in environmental stimulation (including that from other humans), retardation of cognitive development, failure-to-thrive physically, insomnia, and sadness. It should be noted that Spitz's work has been severely criticised for methodological and other weaknesses. Nevertheless, it proved (with Bowlby's work) to be significant in a heuristic sense and has generated research and radical reform in child-care. Non-organic failure-to-thrive children living at home do not, as a rule, present such an alarming picture, although there are cases of acute neglect. Widdowson (1951) replicated Spitz's findings that adequate calorific provision in an unfavourable psychological environment due to the harsh and unsympathetic handling may seriously curtail growth rate. Widdowson studied children in two German orphanages just after the war. A dietary supplement which was expected to produce faster weight gain was introduced as an experiment in one orphanage, using the other as a control. Contrary to expectations, it was the control group which gained weight and grew a little faster during the experimental period of six months. Afterwards it was discovered that the matrons of the two orphanages had swapped over at about the time of the start of the dietary supplement. The matron of the first orphanage had been kindly, but the matron of the control group (who had transferred to the experimental group) was harsh, and harassed the children at meal-times. This could well have caused some achlorhydria and also anorexia (though it is unlikely that the children would have been allowed to leave anything on their plates!). One may speculate, therefore, that the dietary supplement was wasted. This study suggests that nutritional intake is not always a guide to growth performance and that non-nutritional 'emotional' factors may have an overriding role. Indeed one of the indices of basic trust and security in an infant (in Erikson's sense) is stable feeding behaviour, and eating, to be beneficial nutritionally (and enjoyable), requires conditions that denote a relatively benign and calm state of psychosomatic harmony.

Over the last 40 years or so (apart from studies on institutionalised children) researchers and practitioners have been grappling with this baffling problem. The questions of 'what' and 'how' along the spectrum of many different investigations brought similar descriptions and observations, but differed more on 'why' questions. The earlier studies (as in cases of physical abuse) looked for answers in parental deviant behaviour (such as personality disorders, family violence, alcoholism, drug-abuse, poverty, family dysfunctions, and so on).

Recent research examined more precisely the provision of nutrition and the quality of interactions during that process. A diversity of opinion still exists when the processes of interactions are examined and explained. For example, why do some parents react to their child in a certain way? Is that reaction instigated by their indifferent (or even hostile) attitudes towards the child, or do they react inappropriately to the child's resistance to take nutrition and to respond to parental attention? There is little doubt that there are many routes leading to under-feeding: these may or may not be deliberate, based on neglect or rejection, or founded on frustration and persistent struggle. There are those who care for and love their charges (but who are unable to manage difficult children), and those who do not. It is not safe to assume that all children who fail to thrive are temperamentally difficult, nor would it be true that all carers in problematic cases simply find that feeding their charges poses an impossible task. Thus the problem may be triggered off by many factors, and, if this process is not interrupted at an early stage, can lead to the distortion of the parent–child relationship, serious attachment disorders, disturbed behaviour, developmental impairment, and stunting of growth.

MATERNAL PATHOLOGY AND GROWTH-FAILURE

In the late 1950s and 60s, studies of growth-failure and developmental delay (similar to those of institutionalised children) were replicated on infants and young children living at home. Studies of such children and their families have shown that the most commonly identified fore-runners to these growth problems are emotional disturbance and environmental deprivation—with the wide range of psychosocial disorganisation that these concepts imply. Deprivation often involves rejection, isolation from social contacts, and neglect. These associations with poor growth have often been delineated in the context of maternal personality problems, stemming from the mother's own early background and family dysfunctioning. Other psychological difficulties have been found in the manner in which the mothers nurture their small infants. Coleman and

Provence (1957) presented detailed reports of two infants from middle-class families in whom they postulated retardation of both growth and development resulting from insufficient stimulation from the mother and insufficient maternal care. In the first case the child was difficult to feed from birth both on liquids and solids: the feeding situation was described as a persistent struggle. The child was otherwise quite unresponsive to any new stimuli and was passive, while its mother found it difficult to rear and enjoy. When the infant was seven-months-old the mother was again pregnant and the latter's father committed suicide. She showed grief, depression, and anger over a prolonged period. In the second case the mother was isolated and detached from her infant: she stopped breast-feeding on the fourth day after birth because she was afraid she would smother the child, and spanked the infant because its crying drove her 'wild'. She alternated between feelings of depression and helplessness over the baby's developmental lag. This baby was not planned or wanted, because of the mother's career. The authors did not make any distinctions between these two infants and mothers: the second case seems to be one of rejection from birth, while in the first case the distortion of mother–child interactions may have resulted from acute feeding problems and lack of responsiveness of the child to its mother's attentions early on in life.

Fischhoff, Whitten, and Pettit (1971) conducted a psychiatric study of 12 mothers of 3- to 24-month-old failure-to-thrive infants. The data base was derived from two extensive psychiatric interviews supplemented by brief contact with mothers on the ward, a social work report, an unstructured interview with all the available fathers, and observations by the paediatrician and nurses. Fischhoff and colleagues summarised the material for each mother under the following headings:

- age and marital status;
- initial appearance and manner;
- affective aspects and mood
- past history;
- past memories;
- self-image and ego functions;
- present mode of behaviour;
- object relationships;
- defences and fantasies; and
- hopes and day-dreams.

They concluded that 10 out of 12 mothers presented enough behavioural signs to warrant diagnoses of character disorders. These women (according to the authors) presented a constellation of psychological features conducive to inadequate mothering, including limited ability to perceive and assess accurately the environment, their own needs, or those of their children; limitations of adaptability to changes in the environment; adverse affective states; defective object relationships; and limited capacity for concern. Since character-disorders (in the view of many) are untreatable, they suggest that some of these failure-to-thrive children may be better off in foster homes. Although most of the mothers in their small sample were found to present character-disorders, it would appear that this may not be true of all mothers of children who fail to thrive. The term 'character-disorder' can also be a facile and meaningless designation, devoid of useful implications.

Nevertheless similar and different signs of psychopathology have been identified among mothers of failure-to-thrive children in other studies. Barbero and Shaheen (1967) found that mothers of infants who fail to thrive are in general depressed, angry, helpless, and desperate, and have problems in maintaining self-esteem. They state that 'in those instances where the malidentification is part of a more pervasive and structured pathology, it becomes obvious to all concerned that these parents should be referred to the appropriate psychiatric and social agencies'. The authors postulate that depriving mothers have lived under significant environmental psychological disruption, such as alcoholism, childhood deprivation, physical spouse-abuse, and considerable strains in their own families.

Leonard, Rhymes, and Solnit (1966), in their very comprehensive study, described some characteristics of 13 mothers of infants who failed to thrive: these included tension, anger, anxiety, and depression, but they found it difficult to disentangle cause and effect, for failure-to-thrive in an infant (for example) might well contribute to such states in the mothers. The latter themselves had received poor mothering, were sexually traumatised as children, or had experienced family instability. Leonard, Rhymes, and Solnit found the mothers lacking in self-esteem, unable to assess realistically their babies' needs and their own worth, and having feelings of loneliness and isolation. Types of psychopathology described by these authors suggest severe disturbances in the character structure of many of the mothers. Spinetta and Rigler (1972) have hypothesised, on the basis of their studies, that the parents of failure-to-thrive children (like parents who have physically abused their children) have themselves been physically abused or neglected in childhood.

Bullard et al. (1967) concluded from their study of 50 non-organic failure-to-thrive children that neglect (described by them as parental uninterest) is the major aetiological factor for that condition. Contributing to the neglect are factors in the parents' lives (such as instability of life-style, severe marital strife, erratic living habits, and inability to maintain employment or to provide the financial support for the care of the children). Alcoholism is often implicated, as well as a history of entanglements with the law. The mothers tend to describe a lack of feeling for the child, and admit to leaving the child for long periods unattended or with strangers. The authors questioned the appropriateness of using the blanket term 'maternal deprivation' when applied to failure-to-thrive children, and felt it should be used more specifically and should refer to possible inadequacies in feeding, holding, and other particular care-taking activities of the mother.

The positioning of failure-to-thrive as secondary to maternal deprivation may rest on evidence that the infant had little physical handling by the mother, or no appreciable social contact: such mothers are said rarely to hold, cuddle, smile at, play with, or communicate with their children. Those mothers may lack positive feelings for the child, or be uncomfortable with it; they might also be insensitive to, and unable to assess, the needs of the child, particularly with regard to hunger. These aspects have been highlighted by several researchers, including Coleman and Provence (1957), Bullard et al. (1967), Leonard, Rhymes, and Solnit (1966), and Fischhoff, Whitten, and Pettit (1971). In these studies feeding has been singled out as a time of major conflict between mother and child.

There are striking similarities in the clinical observations of the personalities and behavioural features of mothers of failure-to-thrive children; these observations, however, are somewhat questionable because of the absence of contrast or control groups (clinic-attending patients make for notoriously biased samples). A further weakness of much of the work is the absence of evidence on the reliability (or validity) of the procedures used for data collection. Far too many of the conclusions in the literature are based upon retrospective data and clinical impressions. Some of the children and parents are seen only in clinics or hospitals. It is well known that people behave differently and present a different picture when away from their natural habitats. There are many examples in the literature and current child-care practice of parents (especially mothers) being labelled as having character-disorders and causing their infants to fail to thrive, with none of this labelling or causal inferencing scientifically justified. Labelling prior to rigorous assessment (and without adequate control procedures) may seriously confound the results and interpretation of some studies.

One of the more convincing and comprehensive early studies of social development, emotional adaptation, and functioning of mothers of failure-to-thrive children was that of Pollitt, Eichler, and Chan (1975). The aim was to determine which mothers of failure-to-thrive children are likely to be psychologically 'maladapted', and whether they create adverse environmental conditions that interfere with the physical growth and psychological development of the children. Results of this detailed study of the economic, social, family, nutritional, and medical causes of failure-to-thrive (based upon 38 mothers of children selected from an outpatients paediatric clinic) indicated that the behaviour of the women (of the failure-to-thrive group) did not show overt psychopathologies. Their pattern of stressful childhood experiences seemed to suggest that they would have a higher chance of becoming maladjusted during childhood and later life, yet (at least with regard to marital history and mental health) they did not differ from the controls. The largest between-group statistical differences were found in the scores drawn from the mother–child interaction checklist. The mothers in the experimental group showed less frequent verbal and physical contacts, and were less positively reinforcing and warm. These differences in verbal interactions were noted on various socialisation tasks. Substantial differences were also noted in maternal affection, described as 'inoperant' in many of the index mothers. The authors concluded their findings by pointing out that despite stressful backgrounds most of the women in the index group were free of severe psychopathologies. The researchers did not find (as suggested by other studies mentioned above) abnormal social behaviour which might have suggested the presence of personality disturbance.

MOTHER–CHILD INTERACTIONS—INCLUDING FEEDING

More recent studies (Iwaniec, Herbert, & McNeish, 1985a; Powell, Low, & Speers, 1987; Skuse, 1992; and Wolfe, 1993) have indicated deficiencies in child-rearing practices and deviant parent–child interaction rather than character disorders in the carers. They also pointed out that a child's individual characteristics and behavioural style might play a role and contribute to the way their parents interact and relate to failure-to-thrive children. Early child-rearing difficulties (like feeding, sleeping, and persistent crying) might prevent the development of physical and psychological closeness and a warm parent–child relationship. Disturbance in parent–child interaction can lead to mutual avoidance behaviour, which in turn can have serious consequences for the child's development and well-being. There is little doubt that an unsupported and young mother, when faced day after day with a child resistant to most of the caring and socialisation tasks, will resent the child. She might also become alienated from it physically and emotionally. These problems are highlighted (in particular during feeding time) by most researchers and practitioners.

There is little disagreement among researchers that feeding/eating difficulties dominate in the complaints of care-givers whose children come to attention for failure to grow, and the present writer's study confirmed this statement. A history of feeding problems in the index sample (Iwaniec, 1983) showed remarkably similar patterns during the early days of the children's lives: an inability, reluctance, or refusal to suck (taking over an hour to take 3–4 ounces of milk); falling asleep every minute or so; crying while being fed; vomiting; stretching out; and suffering from diarrhoea. This pattern of behaviour was consistent in all cases while the children were on liquids, but it appears that most cases of acute feeding difficulties commenced from the time when solids were introduced: all the children studied persistently refused to take solids; tendencies to vomit and suffer from diarrhoea increased; and screaming while being fed was similar in duration and intensity. Regurgitation and heaving often occurred, children frequently retained food in their mouths, and they demonstrated an inability to swallow and chew. Feeding/eating time (as can well be imagined) became a battle-ground with heightened stress for both parties: anxiety, frustration, and anger were experienced by the mother; and fear, apprehension, and tension by the child. This negatively-charged interaction (manifested by force-feeding, screaming, shouting, shaking, smacking, or sheer anxiety) did not facilitate an atmosphere which was beneficial to growth and to the development of a warm and secure relationship between mother and child.

Feeding difficulties usually include:

(1) poor sucking;
(2) excessively long feeding time;
(3) poor retention of liquids;
(4) vomiting;
(5) prolonged refusal to take solids;
(6) poor swallowing;
(7) poor chewing;
(8) heaving;
(9) complete refusal to take food (usually from the mother); and
(10) no indication of hunger.

Sadly, feeding situations were only too often mismanaged: there could be unrealistic expectations on the part of parents that the child's eating behaviour would change soon (if not immediately) after the physical examination or treatment. The possibility that the child learned to fear broad aspects of the feeding process was often overlooked, while additional stress and fear were imparted to the child by the parents' anxiety and anger. Mothers in the sample were inclined to push food at the children, to shout and smack, and demand normal appetite and normal feeding behaviour. Of course (given the exclusion of organic factors), mothers frequently assumed that there was no longer any reason for the child to resist and reject food: these parents were not told what to expect, or instructed how to feed the recovering child once it was discharged from the hospital. Such instructions and explanations, if provided sensitively, could have changed parents' perceptions to a significant extent.

What is the essence of these tense relationships? To have a child refuse food (when the act of feeding is so permeated with meaning and significance, notably the giving of basic care and affection) is a devastating repudiation for a parent. For a child to fail to thrive in our weight-obsessed culture and to appear neglected in our child-abuse sensitised society is a severe blow to a mother's self-esteem: it is a highly public and deeply humiliating condemnation for those who try to do their best, but are not successful in doing it. Invariably this can lead to a serious distortion of a relationship, and, quite often, after a long chain of events, to rejection. Those mothers feel defeated and rejected by the child, becoming preoccupied (sometimes to the point of obsession) with getting the child to eat at any cost in order that it will gain weight. Some give up and retreat into inertia (passive neglect and emotional indifference), while others might move to active hostility and rejection. Some parents meet with frequent criticism and rebukes, not only from health and child-care agencies, but also from their partners, families, friends, neighbours, and, at times, complete strangers. Mothers often feel that they are being blamed unjustly for their child's condition, and some turn their anger on the child for causing them so much misery. Children, in turn, become withdrawn, apathetic, lethargic, unresponsive, fearful, anxious, and socially and emotionally isolated, so a vicious circle is created. More often than not, the child's participation in the problem-creation is dismissed or overlooked. However, some studies (Iwaniec, 1983) emphasise that the quality of mother–child interaction is often dictated by the temperamental characteristics of the child, and by the carer's and parental attitudes towards the child.

Iwaniec (1991) identified four interactional styles between carers and failure-to-thrive children, which are set out with characteristic interaction behaviour in Table 1.

Table 1: Interactional styles and characteristic behaviour

CARER	DESCRIPTION OF INTERACTION BEHAVIOUR	
	BEHAVIOUR OF CARERS	REACTIONS OF CHILDREN
Forceful, impatient, and angry	Frequent force-feeding, screaming, shaking, smacking, urging child to hurry when eating, and getting frustrated and angry	Fear, anxiety, apprehension, refusal to eat, crying, heaving, and vomiting. Food-avoidance
Unconcerned and neglectful	Inadequate calorific provision, failure to provide appropriate food, and signals of hunger ignored or misunderstood	Loss of weight, lethargic and withdrawn, developmental retardation, sadness, and passivity
Non-persistent and passive	Easily affected by feelings. Depression, low self-esteem, helplessness, anxiety, and desperation	Poor physical growth and delayed development (especially in language and social behaviour)
Determined and coaxing	Resourceful, flexible, patient when managing difficulties, and tries different ways to overcome the child's resistance	Long feeding periods, faddiness, spitting, storing food in mouth, and heaving

It would appear that there were sub-groups in failure-to-thrive interaction, ranging from passive neglect and ineffectual parenting to a more active angry style of interaction. There are also those whose management of the children is positive. Those types of interaction were observed in other types of caring and rearing activities.

However, some infants and children fail to thrive simply because they are underfed, understimulated, and generally neglected. As a result the child is persistently undernourished and fails to thrive. Passive neglect can also stem from maternal depression, family frictions, alcoholism, and various environmental and economic stresses. In those circumstances parents are not able or willing to provide adequate physical and emotional care. Yet indifferent, neglecting parents need not necessarily be hostile towards their children: they might be simply unsympathetic, cold, and distant, and give the impression they are physically and emotionally unavailable or inaccessible to their offspring. In such cases these parents tend to be unresponsive to their children's needs and wishes, and show a restricted concern for the welfare of their young: they pay little attention to the children, and spend the minimum amount of time interacting with them.

We must be alert constantly to the possibility of physical abuse in cases where neglect is caused by disharmony, irresponsibility, alcoholism, and stress. There is no clear differentiation between neglected and abused children: in fact, many children identified at first as victims of battering are discovered later to be seriously neglected as well. Two clear examples are given in the inquiry reports following the deaths of Kimberley Carlile and Jasmine Beckford (*Carlile Report*, 1987, and *Beckford Report*, 1985). The notes of the former state:

> It was one cardinal feature of the failure in standards of care as provided for Kimberley that such (centile) charts were not properly used in her case. Had they been used and interpreted properly, the outcome for the ill-fated child might so easily have been different. (p. 39)

The conclusion of the latter report was that:

> While Jasmine's weight did not go entirely unnoticed, it was never properly taken on board by the doctors or the health visitors and never at all by the social workers. (p. 74)

Weight and quite often physical appearance and psychological expressions are very striking in more acute cases, and when they are spotted they need to be investigated as a matter of prevention to stop further deterioration and subsequent harm.

A recent epidemiological study (Skuse *et al.*, 1992) identified that children referred for failure-to-thrive during the first year of life were, four years later, at six times increased risk of subsequent abuse and/or neglect than those who had not failed to thrive. They found that one in 12 cases had been abused or neglected by four years of age and were put on the Child-Protection Register for reasons other than the growth problem. It is apparent that non-organic failure-to-thrive children are at risk of further abuse of various natures if the problem is not dealt with during the early months of their lives.

Iwaniec (1994) has made the following comments on the basis of a 10-year follow-up of failure-to-thrive children. Firstly, there is a substantial lack of awareness and understanding among the medical and social-work professions about this problem and its long-term implications for the child and the family. Secondly, a child's poor weight-gain and persistent loss of weight, poor physical appearance, and delayed development are often not dealt with at the onset of the problem. Thirdly, some mothers seeking help and advice were dismissed as worrying about nothing: 'he or she will grow out of it' was a common panacea offered to the hapless parents. Repeated visits did not usually register in the form of mental 'alarm-bells' until the child was so wasted that it had to be admitted to a hospital: indeed, several children studied were originally admitted through casualty departments! Fourthly, early intervention is crucial. Children referred during the first year of life did very well on short- and long-term bases, but children with a long history of failure-to-grow, and referred between two to six years of age, showed only moderate improvement or no improvement on a short- or long-term basis. The prognosis is poor if a child is referred only after prolonged difficulties at home. It was somewhat disturbing that only 10% of children were known to the Social Services Department in spite of two (on average) admissions to the hospital for non-organic failure-to-grow. It is important to establish that children with problems outlined above should be dealt with on a multidisciplinary basis, and it is essential that every discipline effectively inter-communicates.

CONCLUSION

It is possible to speculate on the basis of research findings that there are several routes to the failure-to-thrive disorder. An original organic lesion may heal, but the subsequent emotional overlay continues to disrupt eating and this, in turn, affects mother–child interaction and relationships. Maternal resentment and ambivalence is, in a sense, secondary. Maternal rejection—be it primary or secondary—is quite likely to be expressed in rough feeding-patterns (and other child-care activities) which lead to food-avoidance on the part of the child. A child with aversive temperamental attributes is predisposed to biological irregularity and resistance to socialisation. Here, too, may lie a precursor to fraught parent–child interaction. The point is that an acute feeding difficulty, no matter how it originates—for organic reasons, temperament, neglect, hostility, etc.—will, if it persists over a considerable time, result not only in the child's poor growth and development, but also (in some circumstances) distort, or more often exacerbate, the parent–child relationship.

3

EMOTIONAL ABUSE AND STUNTING IN GROWTH

Better is a dinner of herbs where love is, than a stalled ox and hatred therewith *

INTRODUCTION

In the ancient proverb quoted above is an accurate pointer to the reason why some children fail to grow and develop even though no apparent disease may be present. It would appear that stunting of growth may occur, not only because of starvation, physical disease, or poverty, but also through emotional factors ranging from passive neglect to active rejection. The issue of emotional failure to grow has not received the attention it merits among child-care practitioners, so the consequences and social and psychological costs have been underestimated.

In order to demonstrate the meaning of the term 'emotional failure-to-grow' at the very beginning of this chapter, the example of twins (identified as Jimmy and Wayne) may be cited to illustrate a painful process of problem development (Herbert & Iwaniec, 1980).

CASE STUDY

The case is of particular interest as it involved two brothers, born five minutes apart, each weighing the same at birth (5 lbs 3 oz (2.355 kg)), being of the same height, and both parents delighted to have two healthy babies. At the point of referral (24 months after

---

*The Bible: *Proverbs*, XV, 17.

birth), however, they were almost a lifetime apart. Jimmy was a chubby, rosy-cheeked, boisterous two-year-old, who appeared to be a happy, mischievous boy, who ran, played, talked, and laughed. He went to his mother for help and comfort and cuddled up to her spontaneously; he responded readily to her attention and affection; she smiled at him, provided comfort, showed concern, picked him up, sat him on her lap, played with him, answered his questions, watched his movements, showed pleasure in his achievements, corrected him in an encouraging way, and warned him when he was in danger. Her voice was soft when she talked to him.

On the edge of the room, like a stranger, stood Wayne, his posture rigid, staring fixedly. He was a sad, lethargic-looking child, very small and extremely thin; his pale face threw into relief the dark shadows under his eyes; he remained in one spot, as if at attention; he gazed unswervingly at his mother, who took no notice of him. When asked to call Wayne over to her she looked in his direction: as she did so her face hardened and her eyes became angry; she addressed him with a peremptory command; when he hesitated she showed irritation and shouted at him.

Observations of his interaction with his mother confirmed that she never smiled at him, never picked him, never sat him on her lap, never played with him, never showed satisfaction when he did something praiseworthy, and never encouraged him in the pursuit of new activities. She told him off for minor misdemeanours, and persistently criticised and shamed him. The only physical contact came about when she fed, bathed, or dressed him, and at such times her handling was rough, and she seldom spoke to him. When she approached him he appeared to be frightened and occasionally burst into tears. He never came to her for comfort or help, and she never approached him, except to carry out the bare essentials of care and control. Living standards in the household were high, and both children were meticulously clean, well-dressed, and materially well provided for. However, Jimmy and Wayne did not play together, but Jimmy frequently pushed his brother and smacked him. The ensuing cries of Wayne were usually ignored by his mother. Looking at Wayne and Jimmy it was hard to believe that they were twins who were the same weight at birth, for Wayne was so much smaller and thinner. From the very start of his babyhood, Wayne was difficult to feed, cried a lot, slept badly, and was difficult to comfort and to distract. The mother found him unresponsive to her child-rearing efforts, and impossible to enjoy and to love. As time went on, she formed the firm opinion that his behaviour was deliberately calculated to hurt and to annoy her, and, furthermore, that he did not like her. Thus, instead of growing closer together, they moved rapidly apart, with much pain experienced by mother and son. At the point when the case was referred to the Social Services (some two years after the birth of the twins) it was impossible to see that they were exactly the same age, or indeed that they were twins at all.

The chart in Figure 2 demonstrates the dramatic differences in the weight-gain of the two boys.

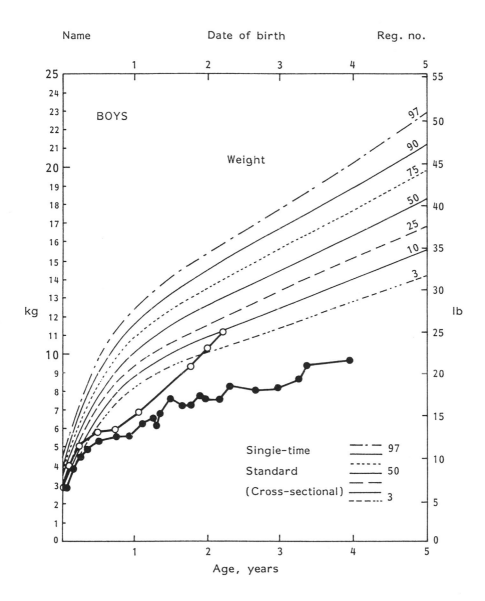

Figure 2: Growth-development chart showing weight differences between the twins Jimmy and Wayne. The peaks in Wayne's case (bottom graph) occurred when he was hospitalised or was in the care of someone other than his mother.
Source: Leicester Royal Infirmary, Department of Child Health (1978)

DESCRIPTION OF PSYCHOSOCIAL DWARFISM

Children who are defined as psychosocial dwarfs are those who are exceptionally short and remain stunted for a considerable time, although there may be no obvious organic reasons for this. Weight is below that expected for the height, though exceptionally that weight may be appropriate for the height, and the child might appear well-nourished, but such appearances may be deceptive because neither weight nor height is normal for the chronological age (Skuse, 1989).

It is believed that prolonged and severe emotional abuse and neglect affect the rate of linear growth and functioning of the secretion of growth-hormones. Although the precise mechanism of growth-hormone arrest is not clear, it can be assumed that emotional factors play an important role. Once a child is removed from an abusive environment, its growth and development quickly accelerate, but if returned to it, a marked deterioration becomes evident, and behaviour worsens. The triggering factors might range from acute rejection and other forms of emotional maltreatment (which might be evident almost from birth) to sexual abuse and particularly cruel physical treatment.

Emotional upheaval in children tends to demonstrate itself in bizarre eating patterns, disturbed toileting, destructiveness, defiant hostility, acute non-compliance, and self-harming behaviour. Relationships of such children with parents or carers are marked by hostility and active rejection: because the children are unloved and unwanted, and because they are reared in an emotional vacuum, their cognitive, language, emotional, and social development is seriously retarded. In such cases serious attachment-disorders are evident, and the relationships are mutually antagonistic: physical and verbal contact is limited to bare essentials, and at such times is hostile or indifferent. Profiles of some of the major problems of psychosocial dwarfism (emotional growth-failure) are given in Figure 3.

CAUSAL MECHANISMS

The controversy about aetiological factors regarding failure-to-grow without organic cause in childhood has been going on for many years. The debate appears to be very lively and far from general agreement on theoretical and practice levels. Questions such as: is psychosocial dwarfism an extension of prolonged non-organic failure-to-thrive or does it occur as a result of emotional trauma like sexual abuse, desertion,

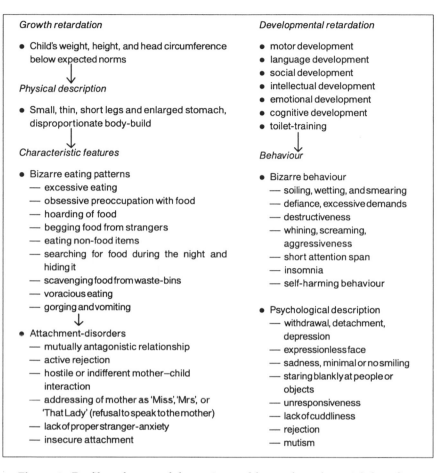

Growth retardation

- Child's weight, height, and head circumference below expected norms

↓

Physical description

- Small, thin, short legs and enlarged stomach, disproportionate body-build

↓

Characteristic features

- Bizarre eating patterns
  — excessive eating
  — obsessive preoccupation with food
  — hoarding of food
  — begging food from strangers
  — eating non-food items
  — searching for food during the night and hiding it
  — scavenging food from waste-bins
  — voracious eating
  — gorging and vomiting

↓

- Attachment-disorders
  — mutually antagonistic relationship
  — active rejection
  — hostile or indifferent mother–child interaction
  — addressing of mother as 'Miss', 'Mrs', or 'That Lady' (refusal to speak to the mother)
  — lack of proper stranger-anxiety
  — insecure attachment

Developmental retardation

- motor development
- language development
- social development
- intellectual development
- emotional development
- cognitive development
- toilet-training

↓

Behaviour

- Bizarre behaviour
  — soiling, wetting, and smearing
  — defiance, excessive demands
  — destructiveness
  — whining, screaming, aggressiveness
  — short attention span
  — insomnia
  — self-harming behaviour

- Psychological description
  — withdrawal, detachment, depression
  — expressionless face
  — sadness, minimal or no smiling
  — staring blankly at people or objects
  — unresponsiveness
  — lack of cuddliness
  — rejection
  — mutism

Figure 3: Profiles of some of the major problems of psychosocial dwarfism

separation from the carer to whom the child was strongly attached, or some other form of attachment discontinuity? Why are the diagnoses confined to the period from two-years-of-age and after? Why do some researchers feel that psychological expression/behaviour in non-organic failure-to-thrive children (as observed in hospital) cannot be one of withdrawal, depression, detachment, sadness, apathy, and so on, while others do? There are many aspects of non-organic failure-to-grow which are not fully understood: this accounts, in part, for the diversity of opinion.

Let us now look at how the ideas about causal factors have developed over the years. The association between maternal deprivation (in particular) and failure-to-grow has led some investigators to hypothesise about the existence of a physiological pathway whereby emotional deprivation affects the neuroendocrine system that regulates growth. Mechanisms of growth-failure are not clear, in spite of many research studies done in this area. It is suggested (Fischhoff, Whitten, & Pettit, 1971) that maternally deprived infants can be underweight because of undereating (which is secondary to being offered inadequate food), or because of the refusal of adequate nourishment offered (rather than as a result of some psychologically-induced defect in absorption or of metabolism).

Several studies have been carried out to test growth-hormone efficiency. The mechanism of the latter in dwarfism was studied extensively in attempts to establish the factors that play a role in growth-hormone arrest and what happens and under what circumstances when growth-hormones are again activated. These studies concentrated on various forms of growth-failure, but particularly on dwarfism without apparent organic cause. Patton and Gardner (1962) postulate that emotional disturbances might have a direct effect on intermediary metabolism so as to interfere with anabolic processes. The production and release of several anterior pituitary hormones are influenced by hypothalamic centres, which are in turn recipients of the pathway from higher neural centres, particularly the limbic cortex. The latter is also thought to be the locus of emotional feeling and behaviour. These authors (on the basis of six very thoroughly-studied children) favoured a theory of emotional influence on growth with secondary hormonal insufficiencies as the main cause of dwarfism.

Apley *et al.* (1971) made extensive enquiries based on paediatric, psychiatric, and social team-work information to discover the truth about food intake of dwarfs in Bristol. Their exhaustive clinical, biochemical, and endocrinal tests on all the children satisfactorily ruled out the operation of pathological causes in the stunting of growth, and (by inference) they point to underfeeding as a triggering factor.

The work of Talbot *et al.* (1947) foreshadowed most of what is now known about these children. They were the first to point to 'chronic grief' as one of the causes of dwarfism. In studying over 100 dwarfs of all kinds (in 25 boys and 23 girls aged 2 to 15 years) they were not able to find any organic cause for the growth-failure. Nutritional histories of these children (as Talbot *et al.* have stated) indicated clearly that there were difficult feeding problems and had been so for the major part of the lives of the children, in many cases since infancy. Talbot *et al.* postulated that the child (having once become undersized) continues with a basically reduced protein and calorie requirement, and that once its pituitary function is reduced, fails to respond when the diet improves: some children, therefore, remain small though apparently well-nourished. Having treated them with pituitary hormones, Talbot and his colleagues found that some of those children (both the well-nourished and the thin ones) were capable of satisfactory growth over many months. Lastly, they discovered through psychiatric and social studies that the background of these children could be grossly abnormal, and they listed the following features in 24 dwarfs:

- rejection 34%;
- poverty 14%;
- mental deficiency 19%;
- chronic grief 14%;
- maternal delinquencies and breakdown 14%; and
- no abnormality 5%.

In studies involving seven well-nourished dwarfs, no abnormality was found in three cases, maternal delinquency or breakdown occurred in three others, and rejection in one. Four of these children with disturbed maternal relationships were dwarfs, but they nevertheless appeared well-nourished. This strongly suggests that consumption of food in terms of calories was not the whole answer to the causes of the dwarfism and led other researchers to pursue the hormone study. The issue of hormones and their effect on growth-arrest is still unclear. What is obvious, however, is that when these children are removed from the maltreating environment, the growth-hormones are 'switched on' again, and the child begins to grow (and at times at a remarkable speed), but when returned once more to the abusive environment there is stunting of growth and the child rapidly loses weight.

Powell, Brasel, and Blizzard (1967) measured growth-hormone response along with other endocrine studies in 13 children. They described many of the common social circumstances in children who failed to thrive, including divorce, marital strife, alcoholism, and extra-marital affairs. They did not study the role of the father as a contributor to the problem, but they stated that in 'no case did the father spend much time' with the children. In addition to their studies of endocrinology, they made interesting and careful observations of the children, and described the following features: encopresis 6/13; polydipsia 13/13; drinking from toilet-bowl 6/13; polyphasia 13/13; stealing food 12/13; eating from rubbish bin 11/13; gorging and vomiting 9/13; getting up at night 7/13;

playing alone 9/13; retarded speech 11/13; temper tantrums 9/13; steatorrhoea 8/13; shortness 13/13; thinness 5/13; malnourishment 1/13; and weight-for-height normal or greater 7/13. Powell, Brasel, and Blizzard concluded that the aetiology of growth-failure and possible hypopituitarism was unresolved.

Charles Whitten (1976) began to challenge some of the concepts mentioned above. He presented evidence in a study of deprived infants where he found that 11 out of 13 gained weight at an accelerated rate when fed adequately while living in a hospital environment. Two children failed to gain weight, but their intake of calories was low. In addition, 7 out of 7 depressed infants gained weight rapidly in their own homes when fed on an adequate diet by their mothers in the presence of observers. Whitten believed that these children were simply starved, and therefore did not grow in weight or height. Whitten was critical of the Spitz, Widdowson, and Freud methodology. He also referred back to the observations in the Widdowson study and commented that 'Fräulein Schwartz must have carried on at such length during meal hours, that the soup became cold or decomposed, so that the children could not eat it even if they were hungry.' Whitten's main criticism was that the other investigators had not properly quantified the calorific intake. However, he was also inaccurate by failing to take into consideration emotional factors.

More recently several studies have emerged which examined medical aspects of growth-hormone function (Green, Campbell, & David, 1984; Green, Deutsch, & Campbell, 1987; and Blizzard & Bulatovic, 1993), and those exploring psychosocial aetiology and manifestations of psychosocial dwarfism (Money, Annecillo, & Kelley, 1983; Iwaniec, 1983; Dowdney *et al.*, 1987; and Skuse, 1992). All these studies support the hypothesis that acute emotional abuse and neglect might contribute to the disfunction of growth-hormones and consequently affect healthy growth and development.

Practitioners should find the following checklist useful, bearing in mind that not all these characteristic features will be present in each case:

(1) bizarre eating behaviour;
(2) excessive hunger-drive;
(3) disrupted sleep pattern;
    (a) wandering around the house in search of food;
    (b) lying awake and motionless in bed for long periods;
(4) disturbed toileting behaviour;
(5) self-harming behaviour;
    (a) head-banging;

     (b) self-biting and self-scratching;

     (c) fire-setting and self-immolation;

     (d) persistent rocking;

  (6) severe non-compliance and stubborn defiance;

  (7) short attention-span (inability to concentrate);

  (8) reluctance to communicate with the primary care-giver (mutism);

  (9) unhappiness, withdrawnness, irritability, and, at times, depression;

(10) destructiveness;

(11) damaging parental attitudes, constant criticisms, rebukes, dismissiveness of the child's achievements, belittling, etc.;

(12) attachment disorders (extremely poor child--parent relationships);

(13) rejection;

(14) possibilities of physical and (especially) sexual abuse;

(15) developmental delays (cognitive, intellectual, emotional, and social);

(16) aggressiveness and temper tantrums;

(17) acceleration of growth when removed from the home environment;

(18) deterioration of growth and behaviour when returned to the home;

(19) age of identification of the problem from the toddler stage to adolescence;

(20) difficult or slow-to-warm-up temperament;

(21) hyperactivity; and

(22) poor relationship with siblings and peers.

It has to be remembered, however, that some children may be very lethargic and withdrawn (slow in movements and activity), while others will practically run from one activity to another, unable to maintain one-task behaviour. Similarly, some will scream and cry, while others will sulk and be irritable.

MANIFESTATIONS OF DISTURBED BEHAVIOUR

Disturbed behaviour can become overt in several ways. Some of the commonest and most striking manifestations are given below.

Self-Harming Behaviour

This usually manifests itself in severe head-banging against the furniture, walls, floor, and other objects, causing bruising and lumps. It usually occurs when the child is distressed or angry: these reactions may be triggered when food is withdrawn as a punishment; when the child is locked up or isolated from the rest of the family; when it is denied a treat for a minor misdemeanour; or when it is unfairly punished. Some of these children bite or scratch themselves to the point of bleeding, usually when they are frustrated or when cruelly criticised and shamed, and also when they are unable to do or to get what they want. Because they suffer from extremely low self-esteem they punish themselves for their misdemeanours, and it could be that they want to draw attention to their pain and distress. Some children will injure themselves by putting a hand or a foot into the fire, or burn personal belongings (like a favourite toy or book or piece of clothing). A girl was given a beautiful coat, bought by her grandmother, and a few minutes later she put it into the open fire and watched it burn. Of course, fire-setting and burning things are also seen as destructive behaviour.

Bizarre Eating

An obsessive preoccupation with food tends to emerge at an older toddler stage (although an early feeding history is that of under-eating). Distorted behaviour around food is expressed by hoarding food in the bedroom, under pillows, in cupboards, under beds and in various drawers, under the settee in the living-room, or behind the furniture. Begging food from strangers is not unusual: some children may stop a person by the gate, street, or in the park and ask for biscuits, fruit, or drinks. At the nursery or hospital they tend to follow a nurse, asking what is for dinner or when they are going to eat, and will not stop until they are told. They will tend to eat non-food items such as pieces of paper, cotton-wool, soil, or cat and dog food (one boy ate all the fabric from the inside of his continental quilt). Getting up at night in search of food is very common, and such children tend to go through cupboards and fridges and will eat whatever they find, even to excess. David, a seven-year-old boy, used to get up in the small hours of the morning and could eat 24 Weetabix with 2–3 pints of milk and a loaf of bread. If he ran out of milk he would go out and steal milk from the doorsteps of neighbours. Five-year-old John, during his first week in the foster-home, ate two big Black-Forest gâteaux at four o'clock in the morning. The foster-mother heard a noise downstairs and thought that there was a burglar in the house, so she armed herself with an iron bar and went downstairs in fear and panic. Instead, she found John in the middle of the kitchen floor with the dog, finishing the second gâteau. The dog was covered with cream (which John had squeezed from the tube). When telling this story, she asked quite seriously if the child would eat the dog as well because he seemed to be preparing the dog for precisely that. Some of these children tend to scavenge food from rubbish bins and search for it: children so affected tend to eat quickly and voraciously (to the point of gorging and vomiting). Parents often complain that they steal food and at times leave other members of the family with nothing to eat for breakfast. Nursery and hospital staff have reported that they take food from other children's plates or eat leftovers. It is not uncommon to find that these children do not eat with the rest of the family: instead, they might be given food while sitting on the floor away from the table, and excluded from conversation and normal family interaction at meal-times.

Why should such children behave in such a bizarre way? One might ask do they eat for comfort to compensate for their distress? Are they being starved as a punishment, since they are frequently deprived of food? Do they hoard food as a preparation to have something to eat when they are deprived of food, or is it a complex consequence of severe maltreatment? It would appear that all these factors are in operation, especially when they coincide with sexual abuse and serious threats.

Toileting

Disturbed toileting behaviour (like deliberately urinating all over the bed, clothing, and furniture; defaecating into pants, corners of the room, under the table, in public places, as well as smearing faeces on walls, toys, and personal belongings, and hiding dirty pants) is a common feature among these children. It indicates a high level of emotional turmoil and distress. It might be aggressive retaliation directed at those who inflict pain in everyday life: this kind of behaviour is very offensive and can lead (especially at school) to rejection by the peer group. Children who are malodorous usually find themselves isolated in both the classroom and playground, thus eliminating opportunities to make friends and to engage in social activities, including swimming and outings. They react to peer rejection either by being aggressive and disruptive, or by being withdrawn and detached. Quite frequently they are bullied both physically and verbally.

Destructiveness

Mindless destructiveness manifests itself by destroying toys, books, clothing, and desirable things. Destructive children tend to tear bed-clothes to pieces, pull down wallpaper, draw or splash paint on walls, set fire to curtains or clothing, or start fires in rooms. Since their self-esteem is extremely low, they might be punishing themselves as not being worthy of owning anything.

DEVELOPMENT

Emotionally abused and neglected children show significant developmental delays, especially in social, cognitive, and language skills: being reared in social isolation where encouragement, instruction, and teaching of new skills (and practising them) are not available, prevents them from acquiring information necessary for optimal development. Lack of individual attention and stimulation and limited verbal and physical contact do not facilitate opportunities to learn, to explore, to reason, or to deal with new curiosities, new observations, and new experiences. Parents are not emotionally and physically available to teach and to answer questions. Because the children are rejected and neglected, they spend little time with their parents, and parental contact is usually limited to bare essentials of care and control. As a result their intellectual, social, and emotional development is retarded. Children who are reared in an abusive environment have their cognitive development curtailed, as they have formed a distorted picture of the world, people, and experiences around them. On the other hand, parents also tend to have distorted perceptions of such children, feeling that it is the child who does not want to be picked up, played with, to be cuddled, or to be in their company. That might be the case with some children due to their psychological make-up (non-cuddly child), but in the majority of cases this type of child's reaction is the result of acute maltreatment which has been present quite often from birth.

SOCIAL AND EMOTIONAL BEHAVIOUR

Interaction between the child and other family members (including siblings) is marked by hostility and dismissal: parents avoid the child, and at times its sheer presence creates a heavy atmosphere of tension and anxiety. Extreme defiance and stubbornness are prevalent, and these children seldom respond to requests or commands. Parents in turn revert to cruel and harsh discipline to exert control and authority: disciplining may involve getting rid of a child's favourite toy or pet; locking the child up in a bedroom, dark cupboard, shed, or cellar for many hours; tying a child to a bed or other piece of furniture; making a child stand for a prolonged period in one spot; smacking and shouting; and putting the child into a bath of cold water as a punishment for soiling or wetting. However, the most common way of punishing a child is withdrawal of food or drink, making a hungry child watch others eat for trivial misdemeanours, sending the child early to bed without being fed, taking food away when the child eats in a messy way, or denying pudding or something special for minor misbehaviour. It is not unusual to see how the child is left out when treats are given to other children. For example, the mother comes home from the shopping trip and gives crisps, sweets, or chocolate to all the children, but not to the child in question, stating that it cannot have them because the child did something yesterday, or that it does not deserve them, or that it must be taught a lesson. Sibling–child relationships are hostile or indifferent: siblings usually ignore the child, do not include it in their activities, and behave towards it in an aggressive and dismissive way. Because parents seldom take the side of the target child, it is smacked, pushed, and toys are frequently snatched from it. It is not unusual to see that the child is being bruised by its siblings (even the younger ones).

It is not an uncommon feature in such cases that rejected children will not speak to their mothers, will not respond to their questions, and seem to dismiss any contact their mothers attempt to make with them. Some children do not address their mothers as 'Mum' or 'Mummy', but refer to them as 'Miss', 'Mrs', or even as 'that Lady'. Yet they will address other people by their correct names, and may be extremely attention-seeking in a most destructive way. One can imagine the devastating feelings of pain and rejection felt by the mothers in such cases. Mutual dislike becomes more acute as the child gets older and the battle of wills intensifies. As an already fragile relationship and a sense of belonging deteriorates the child becomes nothing more than an intruder in the family, and everyone suffers. To quote one of the mothers:

> John will not speak to me (I know he can—he speaks to other people). I heard him swearing at me when I put him into his room. When I asked him to repeat what he said, he would not—even a swear word from him is better than nothing. He would not answer my questions—he would just stare at me. He refers to me as 'Miss' or 'this Lady'—he never calls me 'Mum'. He would position himself in a provoking way, for me to see him. He makes this awful noise, in a high-pitched, squeaking voice, which drives me mad. I just cannot stand him, I cannot bear having him near me—he deliberately behaves like that to hurt me—so for his own good I put him into his room, for his safety and my sanity, so that I do not have to look at him. I cannot allow him to annoy me so much. And yet, I worry so much about him— even though I do not like him. I keep wondering where I went wrong, what has happened. I get on so well with my two other children. I feel so guilty and ashamed and desperately unhappy. People like my family do not believe me, that he is, and has always been, so difficult to care for and to enjoy. I went through hell trying to feed him when he was a baby. My whole life evolves around feeding John and coping with his crying and screaming. I tried to defeat him but he has defeated me instead. He does not want me and I do not want him. One of us has to go. He does not fit into this family: I

feel that someone has dumped him on me and forgotten to take him away again.

MATERNAL CHARACTERISTICS

On the parents' side, mothers of such children are hostile and angry on the one hand, and demoralised, depressed, and defeated on the other. A common cry from such mothers is to ask where they went wrong, or to enquire in anguish what they have done, what is wrong with the child, why is it so difficult to rear, and why is it so difficult to love. The mothers tend to be isolated and lack support, constructive advice, guidance, a helping hand and reassurance: they often feel ashamed, embarrassed, and guilty for their contribution to the child's state, so often (for those reasons) they tend to avoid doctors, health visitors, and social workers. They are also resistant to help, and tend to miss appointments, make excuses for not being at home as arranged, and seldom follow instructions or advice, or complete tasks they were asked to do. Most of them suffer from anxiety and bouts of depression. Their energy-level tends to be low, and at times they seem to have no strength or the mental capacity to try to turn the clock back.

Fathers appear to have better relationships with these children, but they tend to spend little time with them. Their help for the mothers is limited, both physically (in terms of caring) and emotionally (by encouraging or supporting). They are quite often critical of the behaviour of their partners towards the children, but do little to change the situation. It has to be remembered that some of them abuse their children sexually and therefore will dissimulate.

PARENT–CHILD RELATIONSHIP AND INTERACTION

The following describes some of the parent–child hostile and abusive interaction that often leads to several forms of maltreatment:

(1) little and hostile physical contact—lack of touch (such as holding, cuddling, picking up, or sitting on lap);
(2) lack of eye-contact or smiling at the child (if eye-contact exists, it is angry and cold);
(3) limited verbal contact (if present, it tends to be in the form of commands, shouting, screaming, criticising, degrading, or putting down);
(4) ignoring the child's presence or avoiding the child;

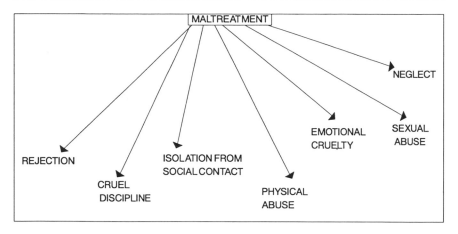

Figure 4: Factors of maltreatment

(5) rejecting;
(6) physically neglecting (such as not feeding, dressing, supervising, stimulating, guiding, teaching, or reassuring);
(7) harming the child (by hitting, shaking, or smacking); and
(8) inflicting psychological pain (by threatening, provoking anxiety, inducing fear, and depriving the child of attention and love).

Maltreatment can take various forms and can contribute to psychosocial dwarfism. Currently recognised maltreating factors are shown in Figure 4.

It has to be recognised that these children are temperamentally difficult and have been difficult to rear from birth. They are irregular in biological functioning, irritable, and difficult to distract or jolly out from bad moods. They are unappealing and difficult to like, not only by parents and families, but also by anyone who deals with them, such as hospital or nursery nurses, teachers, doctors, and foster-parents.

CONCLUSION

It would appear that stunting of growth, as described in this chapter, is the result of severe emotional maltreatment, which, in many cases, was present from birth. Most of the children so affected have been rejected and unwanted by their parents, and for these reasons they developed acute emotional and behavioural disturbances. Psychosocial dwarfism can also result from acute trauma, such as sexual abuse, and when it is investigated, attention should be given to the possibility of such abuse.

4

EMOTIONAL ABUSE AND NEGLECT: EFFECTS ON THE GROWING CHILD

*The greatest respect is owed to a child; if your imagination harbours disgraceful thoughts, do not forget the youthful years of your son**

INTRODUCTION

Human development is viewed in terms of the accomplishment of crucial socialisation tasks. Those tasks will be learned and skills acquired if the socialising agents (such as parents) create an atmosphere and opportunities for the child to learn to the best of its ability. We have seen in Chapters 2 and 3 how neglect and abuse can interfere with a child's physical growth and development: however, not all children who are emotionally neglected or abused show growth-failure, but most of them show developmental delays and various behavioural and emotional problems.

Emotional abuse and neglect affect the speed and quality of development, especially during the early years of a child's life. The question of whether emotional abuse and neglect have long-lasting consequences is still inconclusive. Since there are few longitudinal studies available it is difficult to state to what degree an early maltreatment of this kind will handicap an individual in later life. However, there are ample data available to suggest that maltreatment reflects itself negatively on a child's developmental attainment and that it differs with age (Frodi & Lamb, 1980; Cicchetti & Rizley, 1981; Belsky & Vondra, 1989; Wolfe, 1988; to mention but a few).

---

*Juvenal (*c.* AD 60–*c.* 130): *Satires*, No. 14, Line 47.

Maltreatment demonstrates itself in many different ways and in varying degrees, from lack of care and provision of basic physical needs to lack of attention to stimulation and encouragement of optimal growth and development of children. It also manifests itself by failure to provide love, affection, and emotional availability to the child. At its worst, the child might be rejected and badly affected by parental hostility and dismissiveness. While physical neglect and abuse are more obvious and easier to recognise (because of distinct marks in cases of physical abuse and observable features in cases of physical neglect), emotional abuse and neglect can go unnoticed for a long time. The child might appear well-dressed, clean, and well provided for, but is seldom played with, spoken to, looked at, comforted, attended to when in difficulties, or cuddled. Verbal and physical contact is limited, and emotional input is insignificant in cases of neglect; while harsh, denigrating, threatening, disapproving, and rejecting behaviour is usual in cases of abuse. When children live in such a hostile, anxiety-arousing, or indifferent atmosphere, their physical, cognitive, intellectual, and emotional development is quite likely to be arrested. In infancy curtailed development will tend to show itself in insecure attachment and delayed psycho-motor development; in pre-school children it will be manifest in disturbance of social and emotional behaviour; and in school-age children it will show itself in serious learning deficits and behavioural problems.

Erik Erikson has argued that each developmental stage has to meet certain social demands. At each stage a conflict between opposite poles in a pattern of reciprocity between the self and others has to be resolved. Table 2 shows the major hazards of achieving age-appropriate tasks and what facilitates happy and healthy development.

INFANCY

Parental physical care, attention, and emotional availability are essential for the child to start off optimistically on life's journey. In order to provide those ingredients parents need to be willing and committed to nurture and to love. They also need to have an environment and means to meet these commitments, as well as guidance and support to exercise their parental obligations and duties.

There are various theories stressing different tasks. Erikson (1965), taking a broad view, stated that the essential task of infancy is the development of basic trust in others. He believed that during the early months and

Table 2: Developmental tasks

APPROX-IMATE AGE PERIOD	CHARACTERISTIC TO BE ACHIEVED	MAJOR HAZARD TO ACHIEVEMENT	FACILITATORS
Birth to 2 years	Sense of trust or security	Neglect, abuse, or deprivation of consistent and appropriate love in infancy; harsh or early weaning	If parents meet the preponderance of the infant's needs, the child develops a stronger sense of trust than of mistrust
2 to 4 years	Sense of autonomy—child viewing self as an individual in his/her own right, apart from parents although dependent on them	Conditions which interfere with the child's achieving a feeling of adequacy or the learning of skills such as talking	If the parents reward the child's successful actions and do not shame his or her failures (say in bowel- or bladder-control), the child's sense of autonomy will outweigh the sense of shame and doubt
4 to 6 years	Sense of initiative—period of vigorous reality testing, imagination, and imitation of adult behaviour	Overly strict discipline, internalisation of rigid ethical attitudes which interfere with the child's spontaneity and reality testing	If parents accept the child's curiosity and do not put down the need to know and to question, the child's sense of initiative will outweigh the sense of guilt

6 to 11 years	Sense of duty and accomplishment—laying aside of fantasy and play; undertaking real tasks, developing academic and social competencies	Excessive competition, personal limitations, or other conditions which lead to experiences of failure, resulting in feeling of inferiority and poor work habits	If the child encounters more success than failure at home and at school, he or she will have a greater sense of industry than of inferiority
12 to 15 years	Sense of identity—clarification in adolescence of who one is, and what one's role is	Failure of society to provide clearly defined roles and standards; formation of cliques which provide clear but not always desirable roles and standards	If the young person can reconcile diverse roles, abilities, and values and see their continuity with past and future, the sense of personal identity will not give way to a sense of role diffusion

Source: Adapted from Erikson (1965) by Herbert (1989).

years of life a baby learns whether the world is a good and secure place in which to live, or a source of pain, misery, frustration, and uncertainty. Because a baby is dependent on others for so long, it needs to know that it can depend on the outside world. If its basic needs are met it is thought to develop a 'basic trust' in the world and thus to evolve a nucleus of self-trust, which is more important for later development.

But how does the trust show itself in a child's behaviour early on in life? The first demonstration of social trust in the baby is the ease of feeding, the depth of sleep, and the relaxation of bowels. Later on it is demonstrated when the infant will let its mother out of its sight without undue anxiety or rage. It is thought that if the maternal child-rearing techniques (such as providing comfort, familiarity of images, satiation, and relief of pain) are consistent and predictable then the child slowly develops a sense of ego-identity based on remembered and anticipated sensations of things and people. According to Erikson, a baby who smiles easily demonstrates trust.

What are these early developmental needs? Babies need to be fed regularly and be given appropriate food, to be kept in a warm and clean place, to be changed regularly to avoid nappy-rash, to be washed and bathed, and attended to if in distress or discomfort. They also need a place of relative calm and a peaceful nurturing atmosphere. If these basic needs are not given attention, the child's health, growth, and well-being will suffer. Infants need attention and stimulation to help them develop basic skills like sitting, crawling, walking, talking, and the social behaviour of participation and sharing. They need sensitive training in bowel- and bladder-control. They need to learn how to eat, to dress, to respond to parental requests, and to acquire self-discipline. They need to develop a sense of belonging and of security, and to build up basic trust for an attachment to their parents and siblings. They need close nurturing physical contact (being picked up when in distress, comforted when they hurt themselves, and soothed when disturbed or frightened). The quality and quantity of basic needs provision will determine a child's development and level of attachment to its carers: it also lays the foundation for future accomplishments and the ways the child will perceive and relate to people around it. Neglected and abused children suffer from the omission of parental care, attention, and affection: as a result their physical and psychological development tend to be impaired. The most common problem resulting from physical and emotional neglect during infancy is failure-to-thrive (see Chapter 2). Additionally, the development of an affectionate bond between parents and children tends to be weak and insecure. Parent–child interaction is often cold, indifferent, and, at times, hostile.

Seriously emotionally neglected and abused infants are observed to be withdrawn, lethargic, apathetic, and, in the most adverse circumstances, depressed. Since they live in an emotional vacuum (unattended and unstimulated) they revert to self-stimulating behaviour like rocking, head-banging, and pulling out hair. They often sit or lie motionless, or are irritable.

ATTACHMENT BEHAVIOUR

Neglected and rejected children do not show distress and do not protest when they are separated from their parents. They tend to go with anybody and do not discriminate between known and unknown persons. While in hospital or in a foster-home, they tend to relate in a similar way to a nurse or a foster-mother. However, they appear to be insecure and unable to move freely to explore the environment in an organised and purposeful way. They either cling to the parents or aimlessly run about in a disruptive fashion. They also appear to be frightened and anxious.

Attachment is assessed in a situation unfamiliar to the child in the presence of the mother, and the child's reactions to separation from, and reunion with, the mother are observed. Two patterns of insecure attachment have been identified: anxious-avoidant infants and anxious-resistant infants (Ainsworth, 1980 and Aber & Cicchetti, 1984). Anxious-avoidant infants treat the mother and stranger alike and avoid the mother upon reunion. Anxious-resistant infants show little curiosity about their surroundings, and they often struggle or become rigid when being comforted. It is suggested that anxiously attached infants are more difficult to care for, and in turn their mothers have been found to be less sensitive and less responsive to their babies. Abused and neglected children will cling to their mothers and/or show negative effects like screaming, fear, apprehension, and rigidity. It has been postulated that maltreatment during infancy produces an insecure attachment over a period of time that adversely affects the child's later intellectual and socio-emotional development (Ainsworth, 1980; Steinhauer, 1983).

EARLY CHILDHOOD

The major developmental task at this stage of life according to Erikson (1965) is the attainment of a sense of autonomy. The child begins to function as an individual, doing its own thing and trying new skills. The child is trying to make sense of the environment and tries to control it:

striving for mastery and control often reaches a peak between 2 and 3 years of age. Children struggle with the conflicting needs within themselves and against parental control. Toddlers and older toddlers (2–5 years of age) are, at the best of times, a handful, and require constant supervision and a lot of patience from their parents. Not for nothing are they referred to as 'terrible twos', and parents often find them demanding and exhausting. Their apparently endless energy, explorations, questions, displays of negativism, temper tantrums, and ambivalence are often perceived by parents as oppositional behaviour and sheer naughtiness, leading to interactional problems and distortion of the parent–child relationship. Pre-school children's cognitive, emotional, and intellectual developments require sensitive and supportive conditions to promote the abilities of those children. Parents should allow the child to persist in trying to experiment with autonomy. This helps to build up a strong foundation of self-confidence and delight in independent behaviour. But, as a child is a learner, parents need to be available for them to give instruction, guidance, offer a helping hand (although this is not always accepted), to teach, cajole, merit, and praise. Parents need to allow the child to try tasks that may be beyond it at that stage, for only by encouraging the child to engage in new tasks can the parents hope to promote the youngster's sense of competence. Continual discouragement and/or criticism of a child by parents inculcate an overwhelming sense of shame and self-doubt in that child. Such children lack confidence in their abilities to perform, and they expect to fail at what they do. In order to avoid criticism they refrain from all kinds of new activities. As a result, the process of learning new skills becomes slow and painful. Feelings of self-confidence, a sense of achievement and self-worth are replaced by constant doubting and consequently developmental delays. Maltreated children tend to develop an unfavourable self-image: they do not like themselves and tend to believe that they are to blame for whatever goes wrong around them. Positive self-attitudes are the basic ingredients of positive mental health, and negative self-concepts are among the critical predispositions of maladjustment. The way parents treat children will determine what those children think about themselves. The expressed attitudes and behaviour of the carers will provide vital information to the children about their achievements, goodness, and worth. Living up to parental expectations (or always failing to do so in the case of over-critical or hostile parents) will become part of their self-concept (Herbert, 1974).

The major hazards for optimal development during this stage are parental unavailability and hostile restrictions (which interfere with the child's acquisition of personal adequacy and development of skills such as speech, locomotion, toilet-training, competencies in eating, dressing, and playing, self-control, and ability to discriminate between emotions in others). Social behaviour with peers and adults tends to be more aggresive on the one hand and withdrawn on the other. Since such children are deficient in social maturity due to persistent abuse, their interaction with other children is fraught and problematic. Their attachment, similar to that of infants, is indiscriminate and unselective. They tend to attach themselves to anybody who shows attention and kindness, and long for physical contact and affection. Neglected toddlers are rather inactive and deficient in social skills.

Severely emotionally abused and neglected children do not communicate with their carers and, at times, are completely mute. They tend to ignore their requests and do not respond to parental attempts to engage them in conversation. Language development appears to be most affected in deprived environments: since relationships between the emotionally maltreated child and its siblings are marked by hostility and avoidance, there is little opportunity to practice language skills at home. These children spend a lot of time in social isolation, away from normal family interactions, and this does not promote communication and the development of interpersonal behaviour. Prugh and Harlow (1962) describe this dilemma as 'masked deprivation', where the child is physically at home but emotionally does not belong there. Home observations show that the target child is seldom included (in a positive way) in everyday family interactions. There is a physical distance between parents and the child, and between siblings and the target child. Siblings do not play or communicate with it, and tend to be aggressive and dismissive. The child usually stands 2–3 yards away from them, watching (when the parents are present) or being disruptive (when the parents are not around). Again, the child is seldom seen being close to the others, is never played with, or placed on the mother's lap. Most emotionally abused children are isolated from the rest of the family in order to discipline them: they are often locked up in their bedrooms for many hours as a punishment for any misdemeanour.

Acute emotional abuse and neglect can affect a child's physical growth in terms of poor weight, height, and head circumference. Rapid improvement and acceleration is evident when they are removed to a caring and affectionate environment, such as a foster-home or hospital. A change in social, cognitive, and language development is also observed, although it is not as rapid as physical growth. There is a need to be alert to cruel punishment which is not always visible, but manifests itself as a consequence of maltreatment (for instance as recurring infections and colds caused by being deprived of bed-clothes because of bed-wetting, or by being put into cold water for soiling).

MIDDLE CHILDHOOD

The most commonly identified developmental deficits among 5- to 10-year-old emotionally abused and neglected children are in the areas of academic achievements at school and their ability to relate to the peer group (Salzinger *et al.*, 1984). These researchers found that the maltreated children in comparison with the control sample were two years behind in verbal performance and maths abilities. They also found that maltreated children were seriously failing in one or more subjects and had to have some remedial teaching. Additionally, they discovered that the siblings of maltreated children were also the subject of poor school performance. The latter seems to suggest that academic achievements might be curtailed by a home environment unconducive to learning. It might also be associated with little importance being placed on academic achievements in these families. Belsky (1980) stated that social and family factors (associated with child abuse and neglect) might contribute to the developmental deficits generally. These factors might include: marital strife, lack of social support, inappropriate supervision of children, and irregular school attendance.

In her study of emotionally abused and neglected children, Iwaniec (1983) found that the parents showed a lack of interest in their children's achievements and performance and demonstrated a serious deficit in stimulating and providing opportunities for these children to learn and acquire new knowledge. Out of 17 children 12 experienced learning difficulties and had poor academic attainments during their primary education. Teachers found that these children were unable to concentrate and to pay attention to the given task. Their problem-solving abilities were poor as was their ability to read and write. Six of these children were educationally statemented for special education. Social behaviour in the classroom was marked by aimless overactivity, disrupting their own and their peers' learning.

Teachers find children like this attention-seeking on the one hand and detached and uninvolved on the other. They desperately try to be noticed and accepted by their peers and teachers, but the way they do this is usually aggressive and disruptive. Therefore they are often excluded from the peers' play in the playground and outside school activities. They are seldom invited to the birthday parties of other children and are seen as not worthwhile to have around or with whom to make friends. In order to compensate for their rejection by peers some of them will try to become particularly close to the teachers or other adults in the school, like dinner ladies or secretaries: they try to offer assistance (like carrying books or equipment), and tend to follow them around just in case they have the chance to be helpful, appreciated, and wanted. They tend to volunteer to do various tasks at school, or to compete in sport or other competitions, even though they have no abilities to do so. Emotionally abused children, in many cases, show longing and desire to belong and to be wanted, but lack social skills to get themselves into a circle of peers. Disruptive and aggressive behaviour as well as an inability to observe the 'rules of play' eliminate them from the peer group. Those children who are not performing well academically and who are criticised by the teachers are not easily accepted by their peers.

Additionally, some emotionally abused and neglected children suffer from encopresis and enuresis, and because they smell they are pushed away and rejected by their classmates. Thus the child who has incontinence problems will be isolated and perceived as dirty and revolting. Teachers, too, tend to view them as unpleasant, undesirable, and impossible to manage in the classroom situation. Sadly, teachers and parents alike tend to believe that soiling and wetting are deliberate and/ or the result of sheer laziness to go to the toilet on time, and not because of emotional disturbance brought about by maltreatment. These children might run away from school as a result of ill-treatment there, or might exhibit self-harming behaviour (like scratching to the point of bleeding, wounding with knives or sharp objects, persistent rocking, head-banging, and burning, to mention a few examples) similar to that of psycho-social dwarfs.

All these children, without exception, suffer from very low self-esteem and low self-worth, and their attempts to be accepted, wanted, appreciated, and loved have been unsuccessful at home and often at school. Low self-esteem demonstrates itself in uncertainty, constant doubting, a sense of guilt, a belief that everything which is unfortunate or problematic is their fault, apologising for everything (whether or not they were responsible for what went wrong) verbally or by writing little notes for parents saying that they love them and they are sorry for being 'bad'. Emotional abuse can also affect a child's physical growth (although not in all cases): it is not unusual to find some children small and thin for their age and showing disturbed eating behaviour (see Chapter 3).

CONCLUSION

It would appear that emotional abuse and neglect may have an overriding role in poor developmental attainment and may contribute significantly to the development of emotional and behavioural problems in children. Neglect and rejection during infancy are associated with insecure and anxious attachment, which (if it persists) may impair a child's intellectual, cognitive, social, and emotional development. At the toddler stage, maltreatment of this kind may delay language development and distort personality formation, peer-relations, and social adjustments. In middle childhood, the maltreatment will contribute to poor performance at school, learning difficulties, lack of motivation, and behaviour problems (Brassard, Germaine, & Hart, 1987; Garbarino, Guttmann, & Seeley, 1986; and McGee & Wolfe, 1991).

5

ATTACHMENT AND BONDING IN CASES OF EMOTIONAL ABUSE

A slavish bondage to parents cramps every faculty of the mind *

INTRODUCTION

Parental bonding refers to a loving, close, and committed relationship with a child which provides the foundation for a child's attachment to its parents. This very special relationship will determine the quality of and ability to form subsequent relationships with other people and provides a base for secure and optimistic learning about the world around the child. The presence and availability of parents to whom the child is attached reduces the child's anxiety in stressful situations. (Bowlby, 1969)

Maternal bonding is typically shown by the mother's behaving in a certain manner towards her baby, such as fondling, vocalising, smiling, picking up, touching, kissing, gazing, responding to the child's signals of distress, and the like. A mother would be considered to be bonded to her child if she looked after it well, gave it considerable and considered attention, saw willingly to the child's physical and emotional needs, and got considerable pleasure out of these actions.

Bonding implies a very special emotional relationship between two people which is specific and endures through time. It implies personal sacrifices given freely and willingly, and a high level of tolerance and patience. It also implies unconditional love and caring attitudes (which, on the mothers' part, are quite likely to last a lifetime). Maternal bonding

---

*Mary Wollstonecraft (1759–97): *A Vindication of the Rights of Woman* (London: J. Johnson, 1792), Chapter 11.

implies a special and focused relationship towards the mother's own child. But one needs to recognise this quality of specialness and to be able to assess it. One assumption of a bond might be based on a mother's own statement of her attitudes and feelings towards the child. The practitioner might feel that a mother is bonded to her child if she constantly (over a period of time) states that she loves her child, and has a sense of mutual belonging. On the other hand, if she reports indifference or hostile feelings towards the child (and does not feel that they belong to each other), she would be judged unattached and rejecting. Words, however, do not always match with action, so bonding should be assessed in terms of deeds. To judge whether a mother or father is bonded to her or his child, and whether they love it, is a more complex problem than meets the eye because bonding has many facets and is not a unidimensional attribute. Some parents are reserved and undemonstrative, so the physical and emotional contact is restricted: this, in turn, might be interpreted as unloving or even rejective behaviour, yet the parents are devoted and deep down do love their child. Some, on the other hand, might be tired and overwhelmed with the new and never-ending responsibilities of child-rearing, and even get depressed, so their physical and emotional availability to the child will be restricted due to their weakened condition and not because of their lack of affection or commitment. Some are outwardly loving but neglect their children. Those mothers could be said to be loving, but their behaviours related to bonding are qualitatively different.

MATERNAL BONDING

It is generally believed by many paediatricians, midwives, social workers, and psychiatrists that mother-to-infant bonding takes place rapidly after birth because the mother sees her offspring, touches it, holds it, feels it, and gazes at it: such beliefs clearly must influence practice. Many writers suggest that if this process proceeds reasonably well, the mother will be 'bonded' to the child by an enduring, responsible, and focused emotional attachment. It is believed that the quality of their future relationship is determined by their physical (skin-to-skin) contact during the first *post-partum* hours or days. In the case of mother-and-infant separation after birth, there is often considered to be a risk of failure on the part of the mother to become 'bonded' to her child (for example, Klaus & Kennell, 1976).

The close-contact, critical-period bonding theory is said to be justified on two grounds: one is rooted in studies of animal behavour; the other has to do with observations of human mothers, comparing those who have had little or no contact with their newborn babies with those who have extended contact.

However, there seems to be no reliable evidence that skin-to-skin contact is necessary for the development of mother-love, and, what is more significant, that mother-to-infant bonding does not depend on such contact occurring during a sensitive but short period after the birth of the baby. Most mothers, of course, want to see and hold their babies after they have given birth. Most mothers will be delighted, and will experience very strong emergent pleasant feelings that they have produced a new human life which belongs to them. Nevertheless there is a substantial number of women (especially first-time mothers) who feel confused and uncertain of their feelings: some say they feel 'nothing'; others that they are relieved it is all over (but do not show any excitement about the baby); while many are exhausted after a long labour, and, at times, difficult pregnancy. In many cases, it will take a while before a mother begins to feel a sense of belonging and love towards the child: mutual awareness and familiarity develop gradually.

Love, the joy of having a baby, and pleasure in seeing it grow and develop take time. Love grows strong as a baby begins to respond to a mother's nurturance and care. It would seem that learning to love and to belong comes quickly for some but for others more slowly; the range of individual differences is wide.

It needs to be recognised that maternal bonds and relationships have their own complex, many-sided developmental histories, stretching over many years. Among the factors which can influence the way a mother relates to and behaves with her child are her age, her cultural and social background, her own experiences of being parented, her personality, her previous experiences with babies, her desire to have the child, and her experiences during pregnancy and birth. It is also important to remember about the support system which is required during the first few months of a child's life. Lack of advice and guidance as well as of a 'helping hand' can lead to excessive tiredness, depression, and distortion of a perhaps still fragile relationship. If the baby happens to be difficult to feed, to get to go to sleep, cries a lot, and gives little rewarding feedback, the bond between mother and child will be weak, and furthermore those difficulties can lead to emotional and physical neglect and abuse. It would appear that successful bonding has little to do with the mother's contact with her baby immediately after birth, but more with the subsequent quality and quantity of interaction between them. The child's reactions to the mother—the joy of seeing her, responding to her care and attention, benefiting from her nurturance in healthy growth and vigorous development—will powerfully influence the way she feels about her offspring and the way the mother feels about herself as a parent. The magic of a secure and unquestionable maternal bond of love will be formed.

DISTORTION OF MATERNAL BONDING IN CASES OF EMOTIONAL ABUSE AND NEGLECT

The absence and/or distortion of mother-to-infant bonding during the early stages of the child's life are often considered to be major aetiological factors in various forms of child maltreatment. Emotional abuse and neglect are commonly hypothesised to result from poor parent–child relationships, and, more specifically, from the inability of parents (the mother in particular) to build up and maintain a significant and loving contact with a child. Emotional indifference is evidenced by the restricted quality and quantity of parent–child interaction. Unreasonable (and often angry and negative) parental child-rearing practices are considered to seriously affect the child's physical growth and psychological development.

Emotionally abused or neglected children do not seem to be attached to their parents, and parents appear to be distant from them. Insecure attachment to parents from these children is observed quite often by a lack of proper stranger-anxiety when they are left with people unknown to them. They can tend to go with anybody and do not show signs of distress when separated from their parents. They may also tend to cling to the parent in an attention-seeking way. Parents are not only emotionally unavailable, but quite often openly and cruelly dismissive. It will also be true to say that usually only one child in the family is disliked or rejected in a more intensive way, and, furthermore, the onset of these negative and damaging feelings starts early in a child's life. It can be said that the child's attachment to the parent is weak and insecure when the parental bond of love has not been established. Why is this so? Why are some mothers, while able to build up a caring and loving relationship with their other children, unable to form the same bond with that particular child? Did the child come at the wrong time into the family? Is there something specific about the child which makes him/her difficult to rear and to love? The fact is that the mechanism and the very nature and conditions of attachment of children to parents are still rather poorly understood in of quite an extensive literature on the subject over the last four (for example, Bowlby, 1951, 1969; Rutter, 1972; Schaffer, vorth et al., 1978).

While the concepts of parental bonding and infant attachment have received considerable attention in literature, empirical research in this domain has been limited to mainly average middle-class populations. Attention to abnormal development has resulted in the observation of only a narrow range of responses, mostly concentrated on emotional development in the first year of life. Such limited conceptualisation (when it comes to considering maternal deprivation) encourages a view of the infant as a passive victim of the mother's distorted or insufficient caretaking and lack of bonding; a view which is at odds with recent risk research on the infancy period (Sameroff & Chandler, 1975). Bullard *et al.* (1967), following Ainsworth (1962), broaden the concept of maternal deprivation to include various forms of 'distortion in the mother–child interaction', giving it a developmental context. These authors note that maternal behaviour which may be 'depriving' for the child at one developmental stage, may be experienced very differently by the child at another. This view stresses the interactional qualities of the infant–mother relationship and raises the question of the infant's contribution to his/her own vulnerability, and also perception, understanding, and attribution of events as the child matures.

Carlsson *et al.* (1979) are among the earliest researchers to study infant-to-mother attachment in emotionally and physically neglected children. Twelve infants, 12 to 19 months of age, and hospitalised during the first year of life (with a diagnosis of non-organic failure-to-thrive), were compared with matched controls and observed in a modification of the Ainsworth 'Strange Situation'. Subjects and controls were matched on age, race, sex, socio-economic status, and social class.

Classification by means of the Ainsworth 'Attachment-Scale' revealed that six of the 12 index-children were classified as insecurely attached while only two of the 12 controls were so classified. In addition, there were no cases in which a non-organic failure-to-thrive subject was rated as securely attached while his/her matched control was rated 'insecurely attached'. While the sample size of the study is quite small, these results indicate that half of the patients with the non-organic failure-to-thrive diagnosis were experiencing conflicts of sufficient severity in mother-to-child bonding to be judged as 'insecurely attached'.

The Iwaniec (1983) study of 17 children who failed to grow (and two control groups) revealed acute problems in maternal bonding in seven cases. Emotional indifference and outright rejection dominated the mother–child relationships, while a further six children were emotionally and physically neglected. Quality of physical and emotional care was poor. These mothers showed little interest in their children, and reported difficulties in caring for and enjoying them. The remaining four mothers reported and demonstrated reasonably strong ties with and concerns about their children. Mothers of children who failed to grow differed substantially from the control groups in terms of affection and sense of belonging, and expressed less pleasure in the baby. There was less sense of the child being lovable; less time was spent interacting with the child; mothers did not find it enjoyable to pick up, talk to, smile at, or play with; and they were less demonstrative in showing affection towards the child.

However, the hypothesis of the sensitive period (e.g., seeing, touching, holding the child immediately after birth) as an essential factor for mother–child bonding, is not supported by this study. Fifteen index-mothers did see their children and were allowed contact with him/her after birth. Only one child was in a special-care unit, compared with seven from the first and three from the second control group: they had no other histories of early postnatal separation, and their birth-weight on average was 6 lbs 9 oz or 2.933 kg (which is slightly below the national average on weight of 7 lbs or 3.17 kg). There were no significant differences between the groups in the way the mothers felt about the child after delivery, yet both control group mothers were 'bonded' to their children significantly more than the index group—in the traditional sense of feeling strong, enduring, affectionate ties. Why should this be? What went wrong in establishing loving, caring, enjoyable relationships with that particular child? Index-group mothers reported several difficulties which they felt contributed to the way they felt about their child:

(1) difficulties in feeding—refusal to eat (they felt that the child rejected them as they would not accept the basic nurturance);
(2) poor growth and development of the child (they felt that they were blamed for it);
(3) lack of child's responsiveness to their attempts to interact with them;
(4) irritability and crying;
(5) poor sleeping patterns;
(6) lack of help, support, and advice during the early stages of the child's life;
(7) inability to comfort the child or to distract it when crying or in a bad mood;
(8) intensity of the child's negative reactions to the socialisation processes;
(9) little rewarding feedback from the child, proximity-seeking, or cuddliness;
(10) exhibition of negative moods—which was persistent; and
(11) the mother's feeling of helplessness and depression.

Learning might be a key to understanding problems of bonding. Specific love tends to develop slowly, providing it is reinforced positively by the child by his/her overtures (of wanting her, needing her, enjoying her, being around), then the bond will grow stronger and stronger. Equally, the mother, in order to enjoy the child, must see the positive effects of her efforts in child-rearing. If that does not happen, for whatever reason, she would perceive herself (as would the people around her) as inadequate, neglectful, and uncaring. She will see the child as a major and deliberate contributor to the creation of miserable feelings and her failure as a parent. As time goes on, instead of growing closer together they will grow apart, feeling mutually resentful and rejective.

PARENTAL REJECTION

Rohner (1986) describes rejection as a form of parental behaviour characterised by the absence or withdrawal of warmth and affection. Rejecting parents often dislike, disapprove of, or resent their child. In many cases they view it as a burden, comparing it unfavourably with other children. Rejection can be expressed in many ways, and can take many forms. For some children rejection means callousness and indifference, neglect, hostility, and even cruelty: for others it may be more subtle and covert, with even more complicated emotional convolutions. Two examples are given below to illustrate two forms of rejection:

(1) a two-and-a-half-year-old toddler was persistently punished by his mother for wetting or soiling himself by putting him into a bath of very cold water even during freezing winter weather, and keeping him in the water for 30 minutes or so until he was blue with cold: at the same time, she would criticise, shame, shout, and scream at him. She would also frequently deprive him of sweets and other treats in order to demonstrate to him her dissatisfaction with and dislike of him;

(2) after the birth of her daughter, the mother (who had a well-established career) became resentful of her new maternal role, and, apart from the bare essentials of feeding and washing (which were in any case of poor quality), she kept the child isolated in her bedroom and would not respond to any signals of distress. As the girl grew older she was often told she was unloved, unwanted, and threatened with desertion whenever the mother felt particularly angry. The child lived in a permanent state of anxiety and fear.

The absence of warmth and affection is revealed in two principal ways. The first is by means of open or disguised hostility or aggression towards the child. The second is expressed by indifference, which is often manifested as neglect. Parental hostility is an internal emotional reaction of anger, enmity, or resentment towards the child, and may reveal itself in forms of overt physical or verbal aggression. Hostile parents, for example, may be irritable towards their child, critically impatient or antagonistic: they may curse it, or speak to it in a harsh, deprecating tone of voice. Hostile-aggressive parents may also be very rough or abrupt in their handling of their child, and they may punish the infant often and severely. Punishment *per se*, however, is a form of parental rejection only insofar as it is a clear expression of hostility or aggression towards the child.

A rejected child is likely to be more dependent, more clinging, more intensely possessive, and more seeking of parental approval, nurturance, attention, and physical contact than the accepted child. All human beings have a basic need for positive responses in others, but if a child's 'significant others' are rejecting, and if its needs for warmth and affection are unfulfilled, the child will, up to a point, increase its efforts to attract love and attention. In other words it will become dependent. Beyond a certain point the dependency-responses may be extinguished. The point here is that the seriously rejected child has no opportunity to learn how to express love, because it has never known a loving parent after whom it can model its own behaviour, and, even though it may crave affection, it may have difficulty in accepting it when it is offered. In order to protect itself from more emotional hurt, it tends to insulate its emotions, and ultimately stops trying to get affection from the people from whom it craves. Thus the emotionally abused child becomes emotionally isolated, unable freely and openly to form warm, lasting, and intimate relationships with others. Its attachments tend to be troubled by emotional constriction or defensiveness: in addition, as a result of the psychological damage brought about by maltreatment, the child will have less tolerance of stress.

Such children are apt to become resentful of, or angry with, their parents, as well as being fearful of more rejection, and thereby evolve a 'defensive' independence of, or emotional withdrawal from, the parents. Such a pattern of behaviour by a child initiates a process of counter-rejection by the parents. Behind a child's defensive independence or emotional detachment can often be an unrecognised longing to re-establish a warm, nurturant relationship with the parents. The child is especially likely to be hostile, aggressive, or passive-aggressive if rejection takes the form of parental hositility. Under these conditions the child is provided with an aggressive model to emulate, and thus its own aggressive responses may intensify. Ineffectual and rejecting parenting is likely to show up in disturbance of eating patterns, toilet-training, and general compliance, as these are the first tasks of every child's socialisation. So if the child is unloved it will become unloving, and the parents and child will become mutually antagonistic (Rohner, 1986).

CONCLUSION

As has been indicated above, attachment disorders, therefore, are strongly evident in maltreated children. Their social behaviour is marked by aberrant features such as withdrawal, detachment, lack of connection with activities in the immediate surroundings, depressive reactions, indiscriminate sociability, apprehension, stupor, irritability, and distress. Their interaction with care-givers is marked by ambivalence, avoidance, or indifference on the one hand, or by attention-seeking on the other.

Some maltreated children become aggressive more quickly when frustrated, show fewer socially-acceptable behaviours when interacting with other children, and show lack of concern when peers are distressed (Herrenkohl & Herrenkohl, 1981). Zeanah and Emde (1994) point to the aberrant behaviours which have been observed in hospitalised infants who are failing-to-thrive. They state that 'there is little question that many of these infants are raised in emotionally deprived environments' and 'exhibit expressionless faces, abnormal gaze' (hyperalert, undirected eyes, avoidance, lack of interest), 'lack of smile', and 'lack of directed' vocalisation. Powell, Low, and Speers (1987) pointed to the intensity and frequency of the behaviours mentioned above, and noted that they are more common in infants who fail to thrive than in a comparison group of hospitalised infants who are growing normally. The same findings were registered in Iwaniec (*Child-Care in Practice*, 1994).

Children diagnosed as having reactive attachment disorders, when removed from the abusive care of their parents, accelerate in their development and gradually establish (but very slowly) an attachment to new care-givers. This can take a long time, as confirmed by the long-term follow-up by the present writer on five children who were removed from the care of their parents (due to rejection).

6

CHILDREN'S CHARACTERISTICS AND PARENT–CHILD INTERACTION

How sharper than a serpent's tooth it is
To have a thankless child! *

INTRODUCTION

Parent–child interaction is a two-way process which powerfully affects the way parents and children relate to each other, perceive each other, and influence each other's behaviour. The quality and quantity of mutual interaction is not only determined by parental behaviour towards the child, but also by the child's input (whether positive or negative) that affects this two-way process. Many research findings demonstrate that children, by the nature of their physical or psychological make-up, can exert an influence on their parents' interactions and feelings (Bell, 1968; Bell & Harper, 1977; Schaffer & Emerson, 1964; Thomas & Chess, 1977; Herbert, 1989).

A number of children have characteristics that mismatch with their parents such that temperamental or inborn factors may (for some parents) make their child difficult to rear and to enjoy. Each child has an idiosyncratic pattern of behaviour (an individual way of responding to its environment) which is not totally determined by the way the child is

---

*William Shakespeare (1564–1616): *King Lear* (1605–6). Act I, Scene 4, Line 312.

brought up, or where, or by whom. Certain in-born attributes can seriously worsen relations between parents and children: congenital characteristics (like irregularity in biological functions, unadaptability, hypersensitivity, withdrawal responses to new stimuli, high intensity, and frequent bad moods), can make them particularly difficult to care for and to rear. The child's characteristics and its responses can arouse pride, or, alternatively, resentment, guilt, or helplessness in parents, and what has started (in some parents) as a willing and well-motivated parenthood might end up in resentment, abuse, much misery, and harm to all concerned (especially to the child).

Of course we cannot blame the child for being born prematurely (and therefore posing problems of care), for having temperamental attributes or intellectual potentials, or for being physically or mentally handicapped (and therefore possibly not very attractive or appealing): these are not the fault of the child, but equally we cannot blame the parents for experiencing at times serious child-rearing and child-care problems. Nevertheless such children are vulnerable to parental mismanagement, and, in some cases, to parental maltreatment. Early recognition of children's vulnerability can serve as a warning of future serious problems developing between parents and children and of later psychiatric disorders (Rutter, 1987).

Parents of children who are difficult to rear need help, advice, support, and understanding if we want to prevent maltreatment and promote a child's well-being. It is the omission of early intervention that often leads to harmful consequences on a short- and long-term basis. Parental pleas for help when faced with difficulties of child-rearing are only too often dismissed (or are dealt with in a cursory fashion), which brings more tension and confusion to struggling parents. It is often apparent that anger, disappointment, or unfulfilled dreams of a perfect child are turned against the child. A downwards spiral of destructive interactions rolls on, destroying even more a weak relationship between child and parents. In order to understand some of the interactional difficulties that can arise between children and parents it would be worthwhile to examine some of the research findings regarding temperamental attributes and their effects on child-rearing, on the development of a warm, loving, and caring relationship between parents and children, and on the socialisation processes.

ASSOCIATION BETWEEN TEMPERAMENT AND BEHAVIOURAL DISORDERS

The debate into the definition of temperament over the last 30 years or so is still unresolved (Goldsmith & Alansky, 1987; and Bates, 1989).

However, a major influence on the study of temperament and behavioural development has been the work of Thomas, Chess, and Birch (1968), based on their New York longitudinal study and elaborated since (Thomas & Chess, 1977; and Chess & Thomas, 1989): they view temperament as neither purely genetically circumscribed nor environmentally determined, but as an interaction between predispositions and external influences. The infant is considered in a much more positive way as a proactive and competent being, and its own contribution to shaping its environment from earliest infancy is taken into account. These researchers conducted systematic interviews with parents to elicit their children's day-to-day behaviour. Nine categories of behavioural style (that is, how the child behaved, rather than what it did) were derived from an inductive analysis of the initial interview protocols. These categories are:

(1) activity level or energy output;
(2) rhythmicity of biological functions (sleep-and-wake cycle, hunger, satiety, etc.);
(3) approach to or withdrawal from new situations;
(4) intensity of emotional reaction (e.g., whether the child roared with laughter or smiled quietly);
(5) threshold of sensory responsiveness;
(6) adaptability (that is how easily a child's behaviour changed in response to altered circumstances);
(7) quality of mood;
(8) distractibility and attention span; and
(9) persistence.

Researchers found they could distinguish three clusters of temperamental characteristics on the basis of these attributes, which were grouped under the terms 'difficult', 'easy', and 'slow-to-warm-up' babies. The difficult child showed irregularity in biological functioning, a predominance of negative withdrawal responses to new stimuli, slowness in adapting to changes in the environment, a high frequency of expression of negative moods, and a predominance of intense reactions. The easy child, on the other hand, was positive in mood, highly regular, low or mild in the intensity of reactions, rapidly adaptable, and usually positive in its approach to new situations: in short, its temperamental organisation was such that it usually made early care very easy. The third temperamental type—the slow-to-warm-up—showed low activity-levels combined with negative responses of mild intensity to new stimuli with slow adaptability after repeated contact. An infant with such characteristics differs from the difficult child in that it withdraws from anything new quietly rather than loudly. In addition, it does not usually exhibit the intense reactions, frequent negative moods, and irregularity of biological functions of the difficult child. The authors found that 65% of their sample could be assigned to one of the three general types of temperament. Some 40% were 'easy', 10% were 'difficult', and 15% 'slow-to-warm-up'. That left about 35% of children showing a mixture of characteristics not fitting into any of the three groups. A factor-analysis based on inter-correlations on the nine categories of behavioural style identified a factor which had high loadings on mood, intensity, approach/withdrawal, and adaptability, and showed relative consistency over the first five years of life.

A comparison of the clinical and non-clinical groups showed that over the first five-year period, and beginning at about the third year, the clinical group began to deviate markedly from the non-clinical group in the direction of negative moods, marked intensity, tendency to withdraw, and unadaptability. Children who possessed these patterns of behaviour became known as 'difficult children', and were far less likely to grow up without behaviour problems. (Of the temperamentally difficult children 70% were reported to develop such problems compared to 31% of the whole group who developed problems.)

Two studies in Britain produced similar results. Rutter *et al.* (1964) followed a group of children from infancy and compared characteristics of behavioural reactivity of the 21 who came to psychiatric notice with the 71 who did not. The clinical cases differed significantly from the others in that they were more irregular, non-adaptive, intense, and exhibited more negative mood. Further, these temperamental characteristics were present before the onset of the overt symptoms, and did not themselves constitute the first signs of behavioural disturbance. Graham, Rutter, and George (1973) assessed 60 children, aged between three and seven years, from working-class families in London (each of whom had at least one mentally-ill parent) for both temperamental difficulties and behavioural disorders. They again found that certain temperamental characteristics (especially low habit-regularity, low adaptability, and high-intensity fastidiousness) were predictors of the development of later psychiatric disorders. They argued that effective prevention is more likely if we can identify which children are most at risk, and suggested that there is a link between adverse temperament and adverse family attitudes and relationships. Their findings supported the notion that a child by virtue of its personality structure requires handling geared to its individuality if it is to stand the best chance of avoiding the development of psychiatric disorder.

Cameron (1977) has measured the interrelationship between various risk dimensions (child temperament-change scores and eight parental dimensions of behaviour) over a 5-year period. The parent dimensions include:

(1) parental disapproval, intolerance, and rejection;
(2) parental conflict regarding child-rearing;
(3) parental strictness (i.e., permissiveness);
(4) maternal concern and protectiveness;
(5) depressed living standards;
(6) limitation on the child's maternal supports;
(7) inconsistent parental discipline; and
(8) large family orientation.

Children's temperamental scores (when correlated with eight parent domains) revealed that parental intolerance, inconsistency, and conflict were associated with negative temperamental changes. Strictness and maternal concern/protectiveness correlated with both positive and negative changes depending on age and sex. Parental disapproval, intolerance, and rejection showed the strongest association with both yearly temperament scores and change scores across the first five years.

Carey (1972) developed a short questionnaire form for parents covering the infancy period and utilised it to study the relationship of temperament to certain behavioural symptoms in infancy. In an unselected sample of 60 infants of six-months-of-age, he found a significant correlation ($p<0.02$) between night-waking and low sensory threshold. He suggested two possibilities to explain this correlation:

(1) that greater responses to stimuli in the day make the infant continue to be arousable at night; and
(2) that the infant is more responsive to internal and external stimuli at night as well.

Carey suggested that 'maternal anxiety, anger or feelings of helplessness' may be the result rather than the cause of the baby's waking.

Ross and Ross (1976) have identified a syndrome of behavioural disturbance which they designate as 'the unorganised child'. According to Ross and Ross this syndrome results from a combination of high destructibility, short attention-span, and low persistence in the child in interaction with disorganised functioning or over-permissiveness in the parent. If the unorganised child also has a high activity level it may show restlessness and a tendency to chatter disruptively. If it is less active it may daydream, and if it is intense in its reaction it is likely to show temper tantrums.

Although some characteristics may always put the child at risk, many may be adaptive or maladaptive according to circumstances. For example, overactivity, as demonstrated in the study by Herbert and Iwaniec (1981), was among the main contributory causes of serious conduct disorders and under-achievement at school. But, in a study of institutionalised infants, Schaffer (1966) found that the most active infants were the ones who were least likely to show developmental retardation. Obviously there are degrees of activity—and up to a certain level an active child has adaptive attributes which are attractive and enhance learning and social interaction. Hyperactivity, on the other hand, is generally disliked, and difficult to cope with, by adults.

TEMPERAMENT AND MOTHER–CHILD INTERACTIONS

Most studies of parent–child interaction have assumed (or at least implied) that it is parents who exert the sole (or major) influence on children. A number of writers (Bell, 1974; Herbert, 1974, 1989; Dodge, Bates, & Pettit, 1990; and Earls, 1994) have argued that interaction is a two-way affair in which children also help in significant ways to shape parental behaviour. The validity of this notion has been shown over the years in a variety of rather different studies. For example, Levy (1958) found in a study of nursing mothers that each mother's behaviour towards her infant was considerably influenced by what state the baby was in when brought for feeding—whether awake or asleep, placid, or irritable. Yarrow (1963) found that the maternal behaviour of a foster-mother was altered by the attributes of the infant placed in her care. Different infants elicited different maternal behaviour so that the amount of stimulation and comfort provided by the foster-mother varied with an infant's temperamental characteristics. Rutter (1977) reported that active infants in a neo-natal nursery got more attention from the nurse than did inactive infants (an observation which helps to explain Schaffer's findings that more active infants were less affected by depriving environments because they elicited some stimulation).

Physical or developmental handicaps in the child may also influence parental behaviour. Chavez, Martinez, and Yaschine (1974) found that malnourished children were often ineffective in gaining parental attention. Similarly, it appears that children with congenital handicaps receive patterns of parenting which are somewhat different to those experienced by normal children (Cummings, Bayley, & Rie, 1966). In addition, there is some evidence that a child's level of language skills influences the nature and extent of parental communication (Siegel, 1963;

Siegel & Harkins, 1963; Spradlin & Rosenberg, 1964; and Iwaniec, 1983, 1994).

There is some evidence that children's temperamental characteristics help shape parental behaviour. Osofsky and O'Connell (1972) manipulated the extent to which children exhibited dependent behaviour by varying the level of difficulty of the laboratory tasks they had to perform. They found that when the children were being dependent their mothers interacted more with them, both verbally and physically, and displayed more controlling behaviour. Thus it is possible to suggest with some conviction that a potentially significant factor in the development of behaviour problems is a temperamental or congenital factor in the child, and one which has powerfully modified the parents' interactions and the manner in which they have reared it. This influence can range from the trivial to the height of significance (see Harper, 1975). Sameroff (1975) was able to find confirmation of the hypothesis that characteristics of the child may predispose parents to aversive interaction with the child, leading to physical and emotional abuse and neglect: he stated that breakdowns in the parent–child relationship can take a great variety of forms.

> ... the most heavily researched and carefully documented of these transactional failures related to the inability of parents and children to work out an interactional style which both guarantees the child a reasonable margin of safety and satisfies the child's basic biological and social needs. This is the issue of child abuse. Physical abuse is dramatic evidence of a disorder in the parent–child relationship ... (Sameroff, 1975, p. 275)

It is not difficult (although one must always be cautious in doing retrospective analyses) to see how the attributes causally associated with a disorder might have had their earlier effects on parents. The highly irregular child who never settles to steady sleeping or eating routines poses particular problems for its mother, who will find it difficult to arrange her life, precisely because her child is so unpredictable. The malleable child who easily adapts to changes and new situations is likely to be very much easier to bring up than its non-adaptable sibling whose behaviour is so tiresomely difficult to alter. Because children with these attributes are difficult to rear, they may well arouse more irritation and the parents may come to expect problems because they have occurred before. Both expectations may become self-fulfilling in their effect on the child, and so a vicious circle is created. Parents become increasingly unrewarding to their offspring; the child becomes increasingly attention-seeking and demanding ... and so on.

Numerous studies have reported a relationship between temperament and a variety of developmental outcomes, especially behaviour disorders of various kinds (Carey, 1986; Garrison & Earls, 1987; Rutter, 1987; Prior & Leonard, 1989; Kyrios & Prior, 1990; and Iwaniec, 1983). It seemed that children with adverse temperamental features were more likely to be scapegoated at times of family difficulty. Parental criticism and hostility were strongly associated with the development of behavioural difficulties and psychiatric disorders in children. Parents were highly critical because of their own difficulties which often were not related to their child's behaviour (many parents were chronically depressed), and tended to blame the child for all the ills in the family. Statements often heard were 'if it were not for him/her, we all would be much happier', or that 'life would be much easier'. We know, however, that children react to painful parental handling in a way that might be perceived by an angry or disillusioned carer as oppositional and deliberately naughty behaviour. Furthermore, carers often feel that the child is hurting them, and does it on purpose to punish them for lack of affection. Some parents perceive an undemonstrative child as rejective and dismissive of parental attempts to create physical and emotional closeness. Often parents tried to justify their limited contact with the child by saying 'she or he is happiest when I leave her/him alone: when I pick her/him up, or just try to love her/him, she/he cries and seems to be very uneasy'. Observation, however, shows that parental handling more often than not is rough, impatient, noisy, and anxiety-provoking. It is not surprising that the child shows resistance and avoidance behaviour when in its parents company or when being approached by them. The misinterpretation of the child's reaction (or the lack of it) is at the core of emotional maltreatment and at the centre of the distortion of a positive loving relationship. The worrying aspect of distorted parental perceptions is the child's social isolation which damages the development of pro-social behaviour and emotional well-being.

Of course some children are much easier to love than others because they are lively, responsive, and interesting. More of an effort may be required to love a passive, inert, and unresponsive infant who seems to 'give little back' or is tiring to look after (Herbert & Iwaniec, 1978; Iwaniec, 1983).

Parental behaviour is not merely instinctive. Parents need the child to look at, to cuddle, to smile and respond to their overtures, and if, for any reason, the child does not do that, being a parent may be more of an effort. The kind of problem that can arise is illustrated for example by the Klaus, Leifer, and Leiderman studies (Klaus et al., 1972; Leifer et al., 1972; and Leiderman et al., 1973), which showed that mothers of small premature babies who were separated from them in the first few weeks of life (because they were in an incubator or an intensive care nursery) tended to be less confident and less attentive to their babies. This effect probably arose, in part, from the fragile, rather unresponsive nature of very premature babies, and partly from the lack of contact with the baby during the early period when mothering skills and familiarity with the baby normally could be developed. Some studies, tangential to those mentioned above, have worrying implications: they suggest that in any one family it is the children born after difficulties in pregnancy or delivery and who were separated from their mothers in the neo-natal period who are disproportionately represented in the population of child victims of abuse (e.g., Lynch, 1975).

The significance of differences in temperament (or behavioural style) is underlined by research which demonstrates the releasing effect and initiating role exerted by the behaviour of the child on its parents (Schaffer & Emerson, 1964; and Bell, 1971). The reciprocal interactions of parent and child are in a state of constant adjustment as each positively or negatively reinforces the other. Willingness to reward or punish, for example, are not qualities inherent in the parent but are elicited in large part by a particular child and its behaviour. These are vital factors in the various learning situations encountered by the child (Herbert, 1978, 1989).

It is not, of course, a simple matter of some children being difficult and some easy. It is also a question of interaction with parental attributes. Although there are some children whom nearly all parents would find rewarding and easy, and some who would pose problems for practically anyone, there are many whose characteristics lead to less consistent responses. Some parents like a lively, active, mischievous child, but others may find it wearing and prefer a quieter and less active youngster. Accordingly, in assessing parent–child interaction it is necessary to determine how each responds to the other, and which attributes they find rewarding and which aggravating. These will not necessarily be the same in all families. Help, in terms of advice and counselling, is needed here to prevent the development of negative attitudes and destructive misinterpretation of a child's reactions. It seems possible that stress resulting from a mismatch between the parents' temperaments (including their annoyance threshold) and the child's behaviour style sets the stage for discord, conflict, nervous exhaustion, and eventual feelings of inadequacy as parents. Frustration, guilt, anger, rage, despair, and worse are likely outcomes.

These concerns have led to efforts to develop ways of measuring sequences of parent–child interaction (see Lewis & Rosenblum, 1974). It is not enough to measure, for example, how much the mother talks to her child; it is also necessary to determine the extent to which she does so in response to cues from her infant. The characteristic of being able to 'read' babies' behaviour and interpret their communications is an important part of parenting (Bell & Ainsworth, 1972). Of course responsiveness is, in part, a function of parental characteristics, but also it is likely to be influenced by the clarity and consistency of the signals provided by the child. These considerations were very much in the author's mind in the observations she made in hospital wards and in the children's homes during assessment and treatment.

TEMPERAMENT AND FAILURE-TO-THRIVE AND EMOTIONAL ABUSE

Serious interactional problems have been found in failure-to-thrive children and their parents (especially mothers) in a few studies (Leonard, Rhymes, & Solnit, 1966; Pollitt, Eichler, & Chan, 1975; Pollitt & Eichler, 1976; Herbert & Iwaniec, 1979; Skuse, 1985, 1988; Iwaniec, 1983; Iwaniec, Herbert, & McNeish, 1985a, 1985b; Iwaniec, 1994; and Powell, Low, & Speers, 1987). These authors reported extreme (and maladaptive) maternal reactions to the rearing difficulties created by various behavioural styles in their children. There seem to be marked individual differences in coping behaviour. Active, vigorous, irritable, hypertonic, stubborn, and demanding children showed severe disturbances in relationships with their mothers, with considerable fighting and anger, especially in feeding situations. Mother–child interaction was noisy, hostile, tense, and often angry, which had negative effects on child food-intake and subsequent food-refusal. Quiet, lethargic, withdrawn, undemanding children were seldom interacted with: there was little physical and emotional contact, and they were often overlooked or ignored. They were described by their mothers as rejective: maternal interaction with such children was passive, silent, or indifferent.

These researchers also reported examples of a 'temperamental mismatch' between mothers and children. Some parents, exuberant and energetic themselves, could cope with—and enjoy—an active, noisy baby, but not a passive withdrawn one. A quiet, rather passive mother might find the former rather tiring and hard work. Iwaniec (1983) found that 60% of the children studied were described by their mothers as difficult to manage, and burdensome from early on in their lives. When the temperamental type and parental style of interaction and attitudes were examined, interesting correlations emerged. Of the index-group 72% adapted slowly to all changes, specifically to changes in food, so probably when solids were introduced they were not given enough time to get used to new tastes and textures. On the carers' side, in the interactional process of feeding, food was pushed in with a high degree of impatience and anger. An active child during feeding makes the task more difficult, for such children dislike being held: many of the children were 'squirmy', and holding by mothers was too firm and restrictive. The children were unpredictable in their biological functioning, so the routines of sleeping, eating, and so on were difficult to establish, the mothers found them tiring, and caring for them was time-consuming. They were difficult to enjoy because of their moodiness, irritability, and high-intensity reactions. Their crying was loud and prolonged, and the parents reported their inability to 'jolly' them out of a bad mood or to distract them. The mothers of these children often said that 'when he/she gets into an awkward mood in the morning, he/she can be like that all day'.

The analysis of the casework data revealed that the most intensive negative reactions to feeding and other child-care duties were shown by the temperamentally 'difficult' children. It is of interest and importance to point out that it was the mothers of these children who manifested the most negative ways of interacting with their offspring, most of whom were disliked or rejected. Maternal handling was forceful, impatient, and angry. The clashes between these mother–child pairs were frequent, intensive, and, as time went on, mutually antagonistic, resulting (in some cases) in the complete breakdown of a fragile relationship. It is of importance to point out that these children developed psycho-social dwarfism, probably due to acute parental rejection. Mothers of the slow-to-warm-up children tended to be passive, lacking in determination, or unassertive and unpersistent; they were inclined to get discouraged, were often reduced to tears, and were unable to cope emotionally with the problem (for example, if the child refused to eat or to sleep, or when it cried). The mother's interactional and caring styles in the cases of 18% of easy children and 12% falling into no particular clear-cut category of temperamental characteristics, were, wittingly or unwittingly, neglectful. They seemed to be unaware of or insensitive to their child's physical or emotional needs, and themselves came from very deprived and neglectful homes. They basically lacked appropriate models of parenting and knowledge of child-care.

Among 34 listed behavioural problems, those of the acting-out (including behaviours such as non-compliance, aggression, commanding, temper-tantrums, etc.) and the 'deficit' kinds were prominent, and a dramatic difference was found between emotionally abused or neglected children and both control groups. The average number of behaviour problems manifested by the index children was 5.9 per child, while there was only 1.8 in the first control group, and 0.9 in the second control group.

Looking at the combination of various forms of the mother–child interactions, plus the child's temperamental characteristics, there is some evidence to suggest that the mismatch between a child's temperament and its parents' ability to manage produces clashes, which over time (if help is not provided in the early stages) leads to serious consequences. Of children classified as difficult 30% gave evidence of:

(1) angry and hostile parental interactions, especially at feeding/eating time;
(2) complete refusal to take feeds from the mother, with resulting starvation;
(3) a high risk of physical abuse of a more serious nature (12% were abused); and
(4) bruising in all cases.

In addition:

(5) 30% were cruelly treated (for example, locked up for several hours, held in dark places (such as cupboards or cellars), denied food, forced to watch others eat, and put into baths of cold water for soiling and wetting);
(6) 12% were committed into care having suffered physical and emotional abuse; and
(7) 27% were on the child-protection register.

These children showed more behavioural problems and emotional disturbance: it is important to point out that hospital staff and some foster-mothers and daily-minders also found them difficult to manage and rather unappealing. However, the old 'chicken or egg question' concerning what comes first needs to be carefully examined. Was the child's difficult behaviour triggered off by parental anxious or hostile reactions towards the child, or were these inappropriate reactions influenced by the child's behaviour? The answer might be that both parties influenced each other, but it is the child who is always a victim of those clashes. These vulnerabilities need to be identified in order to prevent further harm to a helpless child: because a child is difficult to rear and to care for does not give parents 'a licence' to abuse and to neglect. A child cannot defend or protect itself: the only way it can fight back and show its uneasiness and confusion is by disturbed behaviour.

Slow-to-warm-up children on the other hand were found to present more serious developmental retardation—most notably in language, social, and cognitive areas. They were also found to be the most emotionally deprived and isolated from family activities and interactions, especially from the mother and siblings. Significant differences in the father–child interactions were found between the groups. Fathers played and talked less often with their offspring and seldom picked them up. The children's unresponsiveness, or frequent negative moods, prevented (as the fathers reported) a close and more enjoyable contact. Additionally, frequent arguments with their partners regarding the child management did not facilitate positive attitudes towards the child.

CONCLUSION

What can reasonably be inferred from these studies is that children differ in their susceptibility to problem-development as they grow older. It is not likely that any precise combination of temperamental characteristics *per se* leads to the appearance of a behaviour disorder—rather it is the interaction between these characteristics and the child's environment which eventuates in psychiatric referral. Parents faced with a temperamentally difficult child tend to find the task of socialising with the child more exacting than the broad spectrum of parents, and they need to be more resourceful and patient from the earliest stage (see Stayton, Hogan, & Ainsworth, 1971).

The mother–child interactions need to be positive and mutually rewarding through the process of positively reinforcing the child's desired behaviours and discouraging undesired behaviours, with the objective eventually of internalising the child's moral and social codes and rules. However, many parents blame their children for being what they are. They tend to interpret their behaviour as deliberately destructive and troublesome. Parental attitudes towards the child tend to become negative as expressed by constant criticism, nagging, smacking, screaming, and shouting, as well as by physical and emotional distancing from the child. One can see how a long and painful journey of emotional abuse and neglect can emerge and intensify.

There is no doubt that some children are more difficult than others in terms of being reared and enjoyed, but those difficulties do not constitute a permission or excuse for maltreatment. The responsibilities lie with the parents and with the child-care services. Parents who are faced with a particularly difficult child need help, and this help should be provided when it is requested, or when attention is being drawn to child-rearing difficulties being experienced and at the onset of the development of problems.

II

ASSESSMENT OF EMOTIONAL ABUSE AND NEGLECT

7

ASSESSING EMOTIONAL ABUSE AND NEGLECT

*If we desire to change something in a child, we should first consider if that
something could be changed with benefit within ourselves**

INTRODUCTION

As we have seen, emotional abuse and neglect are not easy to recognise,
and they are even more difficult to prove. Assessment, therefore, in terms
of evidence-collecting and arguing their harmful effects on children, is of
great importance. Assessment is usually based on semi-structured
interviews, direct observation, and occasionally on psychometric tests
and questionnaires. The latter, however, apply more to research projects
than day-to-day practice.

Interviews with parents and children (of appropriate ages), as well as with
those involved with the family, can provide significant information. Direct
observation of the family in its natural environment is necessary to assess
living conditions, the level of functioning, and the quality of physical and
emotional care provided for the children. Home observation also provides
data on family interaction, and especially on the target child and its
parents. Comprehensive assessment requires a few sessions, gathering
information from the family and agencies involved in the case (if any).
Since referrals involve investigations of the alleged emotional
maltreatment of the child, it is essential to explore parental attitudes
towards the child, child-rearing practices, parental experiences stemming
from their own childhood, parental expectations of the child, commitment
as parents, and various life-stresses. Listening to and hearing the parents,
observing family reactions and behaviours (the ways in which, how, and

*Carl Gustav Jung (1875–1961): 'Vom Werden der Persönlichkeit' (1932), *Gesammelte Werke*
(Olten: Walter-Verlag, 1972), Vol. 17.

what they communicate to each other and how they relate to each other) are at the core of trying to make sense of what is going on in the family system.

If assessment is to provide relevant information for planning intervention- and treatment-strategies, then parental expression of difficulties experienced with the child and perceptions of the various problems need to be taken seriously in order to create the required change for the sake of the child. The assessor needs to be open-minded, objective, and non-judgemental. Assessment should identify parental and family strengths and weaknesses as well as capacity, willingness, and ability to get actively engaged in the therapeutic process. Resources and support-systems should be identified at this stage as well. Honesty, clear free-of-jargon communication, and full engagement of parents in the assessment process help to elicit relevant information about a child's dilemma and its parents' predicaments.

Assessors, however, need a sound knowledge about emotional abuse and its effects on children in order to gauge what he/she is looking for and how to provide well-informed arguments in courts, care conferences with other professional groups, and, above all, for parents and children.

Manifestation and identification of emotional maltreatment have been discussed in previous chapters. Many assessment issues have already been dealt with, so this chapter will provide a framework for the assessment task. Some useful checklists and a typical sample of an emotional-abuse assessment report will be provided.

FRAMEWORK FOR ASSESSMENT

- *Reasons for referral*:
  —who referred the case?
  —what were the concerns expressed?

The Family

(1) *Family composition*:
   (a) description of the family (parents' age, occupation, employment, place of work); and
   (b) number of children (with age, sex, date of birth and school).
(2) *Living conditions*:
   (a) descriptions of accommodation, cleanliness, space, and material standards; and
   (b) description of the neighbourhood and facilities available.

(3) *Financial position*:
    (a) earnings and benefits (some families may need help to supplement existing earnings, or are entitled to benefits of which they are not aware);
    (b) management of money and budgeting; and
    (c) prioritising of spending.
(4) *Family background*:
    (a) length of the marriage or living together;
    (b) family movements (the number of times they have moved house and the reasons for them);
    (c) employment- and education-history;
    (d) health of each member of the family or other significant problems;
    (e) relationships with parents and siblings when the parents were children (their experiences and memories of being neglected, unloved, rejected, or abused);
    (f) child-rearing experienced by the parents as children;
    (g) similarities and differences of child-rearing (the ways in which the parents were brought up, and the ways in which they are bringing up their own children);
    (h) expressions of affection and care within the family;
    (i) family unity and closeness; and
    (j) do the parents keep contact with their parents and siblings and do they ask them for help and support when they are needed?
(5) *Marital relationship*:
    (a) stability and length of the relationship;
    (b) mutual support and help in every-day tasks;
    (c) communication and affection;
    (d) role-distribution regarding child-rearing;
    (e) history of violence and abuse between spouses; and
    (f) alcohol- and substance-abuse.
(6) *Support and help available for the family*:
    (a) frequency of contacts with neighbours and friends;
    (b) use of local resources and facilities;
    (c) use of child-welfare agencies;
    (d) use of child-rearing literature;
    (e) activities, hobbies, and use of opportunities of outside contacts; and
    (f) use of recreation facilities for children.
(7) *Physical and emotional state of the parents*:
    (a) health problems, if any (recent operations or treatments);
    (b) depressive moods;
    (c) clinical depression;
    (d) apathy and dissatisfaction with life;

(e) loss of career or income; and
(f) current stresses in the family.

Parents and Children

(1) *Parent–child relationship and interaction*:
   (Direct observation and guided semi-structured interview)
   (a) how much physical and emotional contact the parents have with the child;
   (b) quality of parental contact with the child;
   (c) nature of parent–child interaction;
   (d) expressed parental attitudes towards the child;
   (e) emotional mutuality between the child and its parents;
   (f) sense of belonging and togetherness;
   (g) sense of security and the child's freedom of expression and movements;
   (h) affection towards the child; and
   (i) commitment to and protection of the child.
(2) *Child-rearing practices*:
   (a) punitive or lax use of discipline (examples of disciplining the child);
   (b) unrealistic expectations (do parents expect too much from the child or too little);
   (c) supervision and guidance;
   (d) clear and fair rules and routines;
   (e) interest in the child and the child's well-being;
   (f) affection, warmth, and support;
   (g) teaching life-skills and -tasks;
   (h) knowledge of child-rearing methods;
   (i) willingness to learn and to change;
   (j) importance attached to child-rearing; and
   (k) family strengths and weaknesses.
(3) *The child*:
   (a) pregnancy and birth:
      (i) parent–child bonding (secure—insecure).
   (b) early child-rearing difficulties:
      (i) feeding and eating problems;
      (ii) sleeping problems; and
      (iii) persistent loud crying.
   (c) child's development and growth:
      (i) psycho-motor developmental delays;

     (ii) poor physical growth (failure-to-thrive); and

     (iii) psychosocial dwarfism.

(d) child's temperamental characteristics:

     (i) difficult or slow-to-warm-up temperament; and

     (ii) child's resistance to socialisation tasks.

(e) child's behaviour:

     (i) non-compliance or overtly compliant behaviour;

     (ii) self-harming and destructive behaviour;

     (iii) disturbed eating behaviour;

     (iv) poor self-control and short concentration-span;

     (v) unresponsiveness and attention-seeking; and

     (vi) irritability.

(f) child's emotional problems:

     (i) fear, severe inhibitions, and apprehension;

     (ii) detachment, depression, and sadness;

     (iii) soiling and wetting;

     (iv) mutism;

     (v) child's pro-social behaviour and strengths; and

     (vi) child's weaknesses and lack of appeal.

REASON FOR REFERRAL

During initial contact with the parents an explanation should be given as to why assessment is taking place, how the referral came about, and how the assessment is going to be conducted. The manner in which information is given should be calm, honest, and showing concern for the whole family. For example, the interview may be started by saying:

> Your G.P. asked us to see you regarding John's difficult behaviour and the way you feel about John. I understand that his lack of speech and his toileting behaviour worries and annoys you, as well as his non-compliance. Your G.P. believes that you both need some help. I will need to see you three or four times to find out more, what the problems are, and how we can deal with them

The type of questions that are going to be asked should be described briefly, as well as stating who needs to be seen regarding the child, such as school teachers, health visitors or other relevant people. Parents may be asked to agree to keep a diary or records of specific behaviours and events. The preliminary interview should be well-planned, especially where resistance and hostility are expected.

The Family

Semi-structured interviews and direct observation usually provide the necessary information about family functioning, current living, and financial circumstances. It is useful to explore financial difficulties, housing problems, and employment at an early stage of the assessment process for two reasons: firstly, these difficulties may genuinely portray why the quality of care is not adequate for the children, and, secondly, the exploration shows parents that the therapists have an interest in them as people with difficulties, and not just in the child. This approach 'opens a door' for further and more personal sharing of information and concerns.

Family Background

This should cover recalling each parent's individual memories and experiences from their childhood—the ways in which they were treated by their own parents; affection, attention, discipline, sense of belonging, and unity bestowed upon them; and parental availability. It is advisable to interview each parent individually, as there might be some aspects of their history that they do not want their partner to know. Sexual abuse as a child is one of them, while a minor criminal record, health problems, and so on are others. Being able to obtain a good background history is important for organising and prioritising intervention. For example, parents who received poor physical and emotional care themselves (and who never had an opportunity to experience a better way of child-rearing), might need help in parent-training on individual and group-work bases, while those who were persistently criticised and degraded by their parents (and suffered as a consequence from a very low self-esteem), may first need cognitive restructuring and help in raising self-efficacy.

Those who strongly believe that inflicting psychological pain on their children as a means of disciplining, and as a method of making them conform and achieve, is perfectly correct (because they themselves were treated in that way as children) might need psychotherapy and cognitive restructuring. Their education and history and some knowledge of their own parents' attitudes towards education may be useful.

Marital Relationship

Information regarding a couple's relationship can be elicited by separately interviewing each partner. Direct observation can also shed some light on the quality of their relationship, conflict regarding child-rearing, communication between spouses, and the level of affection shown in everyday life. It is important to tease out information regarding physical violence in the relationship, such as threats and cruelty inflicted by one partner on the other. Physical violence on wives and the emotional cruelty and restrictions imposed on some women are substantial, and these in turn dramatically affect children and therefore need to be brought to the surface. Use of alcohol and drugs needs to be considered.

The interview should include a discussion of task distribution between parents and their perception of how they should help each other, and of who should do what. The husband's time spent with the family, his engagement in household tasks, and his support and affection for his wife need to be explored. Deficiencies in these areas can be successfully dealt with if identified as problematic.

Support and Help Available for the Family

Available support-systems for the family need to be identified. For instance, do the parents use their extended family, friends, and neighbours when they experience personal difficulties or have problems with their children? Do they feel confident and assertive enough to request help from the child-welfare agencies, or church and community organisations? Do they feel lonely and isolated in the community in which they live? Is this isolation due to the lack of interest of people living in the neighbourhood, or is it due to a lack of social skills and assertiveness on the part of the parents? (It is useful to find out whether the parents would like to use volunteers as befrienders and helpers: to whom do they turn when in need of help and company?)

Physical and Emotional State of Parents

Many parents, and particularly mothers, suffer from chronic illness, anxiety-states, and bouts of depression, and might have gone through operations or difficult treatment which might have rendered them less able to deal effectively with everyday tasks and stresses. Some women suffer acutely from pre-menstrual tension, while some might find disruption of their professional career depressing and feel resentful as a result. Employment might bring stress, frustration, and a sense of helplessness, while loss of a job and inability to find a new one are found to be major stress factors affecting all the family. Ability to cope with stress and capacity in problem-solving strategies need careful assessment in order to provide training and help in these areas.

Parents and Children

Child-rearing practices and parent–child relationships and interaction are at the core of child-protection and well-being, and therefore require both careful interviews and direct observation. What parents think about their children, the ways they feel about them, and the ways in which they care about them can be observed, even when parents deny cruelty and maltreatment. Some of the questions to cover this area (with checklists examining parent–child interaction and reactive and proactive behaviours) are given below:

(1) What kind of problems do you have with John?
(2) How do you handle these behaviours?
(3) How do you discipline John?
(4) Describe rules and routines in your family;
(5) Do you praise John and show pleasure in his achievements?
(6) Do you hug, cuddle, or kiss John?
(7) How often do you speak and do things with him?
(8) What do you like about him? Describe those likeable qualities to me;
(9) Do you enjoy his company? If so, why?
(10) Are you proud of him? Why?
(11) What are your expectations of John?
(12) Do you correct and guide him?
(13) How do you help him to learn different life-skills and tasks such as eating, dressing, toilet-training, playing, and speaking?
(14) How much time do you spend with him, and what do you do when you are together?
(15) Can you describe John to me? What is nice about him, and what do you find difficult?
(16) What do other members of the family think about John? How do they get on together:
   (a) mother?
   (b) father?
   (c) siblings?
(17) Did you want John? Was he planned?
(18) What kind of pregnancy, labour, and birth did you have with John?
(19) What was he like as a baby in terms of: feeding, sleeping, contentment, crying, and health?
(20) Did you feel very close to him when he was a baby?
(21) Can you tell me when he sat, crawled, walked, said his first words, made his sentences, and became toilet-trained?
(22) What were the major difficulties when he was a baby?
(23) What are the major difficulties now?
(24) How would you like to change the present situation?
(25) What assistance and help do you need to make things work for John and the family?
(26) Would you be prepared to work towards improving your relationship with John?

EVENT-RECORDING OF PARENT–CHILD INTERACTIONS

Visit No _____ Assessor _____ Name of client _____

CHILD'S REACTIVE AND PROACTIVE BEHAVIOUR	OFTEN	SELDOM	ALMOST NEVER
1. playing freely 2. laughing/smiling 3. running 4. talking freely 5. coming for help 6. coming for comfort 7. cuddling up to parents 8. responding to affection 9. responding to attention 10. at ease when parents are near 11. joining in activities with other children 12. not frightened when approached by parents or corrected			
FATHER'S/MOTHER'S REACTIVE AND PROACTIVE BEHAVIOUR	OFTEN	SELDOM	ALMOST NEVER
1. talking to the child 2. looking at the child 3. smiling at the child 4. making eye contact (loving) 5. touching (gently) 6. holding (closely, lovingly) 7. playing 8. cuddling 9. kissing 10. sitting the child on the lap 11. handling the child in a gentle way 12. giving requests (as opposed to commands) 13. helping the child if it is in difficulties 14. encouraging the child to participate in play and other activities 15. being concerned about the child 16. picking the child up when it cries or when it is hurt 17. answering the child's questions 18. not ignoring the child's presence 19. emotionally treating the child the same as other children 20. handling children consistently			
SIBLINGS' REACTIVE AND PROACTIVE BEHAVIOUR	OFTEN	SELDOM	ALMOST NEVER
1. playing with the child 2. talking to the child 3. participating in activities 4. accepting the child 5. treating the child well 6. pushing the child away and rejecting it 7. blaming the child for everything that happens 8. protecting the child 9. helping the child when in difficulties or in trouble 10. scapegoating the child			

Source: Iwaniec (1983).

ASSESSMENT OF PHYSICAL AND EMOTIONAL NEGLECT: QUALITY OF CHILD-CARE AT HOME

Physical Care of the Child

(1) is the child appropriately dressed for the weather?
(2) is the child's clothing clean?
(3) is the child's clothing regularly changed?
(4) is the child washed and bathed?
(5) is hygiene at home reasonable?
(6) is a cot/pram/bed available and clean?
(7) are sleeping arrangements appropriate?
(8) is the room warm?
(9) is safety observed, such as fire, electric-points, sharp objects, medicine, chemical substances, etc.?
(10) are supervision and guidance for the child provided?
(11) is medical attention provided when the child is not well?

The questions below may help to assess non-organic failure-to-thrive and nutritional neglect. Failure-to-thrive assessment should also include parent–child interaction during the process of feeding and other child-care activities.

Nutrition

(1) is the child regularly fed?
(2) is the child given enough food?
(3) is the child given appropriate food?
(4) is the child handled patiently during feeding/eating?
(5) is the child encouraged to eat?
(6) is there reasonable flexibility in feeding/eating routine?
(7) is there evidence of anger, frustration, and force-feeding during the feeding/eating period?
(8) is the child punished for not eating?
(9) is there awareness that the child is too thin?
(10) is there concern about the child's well-being?
(11) is there evidence of seeking help and advice?
(12) is there evidence of responding to help and advice?

SAMPLE OF AN ASSESSMENT REPORT

Bob (age 8 years)

Reason for Referral

Bob was referred by the health visitor, followed by the headteacher, as a result of growing concern about his well-being and acutely disturbed behaviour at school and at home.

Family composition

Mrs S.—24 years, single mother, housewife.
Bob—8 years, at school.
Brian—4 years.
Liz—2 years.

Living conditions

The family occupied a 3-bedroomed town-house type of council property on a comparatively new part of an estate. The small open-plan downstairs living accommodation was clean and reasonably tidy. The furniture bore scars from Bob's behaviour. The bedroom shared by the boys was badly marked and damaged by Bob.

Financial position

Mrs S. relied on D.H.S.S. payments and 'manages'. Bob's eating habits put a strain on the food budget; she sometimes ran out of food during the week because of this.

Family background

Mrs S. came from a working-class family of three brothers and three sisters. She described her childhood as very unhappy and stressful. She and her three sisters were sexually abused by her father from a very early age. The father was not legally challenged for his behaviour, but the parents divorced with the mutual agreement that he would not see his wife or the children again. Mrs S. did not remember her age at the time of the parental divorce, but put it down to a pre-teenage period. She described her father as a violent and demanding person who ruled the house by fear and terror. Mrs S.'s mother openly planned to pick up men to arrange marriages for her daughters. She tried to get her daughters off her hands as soon as possible after they were 16 years old, and apparently succeeded with two of them. Mrs S.

met the man picked for her when she was 12, and the mother encouraged a sexual relationship with him. Mrs S. conceived Bob when she was 15. Soon after Bob was born the relationship with the man broke down, and Bob's father left. Mrs S. moved to live with her mother. When Bob was two, Mrs S. met another man and moved with Bob to live with him at her mother's insistent request. She described the first year of that relationship as good. When she conceived Brian her partner became violent and resentful of her and of Bob, and she and Bob were beaten by him. After Bob received a fractured collar-bone, Mrs S. fled to a women's refuge, fearing that the Social Services would take Bob away from her. The cohabitee pursued them there, so they were moved to another one in a different town, but were pursued by him there as well. Eventually they were given a house 50 miles away and she ceased contacts with her family, as she felt it was her mother who directed her partner to her each time she tried to escape from him. Mrs S. had another short liaison with yet another man, resulting in the birth of Liz. When Liz was one year old Mrs S. met a new boyfriend, but they did not live together.

Mrs S. described her inability to trust men, having been sexually and physically abused by her father, but this mistrust became more acute after the episodes of violence with Brian's father. She deliberately broke off the relationship with Liz's father (because she was frightened of a permanent relationship) when her pregnancy became obvious and Bob began to show signs of distress. Mrs S.'s latest relationship was also difficult because she could not show any sign of affection to her partner, and began to treat his demonstrations of affection as a joke, although there was no evidence to suggest that he was not genuine about his feelings and commitment.

Mother's health

Mrs S. was having complications with an inter-uterine contraceptive device. She suffered frequent heavy bleeding and pain. She was waiting to have the device removed when the bleeding stopped. She frequently felt unwell and listless, and this affected her ability to cope with Bob's difficult behaviour.

Availability of support and social contacts

Mrs S. had a good working relationship with the health visitor, and maintained constructive contact with Bob's school teacher and headmaster. She had extensive contacts with her neighbours, babysitting and doing various tasks for them. This help appeared to be one-sided, and she was apparently being used by some of her friends to a great extent. They borrowed things and seldom gave them back, and she babysat, did shopping or even cooked meals for them, with little return. She recognised this, but felt that, on balance, she was not lonely and had a lot of people around her.

Bob's history

Pregnancy and birth—no problems throughout, but delivery was by Caesarian Section.

Development

Bob was described as a very placid and easy baby. He rarely cried and he fed well. His motor and language skills, social development, and toilet-training were achieved within the normal range, and no specific difficulties were experienced during the first two years of his life.

His mother described Bob as an attractive and cuddly baby and toddler. She spent a lot of time playing and doing things with him (which they both enjoyed), and he seemed to respond well to the stimulation and mutual contact. When Bob was two-years-old Mrs S. moved to live with Brian's father, and although they got on well for the first few months all that changed when she became pregnant with her second son. Bob's behaviour changed suddenly and dramatically. He became withdrawn, confused and almost mute. He appeared to be terrified all the time, and used to cringe when approached (especially when by his step-father). When they moved to the first refuge, he was still withdrawn and refused to speak, and in the second refuge he became aggressive with the other children there. He also had serious sleeping difficulties, waking frequently in a panic, slept only for short periods, and eventually refused to go to bed. During investigations a few things were disclosed. His step-father tried to drown him in the bath, and killed his dog by hanging it on a door-handle to show him what was going to happen to Bob if he said anything to his mother and other people. It was believed that Bob was sexually abused by his step-father, but no conclusive evidence was produced to support strong suspicions. The fact that Bob's step-father vanished and could not be found prevented further investigation. Bob's mother (feeling responsible for Bob's maltreatment) used to let him have whatever he wanted, as she was trying to compensate for what had happened to him. Bob's behaviour become progressively worse and more disturbed. He would stop strangers in the street and say that his mother was ill-treating him.

With the help of the health visitor Bob was admitted to a school for disturbed children, where his behaviour continued to be difficult. When the family moved to their own house (he was four-years-old then) Bob killed the canary and seriously hurt a puppy which had to be given away for its safety. Bob was also expelled from a play bus because of the level of violence of his attacks on other children. At that time the health visitor referred Bob to a child psychologist who found Bob severely emotionally disturbed. A behavioural programme was introduced, but the psychologist then left the area and treatment was abandoned.

Bob started overeating at the age of four, which coincided with the onset of other behaviour problems. He hid food all over the house, searched for food at night, and ate everything in the house, leaving other children short of food.

Bob's behaviour at school

Bob's behaviour at school was very disruptive and aggressive. He could be violent to other children if they said anything he did not like, or if he could not get his own way. His academic progress was quite good: he read well and enjoyed reading, liked writing stories, and his number–work was excellent. His teacher reported that if he was given plenty of work and placed away from other children his work and behaviour were good. Bob ran away from school on four occasions, apparently when he was told off and punished (by not being allowed to play in the playground) for fighting with other children.

Mother–child interaction (from mother's account)

Described as very difficult. Mrs S. said she tried to show affection to Bob, but he either rejected or questioned it, and she found it increasingly difficult to show him love. Some of his behaviour made her very angry, and she sent him out of the room because she was frightened of hitting him too hard.

Mrs S. described his behaviour as extreme, either very, very good or very, very bad. When he was good she warmed to him, and when he was bad she 'blew her top' at him. Mrs S. described a recent incident when she was ill and Bob showed great concern: she was able to talk to him and enjoy his concern for a short time, but he then went and started hitting the other children. Mrs S. felt that some of Bob's bad behaviour was a deliberate attempt to hurt her. She publicly criticised him and tended to put him down. He was also given responsibilities inappropriate for his age (for example, to supervise Brian and Liz during the day and, at times, at night).

Child-sibling relationship (from mother's account)

Bob's relationship with Brian was good until recently; now that Brian is more of an age to be a rival, there is increasing friction.

Bob's relationship with Liz is described as good and protective.

Attitudes to Child-Rearing and Discipline

Described as confused and inconsistent by Mrs S. Particularly in relation to Bob, she tried many different approaches: she said she tried to be firm and kind, but admitted to outbursts of temper and 'letting him get away with things'.

List of Target Behaviours

(1) *Stealing food and overeating*: Bob was given regular meals, which he ate very quickly—these were described as large for his age. He was also given snacks (crisps, sweets, etc.) in between. However, his extreme overeating took place in secret when he stole food (mainly during the nights and in the early hours of the mornings).
(2) *Destructiveness*: smashing furniture, ripping wallpaper, destroying toys, etc.
(3) *Defiance—cheek—showing off*: Bob was no longer taken out because his mother felt his behaviour was so extreme and embarrassing.

(4) *Aggression and violence to other children*: kicking, smacking or pulling hair at school, on the street, in the house, and in the neighbourhood.

(5) *Fire-setting*: Bob set fires twice in the sitting-room, and on other occasions in his bedroom: at one time he set fire to the curtains in his bedroom and burned all his toys.

Functional Analysis

Target behaviour 1. Bizarre eating behaviour

Antecedents	Overeating was apparent most of the time, and occurred both at home, at school, and in other people's houses, more acutely so when his mother was present. Searching for food, and eating enormous amounts of it, usually took place very early in the morning when everyone was still asleep. It happened more often after his mother lost her temper with Bob and punished him.
Behaviour	Bob searched the cupboards for food, he ate large quantities: e.g., 24 Weetabix, two–three pints of milk, a loaf of bread, and jam. If he ran out of milk, he would pick up milk from the neighbours' door-steps. He hid bread, biscuits, sausages, and chips in corners, under pillows or under beds, not only in his own room, but all over the house. He ate quickly and voraciously. At school he would eat left-overs from other children's plates or would put food into his pockets to eat later.
Consequences	The mother tended to react in two ways: either she shouted, smacked him, and sent him to his room without his meal, or her reaction was quiet when she felt low and depressed (particularly if his 'night raid' meant there was nothing for the other children to eat). In both cases Bob showed little response or concern.

Target behaviour 2. Destructiveness

Antecedents	Destructiveness usually occurred after Bob was sent to his room as a punishment, but it happened in other rooms. It was seldom manifested at school or in other places.
Behaviour	Bob smashed things belonging to him (like toys or books), and ripped his clothes and his bedding. He scribbled on the walls or tore the wallpaper (his doodles were usually the same, and resembled a house).
Consequences	His mother's reaction depended on her mood at the time. She shouted, cried, smacked him, deprived him of food, threatened to put him into care or to leave him, and almost always told him that he was no good and was wicked.

Target behaviour 3. Defiance

Antecedents
Defiance could occur anywhere, but most acutely when with his mother and in other people's houses, when he was asked to stop doing something he would do the opposite of what was requested, or ignore the request.

Behaviour
When asked by his mother to do something or to stop an activity, Bob would shout and throw himself about, constantly interrupting his mother's conversation, would be rude to his mother, and, when reprimanded, he would intensify his disruptive behaviour. When his mother was not there he was described by neighbours and friends as very obedient and pleasant.

Consequences
If defiance occurred in the houses of other people, the mother would get very embarrassed and would take him home. At home she screamed, called him names, told him that she could not stand him, and did not love him, or would let him get away with the bad behaviour, depending on how she felt and who was with her at the time.

Target behaviour 4. Aggression and violence to other children

Antecedents
Aggression and violence frequently happened at school (in the classroom or in the playground), when adults were not around, and when Bob got very frustrated (usually when other children would not play with him or when he could not get his own way). They also occurred in the garden or on the street.

Behaviour
Bob hit, punched, and kicked other children (in games, e.g. 'Mummies and Daddies' he usually took the role of the angry Daddy or naughty child).

Consequences
If his mother did not hear about it until much later (e.g., from school), nothing as a rule would happen, but occasionally she would tell him off and would shout at him. When she was told about his violent behaviour by the mothers of chidren with whom he played, she would send him to his room and deprive him of food that day.

CLINICAL FORMULATION

The evidence gathered during the assessment suggested that Bob's severe emotional and behavioural problems were the results of physical and emotional maltreatment, and possibly of sexual abuse.

Frequent moves and the associated fear and anxiety of being pursued by a man who was violent to both mother and child aggravated Bob's already severe emotional disturbance. Mrs S., having run away in order to protect Bob and herself, was unable to understand and to support Bob during this difficult period. His behaviour annoyed and angered her, and more often than not she punished him by withdrawing love, persistently threatening him, and physically pushing him away from her. Mrs S.'s frequent changes of partners and her inability to build and maintain any permanent relationship further reduced Bob's already poor sense of security and permanence: she herself needed help to come to terms with her appalling childhood and long-lasting sexual maltreatment which she experienced then. She had had no true childhood, and the model of child-care she had received ill-prepared her to provide adequate nurturance for Bob after his traumatic experiences when mother and son eventually escaped to safety. Unfortunately, no help was provided for either Bob or his mother at the very time when the child's emotional and behavioural problems began to surface.

Bob's wounds never healed; nor did those of his mother. She was never in a position to help her son by giving him the necessary reassurance, affection, and emotional protection. Bob's behaviour gave cause for serious concern, and it was recommended that he should spend time away from home in a specialist foster-home (on a voluntary basis), and that his mother would receive specialist help and psychotherapy in order to try to resolve her deep-seated problems.

CONCLUSION

Assessment of emotional abuse and neglect covers a wide range of problems associated with family functioning, attitudes towards the child and child-rearing methods, the carers' preceptions and understanding of the needs of the children, and the level and quality of care within the family. There is a need to identify and analyse harmful parental behaviour which damages a child's development and well-being. There is also a need to explore a child's behaviour and individual characteristics that can make it vulnerable to parental mishandling. It is well-known that environmental factors, the physical and mental health of the parents, unemployment, drug- and alcohol-abuse, and the lack of a support-system often contribute to emotional abuse and neglect of children, and therefore have to be taken into consideration during the assessment process.

In order to work out an effective care-plan for a child and its family, we need to have a good understanding of what happens to the child within the family and of what triggers inappropriate reactions in the parents towards the child. Relationships and interactions need to be examined, it is also necessary to establish how these problems have evolved, and how they are maintained. Three penetrating questions (What?, How?, and Why?) should guide the process of assessment. The 'What' question covers identification of the nature of the problems; the 'How' question deals with the manifestations of behaviour by parents and child as well as with expressions of emotion; and the 'Why' question leads to possible explanations for the origins and evolution of the problems.

A wealth of information can be obtained from interviews with parents (and with children of appropriate ages), from direct observation, from clarification of observed behaviour and family functioning, from examination of medical and psychosocial reports, and from communication with the agencies and individuals to whom the child and its family are known.

Emotional maltreatment can occur on its own, but it is always a part of the phenomenon of physical and sexual abuse, and requires assessment of the emotional impact on the child. Comprehensive assessment is essential in cases of suspected emotional abuse and neglect: conclusions should be based on factual data, free from assumption, prejudice, and issues that are not properly understood.

III

INTERVENTION AND TREATMENT

8

STARTING INTERVENTION AND TREATMENT WITH FAMILIES

... The childhood shows the man,
As morning shows the day *

INTRODUCTION

Intervention strategies involving treatment of emotionally abused and neglected children (as well as their abusing carers) can take many steps and forms, follow different routes, and may require several methods and approaches in order to deal effectively and comprehensively with the problems. Intervention in this book is described in four phases as a framework for helping children and parents. The selection of methods will depend on individual needs as well as on the nature and severity of the presenting problems.

INTERVENTION AND TREATMENT OF EMOTIONAL ABUSE AND NEGLECT

Successful intervention and treatment may include the child, the family, groups of parents, and the environment in which they live. Interdisciplinary professional involvement is necessary, as is the use of

---

*John Milton (1608–74): *Paradise Regained* (1671), Book 4, Line 220.

community resources, volunteers, neighbours, and friends. The greater the range the better, as intervention strategies need to be tailored to the specific requirements of the individual families and circumstances. The severity of the presenting problems vary from one family to another, as does the capacity of families to work towards the resolution of those problems.

Resource provision differs from one community to another, as does the availability of back-up services. Intervention and treatment, therefore, should be carefully planned, and negotiated, and a care-package worked out in a way which will address all aspects of child and family welfare. Intervention and treatment may be arranged in four phases according to the individual needs and circumstances of each case. A framework of four phases is outlined below.

PHASE I—CRISIS INTERVENTION

(1) Dealing with developmental deficit and providing safety for the child by:
  (a) arranging attendance at a day nursery or family centre (in part as a safety measure and protection from further harm);
    (i) to provide appropriate stimulation, care, and attention for the child;
    (ii) to facilitate opportunities to learn various socialisation tasks (e.g., play, sharing, toileting, eating, and dressing); and
    (iii) to build up self-confidence and self-reliance when with adults and other children (see Chapter 7).
(2) Counselling:
  (a) helping parents to understand what is going on, helping them to find a way out of the problem and assisting them to look for solutions (empathising, reflecting, and sympathising); and
  (b) raising awareness and insight.
(3) Marital work:
  (a) dealing with dysfunctional relationships, distorted communication, violence, and lack of support or help.
(4) Cognitive restructuring:
  (a) dealing with faulty attribution;
  (b) countering negative beliefs and attitudes;
  (c) correcting unrealistic expectations; and
  (d) helping to generate alternative solutions to self-defeating strategies.
(5) Developmental counselling:
  (a) advice regarding children's needs;

(b) advice regarding developmental needs;

(c) advice regarding norms of development;

(d) identifying milestones, psychosocial development;

(e) coping with development hazards and crises; and

(f) helping children with developmental tasks (stimulation, attention, and encouragement).

PHASE II—CALLING ON COMMUNITY RESOURCES

(1) Volunteers (Home Start; family advice centres; mother and toddler groups; play groups; drop-in-centres; community work centres; neighbourhood centres; babysitting circles; mothers' groups attached to churches; Parents Anonymous—stress line; Family Centres— mothers' and parents' groups; and interest groups for women); and

(2) neighbours, friends, and extended families to provide a helping hand, support, and company.

PHASE III—IMPROVING INTERACTION AND RELATIONSHIPS

(1) Building a child's self-confidence by:

(a) increasing positive interaction by play and other activities; and

(b) reducing negative feelings and avoidance behaviour by getting engaged in mutually rewarding activities and structured interaction. Play and play therapy.

(2) Building a child's sense of belonging by:

(a) increasing physical proximity and emotional togetherness (by holding the child, sitting it on the lap, reassuring, showing tenderness and love, story-reading, and other mutual activities); and

(b) drawing the family together (both parents and siblings) in mutual activity (e.g., play, outings, meals, etc.), paying special attention to the target child.

(3) Building a child's self-esteem and a sense of achievement by:

(a) increasing positive reinforcement by introducing:

(i) *social reward*: praise, show pleasure in the child's achievements, pride, smile, hug, kiss, laugh, etc.;

(ii) *symbolic reward*: child gets a sticker or a token as a symbol of achievement. Stickers should be displayed for everyone to see and praise; and

(iii) *tangible reward*: extra story or game with the parents or siblings, trip to the cinema, swimming pool, football match, or extra pocket money.

PHASE IV—DIRECT WORK WITH PARENTS

(1) Parent training in groups, involving:
  (a) Self-control and relaxation training;
  (b) Stress-management training;
  (c) Assertive and social-skills training;
  (d) Problem-solving training;
  (e) Modelling of tasks and behaviour-management; and
  (f) Rehearsal of tasks and behaviour-management.

Counselling

The main task of counselling is to help parents reflect on the problems they are experiencing and to direct them to a better understanding of themselves and their behaviour. The therapist's aim is to direct clients to personality and behavioural change. Such change arises from the client–counsellor relationship, built on trust and frank discussions. Thus counselling involves rigorous exploration of difficulties, clarifying conflicting issues, and searching for alternative ways to understand and deal with problems. Counselling aims to help people to help themselves. The emphasis is put on self-help, similar to the problem-solving approach, calling on the inner resources of the person who is in difficulties. In order to facilitate the required changes the counsellor should be warm, non-judgemental, empathetic, and respectful to the person involved. The process should not be rushed and assumptions should not be made. Counselling can promote personal growth and more mature ways of acting and reacting, thinking first and responding in a more thought-through way. The therapeutic process here enhances the socialisation and education of parents. Starting the helping journey with counselling is advisable for several reasons:

(1) it lays the foundations for further work and commitment to co-operate;
(2) it provides a forum for the parents to be heard, to describe the way in which they see themselves, and to describe the problems in which they are trapped;
(3) it reassures parents that their needs (and not only those of their children) have been addressed;

(4) it makes them feel cared for and listened to;
(5) it builds up trust and a good working relationship;
(6) it provides the worker with a better understanding of the capacities and inner resources of parents;
(7) it helps to identify their limitations as well as their strengths;
(8) it helps to make realistic decisions regarding therapeutic needs and approaches; and
(9) it helps to make decisions about the children's future, and in which direction intervention should go.

Emotionally maltreating parents are often themselves emotionally and socially deprived, and they have no one to turn to for help: they might be reluctant to approach child-welfare agencies for fear of losing their children. Counselling often helps to reduce that fear and might 'open a door' to more sincere, anxiety-free sharing of true feelings and difficulties. Of course not all parents who maltreat their children can benefit from counselling: disturbed people who have little insight are unable to see or to accept their faults and the point of view of others.

Counselling can also be used in small group work, where a situation or a case is described and group members with their counsellor look for explanations and possible remedies: they are encouraged to view the situation through the eyes and hearts of the children. They are encouraged to recall memories of their own childhood—those which were pleasant and those which were painful, frightening, and anxiety provoking—and their feelings of helplessness and confusion. They are asked to link their early experiences to those of their children in order to make them aware of their children's pain and suffering. The aim is to raise empathy with and insight into what is happening to their children, and to show how things can be improved.

Transfer of Feelings

It has been found useful to put forward a scenario of a fictional child's dilemma, and then to discuss it with parents, pointing to the possible pain and difficulties that the child might have been experiencing. Usually, parents make a critical statement of the way in which the child was treated, and some can identify unfair and maltreating aspects of parental behaviour. Parents are then encouraged to explore with the counsellor similar problems with which they and their children are faced. The aim is to raise an awareness of and insight into what is happening, what the child may feel and experience, and how those experiences may affect the child. Parents are also asked to put themselves into the 'child's shoes' and try to recognise those feelings and begin to empathise with the child. Let us look at the process and content of counselling in the transfer of feelings.

Norman is six years of age. Both parents are very strict and demanding. The child is not allowed to bring any of his friends home or to play outside. He is only allowed to play in his bedroom, and, even then, he is restricted to what he can do and to what toys he can use. He is persistently told off if he asks questions or tries to talk to his parents. He is never cuddled or comforted when upset or not well. He is often criticised in a demeaning manner and punished by being sent to his bedroom for long periods, even for minor misdemeanours. Norman looks very nervous, doubtful, and anxious when in his parents' company.

The parents are asked to build up images of a child who is denied freedom of play and expression, who is frequently criticised and denigrated, and for whom parent–child physical proximity and emotional acceptance are absent. They are then asked to transfer these images to Norman's dilemma in order that they should see and realise how their child-rearing practices affect Norman's well-being. Finally, the parents are encouraged to look at and explore alternative ways of child-rearing with the counsellor.

Recalling Early-Childhood Memories

In order to identify better with the child's plight it is useful to ask parents to try to remember one or two of the most pleasant experiences from their own childhood, and one or two of the most painful. The counsellor tries to link those hurtful (and often still quite vivid) parental memories to the current situation involving their child, pointing to the anxiety and fear-provoking effects of their behaviour on the child. Again, pleasurable memories are linked to future desirable and hopeful parental behaviour towards their child.

Parents tend to remember past unpleasantnesses: examples might include a violent father, deep embarrassments of being shamed and unfairly criticised in front of other people, loneliness and lack of affection, inability to please their parents, being blamed for all ills in the family, being treated differently to their siblings, not being heard or listened to, and so on.

Pleasurable memories of parents tend to cover a wide range: among them might be being taken by parents to the cinema, picnicing, outings, special occasions where they were given attention and felt important or appreciated, feelings of being protected, being played with and read stories at night, and comforted when feeling frightened or ill. What becomes apparent is that those pleasurable experiences were rare, and that the parents felt unloved and unsupported when they were growing up. For some the negative experiences became a norm of child-rearing (as they did not know any better); for others, however, those experiences were seen as correct and appropriate as models for child-rearing. The statement that 'it did not do me much harm, I survived—why should not my child do so as well?' is commonly heard. In most cases, however, a child-rearing deficit is common, which in turn distorts the formation of affectionate and caring relationships between parents and children. Counselling can raise insight-awareness and empathy, which can lay foundations for further work, using a variety of approaches and methods.

Marital Work

Emotional abuse and neglect can come about as a result of marital conflict and a dysfunctional relationship between spouses. If parents treat each other badly, if the atmosphere at home is one of tension, anxiety, and resentment, or if there are frequent quarrels or violence, children will be affected more than parents realise. Such children live in permanent fear, insecurity, and exposure to threats of, and active scenes of, violence. When parents are unhappy and angry with each other they will not attend to their children's needs and emotional nurturing. They might fight about the children, using them as tools to justify their behaviour and reactions. Marital conflict fluctuates between fights and quarrels to 'silent days' when communication does not exist: there is constant tension and a build up of resentment. Emotional maltreatment of children under these circumstances is unavoidable, and therefore intervention is necessary to minimise its affect on them.

There is a variety of techniques available to help families 'at war'. Some counsellors use the 'exchange-theory' approach to deal with marital difficulties: in this theoretical model social interaction and relationships are compared with economic bargains or the exchange of gifts. One partner's activities which may benefit the other are seen as 'rewards', while negative activities, such as hostility and tension, are seen as 'penalties'. The partners are asked to draw up a balance sheet, stating the debits and credits in the relationship. Debits might include criticism, hostility, violence, anxiety, neglect, embarrassment, and so on. The debit–credit outcome must be above the 'comparison level', a standard against which satisfaction is judged (Herbert, 1988). A contract is usually drawn up to obligate the couple to work towards set goals in order to improve their relationship. The counsellor serves as a mediator during negotiations and discussions. Each partner states his or her expectations, desired outcomes, and willingness to meet the other half-way. Compromises need to be negotiated to make the therapeutic process work in a balanced and fair manner.

Greene (1965) proposed the use of Classical analysis, Gestalt therapy, and transactional analysis to help with marital difficulties. Beech (1985) stressed the importance of improvement in the communication between spouses, involving openness and the voicing of dissatisfaction at an early stage so that problems do not accelerate to the point where there is no way back. He suggested techniques such as self-instruction to prepare individuals to deal constructively with confrontations, relaxation-training, and stress-management, as well as the all-important technique of self-control. The art of compromise and the use of positive reinforcement techniques must be learned in order to draw couples together in the enjoyment of each other's company. Sharing tasks and responsibilities on an equal basis and saying pleasant things to each other can only help. If there is commitment and goodwill, those behaviours might be developed or renovated where they have been lost. A skilful counsellor can help some couples to find the way out of a self-destroying maze. In the long run such help will also assist the children, trapped, like their parents, in the downwards spiral of misery and hurt.

Developmental Counselling

Much work with parents involves counselling: this aspect is educational and informative in the sense of disseminating knowledge we have of child-development (for example, what is normal or appropriate to the child's age, sex, and level of ability, and suggesting to parents what are reasonable expectations for their child). The transmission of information about normal child-development and basic child-needs for 'optimal' development is often as important as suggestions about ways of dealing with worrying behaviour. The primary aim is to educate parents, and it is hypothesised that the bringing up of children is itself a skill. Unrealistic expectations on the part of parents as to what the child should, or should not, do often leads to parent–child relationship problems and mal-treatment. When pressure is put on a child to perform certain tasks which it is not developmentally ready to perform, then the child will get anxious, confused, and nervous, which, in turn, may bring about behavioural and emotional problems and a sense of helplessness. Parents often perceive a child as lazy and disobedient, and punish it for non-compliance with their requests: emotional abuse can start here, when parents, dissatisfied with a child's performance, constantly criticise, deprive it of affection and treats, and tell the child off for being stupid, thick, ignorant, or good for nothing.

Parents often compare their children, or compare a child, with those of friends and neighbours, so it is essential to counsel them about individual differences in speed of development and how to encourage a child to learn different skills. Sometimes a simple reassurance that there is nothing wrong with the child, or that a type of behaviour is normal for a particular developmental stage, is enough to change parental perceptions of (and consequently attitudes to) the child. In the case of emotional and physical neglect, where a child's development might be delayed due to lack of stimulation, attention, and proper care, parents need to be guided and instructed on what to do and why. This is often the case with toddlers, when temper tantrums and oppositional behaviour are interpreted as sheer naughtiness and wickedness, and not as inner frustration when striving to master a skill. Bowel- and bladder-control is another example of often unrealistic expectations and faulty perceptions on the part of the parents. To illustrate this problem, let us look at Alan's case.

Alan was two-and-a-half years old. He looked withdrawn, and he was unwilling to engage in any activities. He suffered from colds and recurring chest infections. The health visitor noted that he was panic-stricken when asked to go to the bathroom, and he cried when he was taken there. His mother complained that he wetted and soiled himself out of sheer laziness, and said that her next-door neighbour's daughter (the same age as Alan) had been clean and dry for some time, as had been her best friend's son (one month younger than Alan). Mother–child interaction was tense, and her attitudes towards Alan were visibly negative. In the organisation of treatment in such cases as Alan's, it is useful to show graphically when certain life-tasks or skills should be accomplished. Parents need to be told what the time span is, and how it differs between children (and for what reasons). An example of bowel- and bladder-control is shown on a developmental ladder in Figure 5.

Cognitive Behavioural Work

Among the commonest characteristics of emotionally maltreating parents are their self-defeating thoughts and beliefs about their abilities to cope effectively with different life-tasks. These dysfunctional thoughts lead to dysfunctional feelings, and consequently to negative outcomes for the parents and for the child. The way in which we interpret things happening around us, and what we tell ourselves, can have a profound effect on our feelings (and subsequently on our behaviour). Many parents who experience some difficulties in bringing up children tend to run themselves down, saying that they cannot cope, are useless, or that whatever they touch goes wrong. The aim of cognitive work with parents

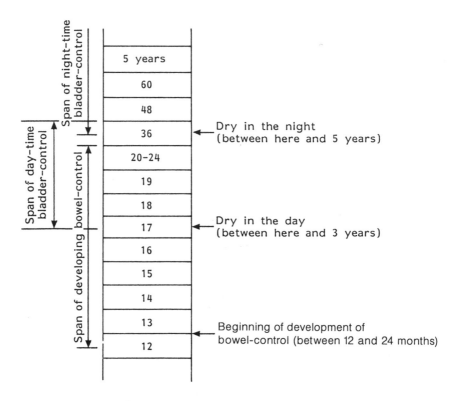

Figure 5: Developmental ladder (bowel- and bladder-control)

is to help them to begin viewing things in a way which generates positive thoughts, beliefs, and feelings about their capabilities of finding a way out of a problem, and to generate emotional energy to take action, based on conviction that they are able to produce change. This therapy points to the successful aspects of clients' lives, so that they can take comfort from those aspects and redirect their thinking to constructive strategies of problem-solving (and feel good about it). For example, a mother who has difficulties in feeding her child (who is failing-to-thrive) usually experiences an overwhelming feeling of inadequacy and failure as a carer. Furthermore, such mothers think and feel that they are the only ones having these difficulties, and therefore they are useless as parents, or, worse, that the child deliberately refuses to take feeds in order to punish them, or because they are not loved by these children.

Table 3: Chain of damaging thoughts, negative feelings, and unhappy outcomes

EVENT	BELIEF	FEELING	BEHAVIOUR	OUTCOME
child fails to thrive	I cannot cope. He/she deliberately behaves like that to hurt me	inadequacy, helplessness, despair	force-feeding, screaming, shouting, frustration, anxiety	food-avoidance behaviour, losing weight
developmental delays	he/she dislikes being picked up or talked to. Dislikes me	depression, frustration, uselessness	do nothing	child is under-stimulated. Emotional neglect
child does not respond to parental requests (oppositional behaviour)	I am inadequate as a parent. I cannot cope	frustration, anger, depression	smacks, shouts, criticises	distorted relationship. Emotional abuse

Table 4: Example 1: Dysfunctional thoughts, beliefs, and alternative ways of thinking

EVENT	BELIEF	FEELING	BEHAVIOUR	OUTCOME
		Self-defeating thoughts and feelings		
child fails-to-thrive	he refuses food to hurt me. I cannot cope	anger, frustration, helplessness	force-feeding, screaming, shouting	food-avoidance behaviour
		Cognitive change—alternative ways of thinking		
child fails-to-thrive	he is a difficult child to feed. There are many children like him	I can try different ways of feeding, and I can manage	being patient and encouraging when feeding a child	child eats more, puts on weight

Table 5: Example 2: Dysfunctional thoughts, beliefs, and alternative ways of thinking

EVENT	BELIEF	FEELING	BEHAVIOUR	OUTCOME
Self-defeating thoughts and feelings				
child is persistently defiant	I am useless as a parent, I cannot do anything right	frustration, anger, depression	smacks the child frequently, gets angry	constant confrontations leading to difficult relationship—emotional abuse
Cognitive change—alternative ways of thinking				
child is persistently defiant	I have brought up two other children. I cannot be that useless	I will ask for advice. I will manage this. I feel I can	I will try different methods of handling the child's difficult behaviour	improvement in child's behaviour. Increased mother's self-esteem

When choosing the cognitive method of working, the first task is to identify such damaging thoughts accurately, and to demonstrate their link with negative feelings and unhappy outcomes. To illustrate this chain let us look at some examples as shown in Table 3.

Dysfunctional thoughts and beliefs are at times experienced by everybody, especially when there is a repetition of misfortunes, so our interpretations and appraisals of events and ourselves are far from the truth, but strongly felt. Beck (1976) suggested that there are certain automatic thoughts which guide our daily lives and 'colour' our feelings. Ellis (1973) went further and said that some of those thoughts are deep-seated, functioning as a 'core-belief', and they need to be teased out in order to be changed. These beliefs might have been in operation for a long time, and therefore became a part of a person's outlook on life: in other words, they are well-established and automatic, and changing core-beliefs and associated feelings is not easy or quick to achieve. Intellectual change might take place, but not emotional change. For example, if a mother manages to improve a child's weight-gain and intake of food and gets a lot of pleasure out of it she may begin to think and feel differently about herself and about her child, but if she has accomplished positive change out of pressure put upon her then cognitive change has not taken place so that when another problem recurs regarding child-management she may feel gloomy, appraising herself in a defeating way, and therefore minimising the possibility of real change. The problem is that parents tend to generalise: one misfortune and difficulties with subsequent misfortunes can generate firm beliefs in parents that they are no good at anything. 'I am a bad mother because I cannot even feed the child' is not an uncommon belief. Being ineffective in one area, or with one child, however, does not mean that the mother is useless at everthing.

Tables 4 and 5 demonstrate dysfunctional thoughts, beliefs, and alternative ways of thinking.

Parents are asked to record unhelpful thoughts that seem to recur frequently, and to link them to the feelings accompanying those thoughts in order to create a realisation of how such thoughts can influence behaviour and well-being, and how exaggerated they are at times. These beliefs and feelings, on closer examination, often prove to be untrue as they stand because they are falsely linked to other areas of life. For example:

(1) being unable to feed a child does not mean being useless at other child-rearing activities;

(2) events can be exaggerated and taken out of proportion, for 'fear has big eyes'. Beliefs may grow that a child will die if it does not take

feeds, a perception is formed that everyone is looking at it because it is so thin and people think it is being starved;

(3) expecting too much and being unable to live up to those expectations: 'My child has to be fully toilet-trained when it is one-and-a-half-years-old'. Failure in achieving this task on time can lead to extreme feelings of inadequacy as a parent and anger directed at the child; and

(4) making irrational inferences unsupported by evidence. For example: 'he cries when I pick him up, because he dislikes me and wants to hurt me'.

These statements and associated feelings are not just ordinary negative thoughts, they are unhealthy, disorted, and damaging to both parent and child. They contain elements of chronic emotional discomfort and maladaptive behaviour, and are self-defeating in nature. Help is needed to generate different ways of thinking and functioning. Parents are asked to produce a balance sheet, worked out alone, with negative and positive statements.

Negative statements	Positive statements
I am useless.	Two of my older children turned out not too badly.
I cannot do anything right.	
I cannot control my child.	They look healthy and quite happy.
I cannot make it eat well.	They are making good progress at school.
I am always anxious.	
I cannot properly organise life.	I am a good cook.
It is my fault I cannot cope.	I can budget my money well.
I am always miserable.	I keep my children clean.
Everyone talks about me.	I try to do things with them.
My neighbours are critical of me.	I read them stories at night.
I am a bad mother.	I prepare one hot meal a day.

Preparing a list like this helps the parent to think more positively and rationally about levels of competence and achievement. Parents are asked to practise positive statements by repeating time and time again what is good about them. The most important task is to help them believe in their strengths and to feel good about them.

Calling on Community Resources

Helping parents should not be limited to direct professional intervention, although this is essential during early stages of involvement. Professional help needs to be backed up by community resources. Good assessment of and familiarity with all local resources will facilitate the directing of parents for further or additional help. The care-plan has to be tailored to the individual needs of parents and children. Isolated parents need to link with other parents in the community through mother and toddler groups, mothers' groups, play centres, parents' drop-in-centres, and parents' training groups run by family centres. Some voluntary organisations and community centres attached to the churches provide facilities for informal meetings run by the parents themselves. Volunteers can be used effectively to help mothers with child-rearing tasks, and to give support, advice, and a helping hand where necessary. 'Home Start' is one of those organisations which trains its volunteers (who are themselves mothers who have brought up children, have experience, and are willing to assist those who need help) in parenting and befriending. Parents tend to relate better, and to feel more at ease with, just another mother who is not there to judge and assess them, but to provide practical help and support. 'Family Aids' (although employed by Social Services Departments) can back up or carry on assigned programmes (of a practical kind) devised by social workers: they provide transport; help with everyday child-care; help with budgeting and planning meals; advise on how to handle difficult behaviour; and show how to play with the child. They assist parents at times when help is most needed (such as getting children ready for school, or at tea-time), and give help in areas where parenting skills are most deficient. Single mothers in particular need occasional breaks from their children, so getting them linked to the local babysitting circle provides that opportunity as well as necessary social contacts.

Calling on neighbours for help and advice may be difficult to achieve as emotionally abusive parents often lack social skills to make and maintain contacts. Because of the low self-esteem of such parents they tend to avoid people around them, thinking they would not wish to have anything to do with them. Many women are at work these days, so they are not available to give a helping hand, even if they were willing to do so. Not all neighbourhoods have a strongly developed community spirit, and although their inhabitants are quick to spot a 'problem family', they are not so quick and willing to offer help: perceptions that they should not interfere in areas 'not their problem' are quite strong in many communities within the United Kingdom. Greater attention is needed to promote a helping spirit among neighbours and friends. Extended families, if within reasonable proximity, should be encouraged to play an active role. Parents can be advised to use telephone advice- and counselling-services when they are particularly stressed and experience difficulties with their children. Family advice centres and Parents Anonymous can alleviate some stress and offer constructive help, particularly for those parents who are in fear of or unable to use official services. One of the most worrying aspects of the child-protection services is the negative image that has been created in the last few years. Some of the criticisms are justified: lack of proper management of the cases, lack of constructive supervision, and inappropriate reaction to child-abuse cases (especially sexual abuse) have all played their parts. But there is also another side of the coin involving the lack of a sufficient workforce to cover the numbers of cases and to deal with them in a helpful way, as well as a paucity of resources in order to provide back-up and preventative services. Child-protection workers are pulled in two directions at the same time. If they take action (based on limited knowledge available at the time) they are criticised; if they do not take action and a tragedy occurs, they are blamed for negligence and malpractice.

'Gate-keeping' policies by some Social Services Departments obstruct preventative work: emotionally abused and neglected children do not appear on the priority lists and are often dealt with briefly, if at all. And yet this type of abuse has more profound long-term consequences than any other form of maltreatment. Greater emphasis on working in partnership with parents, and with all the professional disciplines concerned with child-protection cases, is the most positive development to emerge in recent years. Sharing professional responsibilities and providing appropriate help and expertise will improve judgement, decision-making, and the provision of well-informed help.

CONCLUSION

Starting the helping process for parents and children in trouble requires first to address immediate needs of those families. Quite often, at the point of referral, the family is in a state of crisis and therefore the processes of help must begin with crisis-intervention work such as making day-care provision for children, dealing with financial and housing problems, helping parents to resolve conflict between them (marital work), personal and developmental counselling, and introduction of community resources to the family.

9

WORKING IN PARTNERSHIP WITH PARENTS: A MULTIDISCIPLINARY APPROACH

The greater the power, the more dangerous the abuse *

INTRODUCTION

Recent child-care legislation in England and Wales (*Children Act*, 1989), and several guidelines regarding child-protection work issued by the Department of Health have brought significant changes to the ways in which we deal with and organise the protection of children and families.

Those changes were introduced and legislated for as a result of numerous Public Inquiry Reports (such as those dealing with the deaths of children maltreated by their carers and those concerned with the cavalier approaches to suspected child sexual-abuse cases).

Firstly, both the *Children Act* and the Department of Health guidance *Working Together* (DOH 1991; 1.8) require a multidisciplinary approach when dealing with child-protection and child-abuse cases, and secondly they require that these cases should be dealt with in collaboration with parents. New legislation gave parents greater power to be involved in decision-making and planning for their children's futures as well as giving them responsibilities to provide appropriate care and to play active roles in the process of therapeutic change. A multidisciplinary approach

---

*Edmund Burke (1729–97): Speech (7 February 1771) from *The Speeches. The Works of the Right Honourable Edmund Burke* (London: Henry G. Bohn, 1854–58), p. 357.

was legislated for in order to improve communication between agencies involved in the same cases and to provide the comprehensive assessment and help needed.

WORKING IN PARTNERSHIP WITH PARENTS

Involvement of parents in assessment, decision-making, treatment, or interaction is essential to make things work, even if the child has to be removed from the home. The ways in which parents are treated and the degree to which they participate in the discussions and decision-making will affect their contact with the child (in cases of different care provision) or their involvement in intervention and treatment. Of course, there are many families and parents who will not get involved and who will reject or ignore every attempt to participate and to take responsibility for their actions or lack of them. Chaotic and dysfunctional families with profound negative attitudes towards any type of authority are unlikely to co-operate and to commit themselves to work towards necessary goals.

Partnership requires collaborative work towards common goals and purposes with mutual obligations and commitments to achieve the desired outcome. The process should be appropriately balanced, negotiated, mutually agreed, and put into action. Whether it is realistic to expect that a partnership can be established under these conditions (and with highly sensitive issues with which to deal) is questionable in some cases. The input of work effort is usually skewed towards the professionals, but then so is the power.

Nevertheless, there are parents and families in trouble, experiencing self-defeating difficulties in child-rearing and relationships with the children, who can be actively engaged and who can fully participate in the therapeutic process. The point is that without parental agreement and commitment to work towards mutually recognised goals, progress is not going to be made at home. Therefore every effort needs to be made to involve parents (at least to a reasonable degree) from the start of the decision-making processes as well as in the intervention and problem-solving work. It is hoped that working in partnership with carers will bring better understanding and realisation of their importance to the case and that they can play a major part in determining future outcomes. Since new legislation has been implemented, parents and children have begun to be involved in the agencies' activities (such as attending case conferences and case reviews). Parents are better informed and have opportunity to put their point of view in the presence of all professionals involved in the case of their child.

CASE CONFERENCES

It is a matter of good practice and professional ethics in child-protection cases to involve parents when important decisions are taken concerning their children. Parents have a right and a duty to be heard and to hear what the concerns are, as expressed by the professional panel, as Brown and Waters (1986) point out:

> can you think of many other areas of life in which such important decisions take place about people, in their absence without their viewpoint being represented and without having the right or freedom to challenge the recommendation, decision, and resulting action. (Brown and Waters, 1986, p. 26)

The case conference has been identified as the primary forum for case co-ordination, and is central to child-protection procedures, based on the inter-agency nature of assessment, decision-making, treatment, and management of the case. The document *Working Together*, under the *Children Act* (1989) guidelines, makes it clear that parents and children (of appropriate ages) should be present throughout the child-protection conference, requiring openness and honesty between families and professionals. It needs to be said that although the guideline promotes parental involvement, it is not required by law (Hallett & Birchall, 1992).

There is much current debate for and against parental participation at case conferences. Arguments against include such issues as:

(1) parental behaviour during the conference cannot be predicted and may disrupt the procedure;
(2) the emotive nature of the subject matter cannot be controlled in the presence of parents; and
(3) decision-making in the best interests of the child may be inhibited, as parents might incriminate themselves by saying something in the presence of police.

Arguments for include:

(1) recognition that assumptions made by the professionals can be challenged by parents;
(2) acknowledgement that parents know their children best and can provide important information to influence decisions;
(3) creation of possibilities for sharing information and concerns;
(4) enhancement of parental commitment to exercising the child- protection plan;

(5) knowledge of what professionals are supposed to do to help parents and their responsibilites for their action or inaction;

(6) increased awareness and understanding of the professionals' roles and duties, so parents can view them in a more positive way; and

(7) formal agreement to play a part in negotiating a working agreement and to observe the rules of the contract (Corby, 1979; and Hallet & Birchall, 1992).

The case conference should decide whether or not to take further action. If it is determined to intervene, this usually involves placing the child on the Child-Protection Register, voluntary admission into care, court action, or the child remaining at home with provision of help. A care-plan is worked out, and tasks are distributed and formally agreed. The service agreement should be written as soon as possible and signed by all concerned. Individual contracts between key workers and the parents should be negotiated and formally written in the early stages of treatment.

AGREEMENTS AND CONTRACTS

Written contracts between therapist and clients have been used in many behavioural programmes designed to decrease child-abuse and neglect (Stein, Gambrill, & Wiltse, 1978; Jeffrey, 1976; Reavley & Gilbert, 1976; Reavley, Gilbert, & Carver, 1978; and Hutchings, 1980b). Some researchers and practitioners have used written contracts as a routine part of practice (Stein & Gambrill, 1976; Sheldon, 1982; and Iwaniec, 1983). There are many advantages in using this method of work: it clarifies agreements between parties, sets up goals, and clears expectations. The contracts in the Alameda Project (Stein, Gambrill, & Wiltse, 1978) identified the parent's goals (such as the return of a child to her care); the consequences that would occur dependent on whether objectives were met; the time limit involved (usually six months); the responsibilities of the parents and the social workers; and the formal agreements of involved parties. All the latter should participate in the formation of the contracts, and entries in contracts are made only with the agreement of all participants. Copies of contracts as well as written descriptions of intervention plans were given to clients. (These served as helpful reminders of agreements made.) Hutchings (1980b) recommends keeping copies of clients' records in their homes to facilitate communications among the many professionals who may be involved with a given family.

Written agreements and contracts began to be widely used in Britain following the implementation of the *Children Act* (1989): they are useful memoranda of mutual obligations and powers in the partnership arrangements with parents.

Service Contracts

There are two main types of contract used with parents: service contracts and contingency contracts. Service contracts are ordinarily used as a reminder for all parties of what is involved, who is going to do what and how, the time span, and statements of expectations and directions. They also provide a useful basis for evaluation and monitoring of work and progress. These contracts cover a wide variety of goals, from resource provision to therapeutic tasks. A copy of the service contract should be given to everyone involved, including parents. Contracts should be signed by all concerned.

Contingency Contracts

Contingency contracts are highly specific, carefully negotiated, and are based on 'Exchange-Rate Theory' principles. They are mostly used in marital work, work with adolescents or family work, where there is conflict, anger, and resentment, and where individuals are at loggerheads. For further reading, see Sheldon (1982).

Whether a service or contingency contract is used, certain principles should be observed. The formal contract should:

(1) be written;
(2) clearly spell out goals;
(3) describe intervention methods;
(4) define the behaviour and obligations of the parties involved;
(5) specify the length of the contract time; and
(6) define the review time and methods.

ADVANTAGE OF USING WRITTEN AND SIGNED AGREEMENTS

A written and signed agreement:

(1) spells out what is expected from care-givers and professionals involved;
(2) clearly states the problems, concerns, and goals of the required intervention;

(3) clearly defines *who* is going to do *what*, as well as the time, place, and assumed duration of an involvement;

(4) provides a structure for the work to be done between care-givers, child, and professionals involved;

(5) enhances communications on a multidisciplinary basis;

(6) disciplines and motivates all parties involved in problem-solving;

(7) is a good reminder of what is intended and hoped for;

(8) obligates all parties to focus on the child's neglected needs and remediation of those needs;

(9) provides dates for regular evaluation and monitoring of the case;

(10) provides a set of expectations and priorities to work on mutually agreed and negotiated tasks;

(11) protects all parties in the event of dispute;

(12) gives care-givers a chance and permission to re-negotiate the terms of the contract (without being seen as awkward or deliberately sabotaging set work); and

(13) involves all concerned in decision-making.

Checklist for Writing Contracts

The following questions can help the recognition of problems in the preparation of contracts:

(1) were the problems clearly specified?

(2) did the contract provide for immediate reinforcement?

(3) did the contract ask for small accomplishments (to start with) for the desired improvement?

(4) did the contract call for task accomplishment rather than obedience?

(5) was the contract fair?

(6) were the terms of the contract clear?

(7) was the contract honest?

(8) was the contract positive?

(9) was contracting as a method being used systematically?

(10) was the contract mutually negotiated and agreed?; and

(11) was the bonus clause included (for example, the de-registration of the child from the Child-Protection Register)?

In order to demonstrate these methods at work, a case of suspected failure-to-thrive will be described, from identification of the problem case conference, decision-taking, preparation of care-plan, inter-agency work in partnership with parents (service contract); key workers' contracts with the parents, and the methods involved in treatment.

CASE STUDY

Referral

A child, aged 18 months, was referred to the Social Services by the health visitor, who was seriously concerned about the child's physical and psycho-social development and general well-being. John looked extremely thin, withdrawn, unresponsive, and physically ill. The parents appeared to be neglectful and dismissive (or unaware) of the child's nourishment and nurturing needs. The social worker visited the family and was alarmed by the child's physical appearance and by the indifferent mother—child interactions and relationship. The mother expressed feelings of resentment and dislike of the child as he was causing anxiety and was difficult to feed and satisfy. The father, on the other hand, did not see anything wrong and was angry that people were bothering them 'about nothing'. A case conference was called, and the child was placed on the Child-Protection Register. Both parents attended a case conference. A protection- and care-plan was drawn up and a contract written and signed by all concerned.

Problems Identified at the Case Conference and as Shared by the Social Worker and the Health Visitor

(1) the child's weight was significantly below third percentile;
(2) the child's development was retarded in all respects;
(3) the mother—child relationship was at best neglectful and indifferent;
(4) the mother—child bonding appeared to be weak;
(5) there was little stimulation and attention given to the child;
(6) physical care was found to be poor;
(7) both parents had insufficient parenting skills;
(8) marital frictions and family dysfunctioning was present; and
(9) the mother appeared to be depressed and without hope.

Problems Presented by the Parents

(1) John was difficult to rear from early on, and was difficult to feed;
(2) he slept badly and cried a lot;
(3) he was defiant and stubborn;

(4) he always preferred to be left alone—when he was picked up he cried and was miserable;

(5) the mother felt that he was deliberately annoying her because he disliked her;

(6) his behaviour irritated her, so she shouted at him a lot and kept him away from her so as not to hit him;

(7) the mother felt defeated and helpless;

(8) the mother did not know how to cope with the child; and

(9) the father did not help, as he did not see it as his duty to do so.

Significant Harm Identified

(1) development of child delayed due to the lack of parental nurturing;

(2) non-organic failure-to-thrive predicted due to parental physical and emotional neglect (failure-to-thrive needs to be medically investigated); and

(3) development of child's positive self-esteem, sense of achievement, sense of belonging and other aspects of socialisation affected by distorted parent—child relationship and hostile interaction.

ACTION PLAN

Case Conference Recommendations

Step I   G.P. to refer John to the paediatrician to investigate any possible organic reason for the child's poor growth and development (for immediate action);

Step II   Comprehensive psychosocial assessment to be undertaken by the social worker;

Step III   Child's weight to be monitored by the health visitor or the G.P. on a fortnightly basis (after medical investigation);

Step IV   Help, advice, and supervision regarding eating (nutritional provision and appropriate management during this process) to be provided by the health visitor;

Step V   Developmental counselling to be provided by the health visitor.

Step VI   Attendance of the child at the Family Centre or day nursery to be organised on a part-time basis (two days a week) to help the child with its developmental deficit;

Step VII   Social worker to help to improve distorted and harmful interaction and relationship between mother and child, and to work towards better family functioning and fair role-distribution between parents;

Step VIII   To review this case in three months time (or earlier if the key worker or any other person involved requests to do so if there is serious concern); and

Step IX   To allocate a key worker responsible for co-ordination for this case.

CARE PLAN—SERVICE AGREEMENT

This agreement is drawn up between *North & West Unit of Management and Mr and Mrs Blank regarding John Blank*, age *18 months*, D.O.B. *18.11.92*, who is a subject of the protection-plan.

In keeping with the requirements of the case conference decision of re-registration of *John*, we agree to work towards the goals set out below.

To improve quality of care and *John's* well-being as evidenced by:
(1) steady weight-gain;
(2) improvement in his general development;
(3) improvement in parent—child interaction and relationship; and
(4) improvement in family functioning.

All people concerned agree to keep the following arrangements:

Mr and Mrs Blank (parents) agree to:

(1)   take John every other Monday morning to the health centre to be weighed;
(2)   take John every Tuesday and Thursday to the Family Centre;
(3)   work with the health visitor (Mrs King) and the social worker (Mrs Smith) to help them to resolve concerns regarding John's well-being, physical growth, and retarded development; and
(4)   keep the appointments and communicate any difficulties that might occur during that time.

Mrs King (health visitor) agrees to:

(1)   be at the clinic every other Monday morning at an agreed time to weigh John;
(2)   help Mrs Blank with John's eating difficulties, and will advise the parents how to help John to catch up in his development;
(3)   visit the family every day at lunchtime for the first weeks (apart from Tuesday and Thursday when John is in the Family Centre), and then twice a week for the next two weeks; and
(4)   keep a weight record, and evaluate the work done jointly with the parents.

Mrs Smith (social worker) agrees to:

(1)   make arrangements for John to attend the Family Centre on Tuesdays and Thursdays;
(2)   provide counselling for both parents to better understand John's physical and emotional needs, and to help them to improve John's care. She will also help them to resolve their marital frictions;
(3)   help the parents to learn how to play with John, how to deal with his irritating behaviour, and how to deal with the mother's negative feelings towards John. She will also help to deal with John's anxiety, fear, and apprehension towards his mother;

continues

continued

(4) provide six sessions over a six-week period; and

(5) keep a record of work done, and evaluate progress. These tasks will be jointly conducted with the parents.

<u>Dr Green</u> (the G.P.) agrees to:

(1) make arrangements with the paediatrician at the hospital to conduct medical investigations; and

(2) see John at the surgery once a month to monitor his physical health and development (more frequently if there is a need or request by parents or professionals involved).

The requirements and objectives are re-negotiable at any time on request by either party.

All parties agree to fulfil their obligations and to observe times of appointments. If for any reason any parties are prevented from keeping an appointment, they must communicate this to the person concerned and make an alternative arrangement.

This care plan will be reviewed in three months' time. All involved should communicate their concerns and progress to the key worker, *Mrs Smith*.

1. Case review *10 June 1994*

Signed: _____ Mr *Blank*

Signed: _____ Mrs *Blank*

Signed: _____ Mrs *Smith*
(social worker)

Signed: _____ Mrs *King*
(health visitor)

Signed: _____ Dr *Green* (G.P.)

Date: _____

Signed: _____ Case-
Conference
chair

The key worker draws up this agreement after the case conference and sends it for signatures. When all signatures are obtained it is sent or given to all parties concerned.

CONTRACT

This contract is drawn up between *Mrs Smith* (social worker) and *Mr and Mrs Blank* (*John's* parents) in the presence of *Mrs King* (health visitor)

Date: _____

In keeping with the requirements of the case conference decision, we agree to work towards the goals set out by both parties:

Mr and Mrs Blank agree:

(1) *to play with John every day after tea:*
     15 minutes for the first two weeks;
     20 minutes for the 3rd, 4th, 5th, and 6th week; and
     25 minutes for the subsequent weeks.
(2) *to talk to John (while playing with him) in an encouraging way, to praise him for each good response, to talk to him in a soft, warm, and reassuring voice, to show pleasure in his achievements, and to thank him if he participates in play;*
(3) *to read a story or to describe a picture while sitting John on his/her lap and holding him close to him/her for 10 minutes every day, just before he is put to bed; and*
(4) *to have their evening meal sitting at the table (not in front of the television), to talk to each other about the day's events, etc., and also to talk to John.*

Mr Blank agrees to help his wife:

(1) *to put John to bed every other night; and*
(2) *to do the weekly shopping.*

Mrs Blank agrees:

to be more open with her husband, and to tell him what bothers her, instead of sulking or screaming at him.

Mrs Smith (social worker), on her part, agrees:

(1) *to help Mr and Mrs Blank with the first three play sessions, to advise them what play material or toys to use, and on how each session will be conducted;*
(2) *to get Mrs Blank some picture books for the story reading sessions;*
(3) *to review with the parents John's progress at the Family Centre; and*

continues

continued

(4) *to see the family every Thursday for six weeks from 3.30–4.30pm to help them with their own difficulties and to help them with John's problems.*

Both parties agree:

To evaluate their work together on a weekly basis (after the counselling session) and to keep records of these evaluations.

The requirements and objectives are re-negotiable at any time on request by either party.

Bonus: *If progress is made, an early de-registration of John will be considered.*

Signed: _____ Social Worker

Signed: _____ Father

Signed: _____ Mother

Signed: _____ Health Visitor
(Observer)

Date: _____

This contract will be reviewed in two weeks from the date of this agreement.

CONTRACT

This contract is drawn up between *Mrs King* (health visitor) and *Mr and Mrs Blank* (*John's* parents) in the presence of *Mrs Smith* (social worker)

Date: _____

In keeping with the requirements of the case conference decision, we agree to work towards the goals set out by both parties:

Mrs Blank agrees:

(1) *to feed John regularly (four times a day): 8am breakfast, 12–12.30pm lunch, 3.30pm tea (snack), 5.30pm dinner;*

(2) *to provide food appropriate for the child's age (as advised by the health visitor);*

(3) *to encourage John to eat by talking warmly to him, and not rushing him or shouting at him when he is in difficulties;*

(4) *to praise John when he has made an effort to eat well and is eating a reasonable amount of food; and*

(5) *to bring John to the health centre to be weighed every other Monday morning at 10am.*

continues

continued

Mr Blank agrees:

(1) to help Mrs Blank with John's eating at dinner-times and during weekends; and

(2) to be sympathetic, warm, and encouraging to John and to his wife.

Mrs King (health visitor), on her part, agrees:

(1) to work out with Mrs Blank a range of menus which will be nutritional and within the family financial remit;

(2) to show and advise Mr and Mrs Blank how to manage John during meal-times, three times at lunch-time during the first week, and twice a week for the following three weeks. Progress will be reviewed and a decision taken as to whether further help is needed; and

(3) to advise Mr and Mrs Blank with John's toilet-training, play, and doing things for himself.

Both parties agree:

(1) to review progress on a weekly basis and to keep the record of that evaluation; and

(2) to keep the appointments and to do the work outlined in this agreement. If for any unavoidable reason an appointment cannot be kept, this will be communicated to the parties concerned and alternative arrangements will be made.

The requirements and objectives are re-negotiable at any time on request by either party.

Bonus: *If progress is made, an early de-registration of John will be considered.*

Signed: _____ *Mr Blank*
                                                    (father)

Signed: _____ *Mrs Blank*
                                                    (mother)

Signed: _____ *Mrs King*
                                                    (health visitor)

Signed: _____ *Mrs Smith*
                                                    (social worker)

Date: _____

This contract will be reviewed in two weeks from the date of that agreement.

The health visitor's and social worker's contracts are negotiated and written when both persons are present: they are going to be the main service providers, so they must know their remit, range of responsibilities, and the approaches they are going to take, so that they do not contradict each other when dealing with the family.

TREATMENT OF FAILURE-TO-THRIVE CHILDREN AND THEIR FAMILIES

Treatment of failure-to-thrive children and their families will depend on the severity of the problems, age of the children, and the duration of the condition. The most important therapeutic ingredient is to deal with the feeding/eating behaviour of the child, parental interaction during this process, and the appropriateness of food provided. In most cases, feeding-related problems will have to be dealt with.

Treatment of failure-to-thrive usually involves four stages:

(1) resolving feeding difficulties and improving feeding style (i.e., modifying parental behaviour and responses during the act of feeding);
(2) deliberately, and in a planned fashion, increasing positive interactions and decreasing negative interactions between mother and child (and indeed between other members of the family) where relevant. We may need to desensitise the child's anxiety and fear with regard to the parent's feeding and other care-giving activities. We may also have to desensitise the parent's tension, anger, and resentment when in the child's company;
(3) intensifying of parent–child interactions; and
(4) some older children with a long history of failure-to-thrive present behavioural problems. These are dealt with once the 'emotional arousal' in the family (especially between mother and child) improves. It is unwise and also unproductive to deal with all presenting problems at the same time. Firstly, some irritating and worrying behaviours resolve themselves once the child is emotionally 'accepted' by the mother, and when her responses to the child are more positive. Secondly, by including all problematic behaviours, therapy could well overburden an already tired, demoralised, and depressed mother, who by this time has very little coping capacity.

During the assessment period we pay attention to immediate needs. It is advisable sometimes to arrange day nursery care for the child. It is beneficial for the social worker dealing with the family to discuss the assessment and the intervention-plan with the mother, and certainly with both parents where there is a father present. It is important to remember that the mother needs help in her own right as well as the father. Most mothers of failure-to-thrive children need to learn to control feelings of anger, rage, and hostility, and to deal with high levels of anxiety. This may be achieved (before any formal programme) by doing relaxation exercises: the child-free period might be used to learn and practise how to relax and also to develop self-control skills.

Stage (1) might require the following to be dealt with:

(a) making sure the right amount of food is given;
(b) ensuring the appropriate food for the age of the child is given; and
(c) ensuring that the feeding style is appropriate.

In cases where carer–child interaction during the process of feeding is tense, anxious, and stressful, special attention needs to be paid to improving the atmosphere. The following methods have proved to be helpful in resolving feeding-problems (Iwaniec, 1983).

Feeding is tackled in a highly structured (and thus directive) manner. Meal-times have to be made more relaxed: mothers are asked (and rehearsed) to desist from screaming, shouting, and threatening the child over meals (self-control training). The period of eating is made quiet and calm, and the mother is asked to talk soothingly and pleasantly to the child. It is extremely difficult for mothers to achieve and maintain this pattern of behaviour. It is essential that the therapist models the feeding, feeds the child a few times, and then helps to reassure the child: she may have to prompt the mother to help the child in a gentle manner to eat when it is in difficulties. The mother is encouraged to look at it, smile, and touch it. If the child refuses food, the mother has to leave it if she is unable to encourage or coax it by play or soft words. Food should be arranged decoratively to look attractive. She should never feed the child when feeling acutely tense or angry. This aspect of the programme is purely instrumental in the sense of encouraging the child to eat by creating less fraught circumstances.

Stage (2) might involve increasing:

(a) stimulation for the child if it has been neglected and suffers developmental delays. Parents would be advised and shown how to talk, play, and generally stimulate the child; and
(b) appropriate and loving caring interaction between the child and the care-giver. Where emotional neglect is evident and parent–child

attachment is weak, especial attention is paid to improving the quality and quantity of interaction between care-giver and child. This can be achieved by specially designed activities and play. In most cases a contract is drawn up specifying mutual obligations and goals between the family and the therapist (as shown above).

Stage (3) might require:

(a) dealing with behavioural problems like disobedience, sleeping patterns, temper tantrums, and so on;
(b) teaching socialisation tasks like toilet-training, dressing, discrimination-training, language development, play, sharing with other children, and self-control; and
(c) intensifying parent–child relationship and interaction by their spending a lot of time together and being involved in mutual activities.

Stage (4) might involve:

(a) placement or activities outside the home environment, such as mother and toddler groups, play groups, or provision of day nurseries or family centres; and
(b) volunteers like Home Start, which would be most beneficial and necessary in cases of social isolation and depressive reactions in the mother. Use of neighbours and the extended family should be encouraged.

It is most important to observe the following stages of involvement when dealing with failure-to-thrive children:

(1) identifying that a child's weight is below expected norms and its general well-being is questionable;
(2) giving advice and help on feeding, caring, and management provided by the health visitor;
(3) if there is no improvement, referral to the paediatrician to investigate any possible organic reason for a child's poor growth and development;
(4) medical investigation;
(5) if a non-organic reason is found for the failure-to-thrive, referral to the Social Services, child psychiatrist or child psychologist for psycho-social assessment;
(6) more serious cases (if there is evidence of rejection, emotional indifference, or more serious neglect) to be conferenced;
(7) treatment/intervention programme to be worked out and negotiated with the care-givers;

(8) monitoring the child's growth and development (outpatients' clinic, G.P., health visitor, etc.);

(9) monitoring of child–care-givers interaction and relationship and general well-being of the child by the social worker; and

(10) case closed when there is evidence of systematic improvement in the child's growth and development and care-givers–child relationships.

Note: Failure-to-thrive children should be dealt with on a multidisciplinary basis. Good communication and co-ordination between social workers, doctors and health visitors, schools, nurseries, etc., are essential.

CONCLUSION

The introduction of a multidisciplinary approach to deal with child-abuse and neglect has increased inter-agency communication and more effective treatment of children and families. Giving parents responsibilites as well as privileges encourages a partnership between protecting agencies and carers: that partnership is demonstrated by the greater involvement of parents in planning for their children's futures, decision-making, and participation in problem-solving. Mutual obligations to evolve and work out a care-plan are generally negotiated and contracted. The use of a care-plan and contracts is demonstrated above in the case of a child who fails to thrive.

10

HELPING FAMILIES

What do the ravages of time not damage?
The age of our own parents ... has borne us ...
who will soon give way
*to an even more vicious generation**

INTRODUCTION

Parent-training is perhaps a major development in helping parents to become better equipped to understand their children's developmental needs and better informed to deal with child-rearing problems as they occur. Strangely enough, and in spite of the recognition of world-wide serious child-rearing and child-management problems, little has been done to educate people and to prepare them for parenthood. Raising children requires not only love and acceptance, but also awareness and skills to do the job confidently and well: one without the other seldom works, especially where there is nobody to advise, to give a helping hand, to show, and to reassure. The increase in numbers of single parents (many of whom are immature in many ways at the time their children are born) domiciled away from immediate family or friends (from whom, traditionally, help was provided), seems to have increased a need for professionals to step in as advisors and helpers. Helping parents to become better carers has assumed greater urgency as a result of growing concern about child-abuse and neglect. As time has passed and further knowledge and understanding of the causation of child-abuse has been gained, it is realised that, in order to prevent children from suffering, parents must be trained and must be helped in child-rearing practices.

In order to help parents to bring up children and deal with the everyday difficulties with which they may be faced, varieties of parent-training programmes have emerged that address child-care issues. Although they

---

*Quintus Horatius Flaccus (65–8 BC): *Odes*, Book 3, No 6, Line 45.

differ in theoretical orientation, emphasis, and actual methods of training, the aims are the same—to help parents to help their children to grow up happily, healthily, and vigorously (Henry, 1981; Dembo, Sweitzer, & Lauritzen, 1985; Herbert, 1988; Brooks, 1991; and Callias, 1994). It would seem that the most developed and researched parent-training methods are based on Applied Social Learning theory and Cognitive Behavioural treatment (Callias, 1994).

Parent-training is usually carried out on individual and group-work bases, but the former is the more usual, more commonly used, and apparently the best developed (Callias, 1994). There are wide variations in terms of type and extent of parental involvement (when training is done on individual home bases), ranging from carrying out simple instructions in contingency management (Herbert, 1988) to a full involvement of the therapists in all aspects of observation, recording, programme planning, and implementation (McAuley, 1982; Iwaniec, 1983; Wolfe *et al.*, 1988; and Azar & Siegel, 1990). The teaching element might range from basic behavioural analysis and practice (Scott & Stradling, 1987) to the mastery of general learning principles (McAuley & McAuley, 1977; and Webster-Stratton, 1991). In some cases the wider family and community are engaged in the therapeutic programme: for example, siblings have been enlisted to give a helping hand (Iwaniec, 1983), as have peers (Clement, Roberts, & Lantz, 1976) and parent groups (Webster-Stratton, 1991; and Patterson, 1982). Children, especially older ones, are also trained to be their own behaviour 'therapists' (Scott & Stradling, 1987), monitoring their own problems and using self-control methods taught by the worker.

Parent-Training with Abusive Parents

Parents who abuse and neglect their children often lack positive child-rearing skills, and the way they interact with, and discipline, their children is inappropriate or even dangerous. A number of studies showed that abusive parents interact with their children in a more positive and constructive manner after training in child-rearing (Sandler, Vandercar, & Milhoan, 1978; Wolfe, 1991; Wolfe, Sandler, & Kaufman, 1980; Wolfe *et al.*, 1988; Iwaniec, 1983; and Azar & Siegel, 1990). A training package consisting of many elements is used to increase skills: those elements include asking parents to read relevant material (which is specially prepared in a jargon-free and straightforward way); showing parents how to pinpoint specific behaviours and how to observe what happens just before and just after behaviours of concern; presenting by modelling effective and ineffective ways to interact with children; practising of skills by role-playing and rehearsing; giving feedback concerning progress; and setting assignments to be carried out at home (such as recording or reading).

Programmes are organised on a step-by-step basis, complex principles and skills being discussed and developed only after more elementary ones have been acquired. In some programmes parents are offered rewards contingent on changes in their behaviour and task-accomplishment (Sandler, Vandercar, & Milhoan, 1978). Training programmes differ in respect of the precise components used: for example what is read, how many rehearsal-trials are offered, types of models presented, whether parents are first asked to describe how to use a procedure (after the principle is explained and model presented) before being requested to demonstrate the use of it. Sandler, Vandercar, and Milhoan (1978), trained a 23-year-old mother (referred to a community agency as an abusive parent) to use more effective positive-reinforcement practices with her four-year-old daughter. The specific aims of the programme were to increase the mother's use of approval and positive physical interactions with her daughter.

Training was conducted over nine sessions. The mother was requested to complete assigned reading and review tests as recommended in *Parents and Teachers* (Becker, 1976), and to carry out suggestions in the text using weekly hand-outs that described specific child-management practices. Incentives were offered to the mother for completing agreed tasks, such as free restaurant meals and free tickets for the cinema donated by local business firms and individuals. Role-playing, in which the mother first played the part of the child and a social worker the part of the mother, was used to develop new skills. These roles were then reversed to give the mother practice in new behaviours. Analysis of the results showed a marked increase in the mother's use of approval, and a decrease in the use of negative commands. These results were maintained over a five-month follow-up period.

There are many different methods of training parents: these may involve the location where training takes place (clinic or home); means of instruction (assigned readings, programmed material, lectures, group discussions, films, direct-training, model presentation, coaching, rehearsal, and feedback in which the parent's behaviour is systematically shaped); the participants who are present (for example, the parent alone, child and parent, parents, child, and siblings, or a group of parents); and the requirements made of the parents in terms of sophistication of learning new ways of interacting with, relating to, and managing their children and their own behaviour and attitudes. Training on an individual basis is preferably carried out in the home, because this helps the acquisition of new skills away from an artificial setting like an office, clinic, or research centre, where the subject may be unduly inhibited and the therapist will be unfamiliar with the home environment. Choices are made largely in the context of training, availability of resources, and time required for the specific programme. At times it is more beneficial to bring a family into a quieter, organised, and well-equipped place to teach necessary skills and then to encourage the practice of those skills, once they have been learned, at home.

Parents are often trained in a set of procedures (for example, how to talk to the child, how to use a tone of voice appropriate to age, and how frequently to offer praise, reassurance, smiles, or hugs when a child does, or attempts to do, something which is praiseworthy). Training in these general principles will help family members to use them in order to deal with other problems in similar or different situations. In a case when one child is rejected by the parents, siblings tend to be rejective as well, simply because they have picked up negative parental behaviour towards the rejected child, so by changing parental behaviour and responses to that child, it is probable that the behaviour of siblings will alter as well. Siblings are also trained by using modelling and instructions as how to interact with the target child.

Iwaniec (1983) trained six excessively rejective siblings in four families by using play as a forum to teach them by modelling how to respond to a target child in a kind way. Operant proceedings were used (praising and rewarding by giving a picture of their choice) to encourage positive responses. Both parents were asked to pay special attention to a rejected child and to correct other children when their behaviour was harsh and dismissive. The results were encouraging in three cases. The positive outcomes were attributed to the fair and good supervision of children by parents and their positive corrections of siblings' behaviour towards the target child. Factors influencing the selection of training format include the age of the child; the perceived potential of the parent to learn new methods of child-management by means of didactic instruction or training; tolerance levels of parents; and resources available to the worker. The focus of training has been typically on altering the behaviour of both parents and siblings towards the abused child, and helping parents to develop strategies of better child- and stress-management.

McAuley and McAuley (1977) report a case in which a mother abused her six-year-old boy. In the latter stages of the treatment programme the father became involved. When the mother and her son returned home from a stay in an in-patient unit, three sessions were arranged in the home during which the father was coached as to how to use the new child-management methods that the mother had learned, and agreements were made between the mother and father concerning child-rearing responsibilities. The father agreed to look after the child when his wife was preparing meals and during other periods of the day: he also agreed to put the child to bed twice a week. He received extra time to spend with his friends on agreed nights out for each successful bargaining episode. Each parent agreed to 'fine' the other for any failure to use appropriate contingency-management procedures.

AN EXAMPLE OF TRAINING PHYSICALLY AND EMOTIONALLY NEGLECTFUL PARENTS

The author and her students have used different parent-training models on individual and group work bases. Families referred for treatment were on the Child-Protection Register for all forms of child-maltreatment (not sexual abuse). All children were developmentally delayed due to poor parenting, presented behavioural difficulties (mostly non-compliance) as well as aggression, toileting, and bed-time problems, and generally exhibited disorganised and disruptive behaviour. Assessment of the families showed serious neglect (mostly due to lack of child-rearing skills and lack of basic knowledge of the children's developmental needs): additionally, marital frictions and disagreements as to how to discipline children were often present. A training programme was organised in three stages taking place in the child's home and occasionally in the Student Training Unit.

Stage I   Developmental counselling included discussion, the use of pictures, instruction, provision of simple reading, and the use of specially devised developmental quizzes. Both parents were involved in this training.

Stage II   Learning in order to improve parent–child interaction and on-task behaviour by learning to play and creating activities that had some meaning for the children.

Parents were taught how to redirect children's disruptive behaviour (which comes about as a result of boredom) towards pleasant activities for which there was a point. Parents were shown and instructed how to play with children, what inexpensive material to use for play, how to make toys, and how to organise creative play by using household junk. Parents and children were actively involved in making things and playing together under the guidance and supervision of a social worker. Some sessions were video-taped and then played back and discussed. Children and parents then reported to the workers what they liked about the activities, what was well done, what could be done better, and how they felt after having fun together. At the end (while the children were playing) social workers and parents drew up a list of positives and negatives from the video. For example:

Positives   the father helped John when he did not know what to do next. The mother smiled at John and showed pleasure when he glued two pieces of paper together. She thanked him when he passed a box to her;

Negatives   the mother shouted at Sue and got angry when the child mislaid her scissors. The father was too critical of Dean when he could not cut figures from a big piece of paper. The mother did not praise Sue when she eventually managed to put things together as she was asked to do.

From the above negatives, demonstrations by means of role-playing were conducted by two social workers in order to show what should have been done and said. Lists of things to remember and to practise were drawn up for parents to encourage appropriate behaviour and responses towards their children. These lists included advice to always praise children when they do things well or respond to requests, because such praise can help children to feel good about themselves and encourage attempts to do better next time. In turn, children will like the parents, because being with them gives them pleasure and a feeling of being appreciated. It is important that parents should not shout at children or call them names and degrade them: rather they should guide children and show them how to carry out tasks, for children are young and need to learn how to do things. Creativity should be encouraged, things should be found for children to do, and help shown or given in organising play or other activities in order to avoid boredom.

Homework

Parents were asked to apply the above principles between the sessions, keeping simple records to indicate the child's responsiveness to their positive approach when interacting with them.

Stage III   Management of behaviour, learning how to discipline children and setting up rules. The use of positive reinforcement to increase pro-social behaviour, use of time-out, extinction, and response-cost to decrease anti-social behaviour.

Methods used: Films, videos, role-play, modelling, rehearsal, and discussion.

Both parents were involved whenever possible in these training sessions. Missed sessions by the father were compensated for by coaching and by giving a set of instructions which were then discussed and negotiated with him. The training package consisted of eight sessions lasting two hours each.

Evaluations showed substantial changes, including:

(1) development of the child (improvement in language, social behaviour, intellectual alertness, and cognitive development);
(2) better ability to provide constructive activities for the child which were both stimulating, educational, and enjoyable;
(3) improvement in parent–child interaction and relationship, as evidenced by evaluation provided by the referring social worker, teacher, G.P., paediatrician, or health visitor. Fewer confrontations with the children were reported by the parents and extended family (when applicable). A decrease of 50% from the base-line assessment in behaviours such as screaming, shouting, criticising, calling names, ridiculing, and hitting was demonstrated in six families, and of 70% in three families: there was only modest improvement of 25% in two cases, but in both of these there were mitigating circumstances (serious illness in one and death in the other);
(4) better physical care, such as the provision of cooked meals and improved cleanliness of children, was evident in all cases; and
(5) parents and social workers reported better functioning as a family, as a couple, and as parents.

New routines were observed and everyday rules set (which were implemented during parent-training), such as bed-time routines (which consisted of set times for going to bed, washing, bathing, and bed-time story) and meal-time routines (consisting of regular meals, cooked dinners, eating together as a family, teaching table-manners, and talking to each other).

SHARING WITH PARENTS

Training in some of the important components of effective reinforcement-practices begins during the initial assessment stage, when parents grasp how to pinpoint specific behaviours they would like to change, learn to record the frequency of behaviours, and to realise how to identify related antecedents and consequences. Ideally, they learn to use observation as their first reaction to a problem (that is, to collect information to recognise how their behaviour influences their children). During intervention, parents first acquire knowledge of how to use positive reinforcements in order to develop and maintain appropriate behaviour. In the cases of emotional abuse, when parents blame the child for the misery and stress created in the family, the use of ABC analyses can help an abusive parent to understand by being shown graphically what is happening and how the child's avoidance-behaviour is being triggered off by parental anger, hostility, and anxiety.

Learning how to shape new behaviours is an important skill for parents to acquire in a way which is well-informed and easy to understand. In abusive situations we will focus on strengthening the parent–child relationship by training parents to respond to the children's needs and socialisation tasks in a more informed and positive way. Instructions, model-presentations, rehearsal, coaching, feedback, counselling, and developmental counselling are used to help parents to learn these new skills. For example, parents might be asked to watch a video-tape of a mother teaching her child, and then required to identify what she did to make learning easier and more fun for the child. Additional teaching-sessions could be modelled for the parents, to include humorous mistakes that can be corrected by everyone involved. The advantage of cognitive-behavioural parent-training methods is that they seem to have 'face-validity' for parents. There is no mystery surrounding the therapeutic process. As one mother said:

> I thought that I would have to do all sorts of things in therapy, which I was frightened of, but what we did was so simple, and I had a lot of fun doing it.

PARENT-TRAINING IN GROUPS COMBINING INDIVIDUAL AND GROUP-WORK

Most work with abusive families is done on an individual basis, or at best during the early stages. But combining individual work with subsequent or alongside group-work has been evaluated positively, especially on a long-term basis (Azar, 1989). Group meetings are used to teach parents management-principles, and sometimes basic child-development. At the same time, during home visits, parents are taught to apply management techniques to their own particular problems like anger, resentment, lack of support, marital problems, financial difficulties, or loneliness (Wolfe, 1988; and Azar, 1989).

A combination of individual and group-work as advisable and effective models was demonstrated by Wolfe *et al.* (1988), and Wasik *et al.* (1990), cited in Callias (1994). Wolfe devised additional group-work training to that already going on in individual parent-training. Young parents of children who matched the criteria for being 'at risk' for child-maltreatment attended an informal self-supporting group, while their children attended day care; 50% of these mothers were given additional behavioural training (Wolfe *et al.*, 1988). Both groups showed improvements, but mothers who received extra parent-training showed better long-term gains, were better prepared for child-rearing, and were regarded as less likely to abuse their children (Wasik *et al.*, 1990). In a study of families with children at risk of cognitive difficulties because of parental, social, and educational disadvantages, children were randomly assigned at birth to:

(1) an intensive intervention, combining family education with centre-based educational day care for the child;
(2) a less-intensive intervention of family-based education only; and
(3) a non-intervention control group.

In a regular assessment up to four-and-a-half-years-of-age, children in educational day care whose families also received family-support work did better than those in groups (2) and (3), and no significant effects on cognitive abilities were noted for the family education group only. These studies suggest that 'at risk' families for child maltreatment require more intensive and more varied training to compensate for parental-skill deficit and to facilitate opportunities for children's early learning.

SELF-EFFICACY THEORY IN PARENT-TRAINING

One of the most striking problems that emotionally abusive and rejective mothers have in common is very low self-esteem and low self-efficacy. These characteristics are expressed in different ways by different women. Some are depressed, inactive, and rather passive, creating an atmosphere of sadness and unspecified restriction; while others are irritable, hostile, and defensive. Once they calm down and realise that one is not there to criticise them or to show them up by snatching their children away from them, it becomes apparent how little they think about themselves as parents, wives, and individuals in their own right.

For that reason self-efficacy training should be introduced early on in the programme, and consciously and persistently applied by therapists. Let us look at the self-efficacy theory first: this attempts to explain the mutual interactional influences of people's self-perceptions and their behaviour. Self-efficacy is a belief in oneself, a conviction that one can produce positive outcomes through effort and persistence. People high in self-efficacy are convinced of their own effectiveness: those who are low in it believe that their efforts are doomed to failure. People with a history of failure in certain situations begin to believe that they cannot succeed. Their pessimism leads them to avoid their fear: avoidance further handicaps them when they are forced to act, and a vicious cycle of fear and performance failure is established. Self-efficacy is particularly relevant to mothers of failure-to-thrive children and rejective mothers. Many researchers have pointed out the lack of self-esteem, feeling of inadequacy as a parent, and helplessness which are experienced by mothers who maltreat their offspring (Leonard, Rhymes, & Solnit 1966; Pollitt, Gilmore, & Valcarcel, 1978; and Iwaniec, 1983).

If a psychological treatment can boost a mother's perceived self-efficacy, then she can approach formerly dreaded situations with new confidence. As we know, mothers of failure-to-thrive children dread to feed them, are unable to manage the situation satisfactorily and confidently, get anxious and helpless, and avoid feeding their children because they believe their attempts will fail. By being shown how to handle feeding, and how to control anxiety and tension when giving the child food, the mother will experience some success, which will be reinforced by the therapist: this, in turn, will give her a sense of achievement and will boost confidence. Repetitions of small achievements produced by the successful re-enactment of the performance of tasks will lead gradually to stronger self-esteem: the heightened self-efficacy leads to more vigorous, persistent, and probably more successful attempts to cope with problems, while successful problem-solving further increases perceived self-effectiveness. Bandura (1981) offers major sources of self-efficacy expectations: these include performance, accomplishments, modelling demonstrations, verbal persuasions, and emotional arousal.

Thus, if a mother succeeds in eliminating or changing one problem of behaviour in her child, then her expectations of further success should increase. If an apprehensive child, fearful of its mother, manages to approach her when in difficulties, or if the rejectful mother manages to sit a child on her lap and cuddle it, then they have learned that they can perform a difficult task and their sense of competence is enhanced. Such self-observed success is the most potent and rewarding source of increased self-confidence. With long-standing distorted mother–child relationships, this can be a turning point for speedy recovery or discovery of mutual belonging and love.

CASE STUDY

Jack was rejected in a visibly hostile way by his mother, and this rejection became mutual by the age of five. According to his mother, this serious distortion in their relationship resulted from his refusal to take feeds from her: everyone could feed him but her, so she felt rejected as he refused to accept the basic care and attention from her (which was food). Their interaction became painful and hostile, so eventually she never touched him or spoke to him unless it was absolutely necessary, while he would never approach her or come to her for help, reassurance, or comfort.

The therapeutic programme in parent-training was slow and at times difficult as Jack had to be engaged in the therapy as well. The aim was to reduce fear, apprehension, and reluctance in Jack, and anger, hostility, and anxiety in the mother. After eight weeks of quite intensive work in trying to bring them closer together (by gradual exposure-training, by play, and by being in close proximity), there was a breakthrough. The weeping and emotional mother telephoned the therapist: it was not possible to make sense of what she was saying and it was thought that she had hurt Jack, or that something dreadful had happened. Eventually she said that Jack had put his arms around her and put his cheek to hers, which was the first loving gesture he had ever made. This overwhelmed the mother, and it was clear the awkward corner, where hate is turned to the possibility of liking (at least), had been turned. This can only be achieved by practice, by trying, and by doing things. It is seldom possible to 'talk people out' of such problems as distorted relationships and hateful interactions, but practising can make this work. It is certainly difficult, if not impossible, to desensitise a child's fearful, apprehensive and also rejective feelings towards the parent. That simple gesture, though hard-earned, increased the mother's self-efficacy and sense of achievement.

Observing others succeed (vicarious success) can also boost an insecure observer's self-confidence (a 'coping' model), but not as strongly as directly experiencing success. After all, the other person may be perceived as braver and more skilled than the observer could ever hope to be. Parents who fail miserably to manage their children tend to doubt their own skills until they have actually succeeded in performing a difficult task. There is a lot of evidence from parent-training programmes (Greist *et al.*, 1982; Wolfe, 1990, 1991; Azar, 1989; Iwaniec, 1990; and Webster-Stratton, 1991) that combined parent-skill training is most effective. Role-playing, rehearsing, discussion, or awareness acquired through reflective counselling at group-work level work best if put into operation at an individual level.

Learning and applying is very important for raising self-efficacy. Many forms of instruction in psychotherapy rely on verbal persuasion, but these seem to have limited value in raising self-efficacy expectations. If a therapist tries to reassure a tired, demoralised mother that a child will behave better when the mother changes her attitudes towards it, and when she begins to manage it correctly, but the therapist fails to provide precise guidance as to the most effective methods, attempts by the mother may fail, with the result that she may feel even more helpless than ever. It is not the precise methods of behaviour-management (those should be tailored to the individual preference of the family), but the building of confidence, encouragement of persistence, and achievement of consistence that are important, so that the child is not confused and knows what is expected from it (see Wolfe, 1991). Attribution is a key factor in any therapeutic intervention. If the client simply attributes beneficial change to the therapist or to 'luck' rather than to the client's own efforts (so-called 'internal locus of control'), then therapeutic objectives have only partially been met and may not generalise over time.

CONCLUSION

A client's own emotional arousal can increase or undermine his/her expectations of success. A child who trembles at the thought of going to school because of fear of being bullied, or of facing its mother when it soils its pants, is less optimistic about its ability to stop soiling than is a calmer child. The observer of emotional states may tend to reach conclusions about personal effectiveness. Extreme anxiety can interfere with many types of performance, which is on a continuum with emotionally abused and neglected children and their carers. When anxiety is reduced, perhaps through relaxation training, systematic desensitisation, tranquillisers, or reassurance, then self-confidence should increase and with it rises the possibility of success.

11

GROUP-WORK WITH EMOTIONALLY ABUSIVE AND NEGLECTFUL PARENTS

Is not the pleasure of feeling and exhibiting power *over other beings, a principal part of the gratification of cruelty?* *

INTRODUCTION

Group-work with parents who experience similar problems may be more cost-effective and can provide additional benefits such as peer-support, modelling, and observations of role-play by others. Because a group-training programme has to be prepared and planned in advance, the theoretical and conceptual content might be better organised and thought about than on an individual basis. The same would apply for teaching different techniques, and using teaching/training aids. Being in a group, members benefit from formal and informal discussions, see how problems are managed by different people by observing role-plays, participate in role-play themselves, and get involved in group exercises. Exchanges of tips and ideas facilitate better coping strategies and fill educational gaps, while group discussions and exercises provide a forum for reassurance and clarification: indeed group-work with abusive parents reduces their feelings of isolation, uniqueness, despair, and hopelessness. Well-motivated members of groups, who have contributed to organisation and even to some content planning, will keep the group going, will make the best out of it, and will create opportunities to develop contacts with each other outside group-work.

---

*John Foster (1770–1843): *Journal*, Item 772 in J. E. Ryland (Ed.), *The Life and Correspondence of John Foster* (London: Jackson & Walford, 1846).

However, the running of effective parent-training groups is not free of problems. Firstly, they are time-consuming to organise (to prepare their content and to provide the necessary teaching material): particular difficulties arise when trying to set up timetables for group-work which will be possible and convenient for everyone concerned—working fathers, for instance, may often find regular attendance inconvenient or even out of the question. Group-work, in comparison with individual parent-training sessions, is, as has been noted above, more cost-effective but has also some limitations, particularly when neglecting and rejecting parents are involved. They feel ashamed, embarrassed, and reluctant to share their experiences with completely strange people, so a combination of group-work and individual work would seem to be an appropriate choice in these circumstances. Parents can be prepared before group-work for 'learning in public' and talking about their negative feelings and difficulties experienced with children: the fact that the group-leader already knows them helps to break the ice. It is also essential to involve them in group planning: they need to 'own' that group, and to feel that they have contributed to its creation. Levels of attendance and commitment to participate and to learn depend on early involvement of prospective group-members in work-planning.

PLANNING GROUP-WORK

Good preparation will determine the success of group-work. There are some general rules that need to be taken into consideration when planning group-work. It is necessary to:

(1) negotiate and discuss specific issues that parents would like to explore;
(2) discuss and learn from the prospective group-members;
(3) list points and work out the logical order, always starting from general, impersonal, unthreatening ones to more complex, challenging, and personal issues and feelings;
(4) find at least one co-worker;
(5) find a group-work consultant (it does not have to be a line manager);
(6) find a private and quiet place for group-work;
(7) make provision for children while parents/mothers have their session;
(8) plan each session before group-work starts;
(9) prepare and organise teaching materials, videos, audio-tapes, materials for play sessions, and other aids; and
(10) work out an evaluation system.

David and Frank Johnson, authors of the book *Joining Together*, have made several suggestions for successful group-work which can be adapted to a particular set and range of problems. For example, when planning and setting up a group for emotionally abusive and neglectful mothers, the following principles should be observed (cited in Herbert, 1989):

(1) *Definition of terms and concepts*: Group-members need to be provided with terms and definitions of those terms (such as reinforcement, stimulation, interaction, discipline, attachment, trust-building, maltreatment, neglect, abuse, modelling, rehearsal, and so on) to help to achieve full participation from all members. Group-leaders should describe each concept, giving examples or providing alternative words (for instance interaction means 'what you do with the child and how you are doing it', involving playing, reading, talking, supervising, instructing, and everyday activity);

(2) *Negotiation and/or establishment of goals*: Goals and objectives should be made clear and agreed for each session (for instance, self-control training would include short instruction, role-play, modelling, brain-storming, discussion, clarification, and giving instruction for homework). Viewing of videos dealing with a topic, or getting a handout to prepare members for the session can be helpful and appreciated, as everybody concerned is given an equal opportunity to participate in the discussions and the exercises. Each session should allow time to review homework tasks for each member of the group;

(3) *Encouragement of free and fair discussion*: In order to learn and to feel a part of the group, each member should be encouraged to freely, openly, and fairly express feelings and ideas, attitudes, and beliefs. Each group should have a few basic rules about what is allowed and what is not (like scapegoating, bullying, and excessive criticism of any one member);

(4) *Integration of the material*: Constant connections should be made where appropriate between topics covered early on and current themes (for example, links between stress-management techniques, problem-solving, self-control, and child-discipline). Parent-training groups should try out practical ideas, such as communicating with children who are apprehensive and fearful of their parents by means of role-play or homework tasks. Discussions or instructions alone are unlikely to be helpful without preliminary sessions to encourage familiarity with methods and applications in practice;

(5) *Encouragement of the application of discussion material*: Group-members should be actively and constantly encouraged and reminded to link what they have learned to their own lives, circumstances, and needs. They should also be prompted to report back to the group the

'feedback' they received from trying different methods and techniques at home; and

(6) *Evaluation of the quality of the discussions*: Group-members should be asked to examine critically their performance as a body and as individuals, and their contributions to the success or failure of the efficacy of the group.

EFFECTIVE GROUP-INTERVENTION

It is extremely important to select the appropriate place for group-work. The room should be bright, with comfortable seating, and should be warm. Seats should be arranged in a circle, so that group-members can see and hear each other. Video equipment, flip charts, cassette players, and other teaching aids should be checked and prepared beforehand, so that no time is wasted and no embarrassing pauses occur during the times allotted for sessions.

It must be remembered that emotionally abusive parents are very defensive and are reluctant to talk about themselves, so the group-leaders should start from neutral topics such as child-development and child-needs, and a dispassionate look at the behavioural problems of children. An early exploration of parental feelings towards children, and an examination of the ways in which parents attempt to manage the behaviour of their children, can be intimidating and consequently may arrest full participation (and learning processes). Once group-members get to know each other and begin to feel more comfortable in each other's company, explorations of feelings and airing of personal difficulties and dilemmas can begin. Group-leaders should facilitate (but not dominate) group-life: they should keep an eye on the group dynamics, they must make sure that every member has an opportunity to speak, and they need to restrain those members who try to dominate or 'hog' the discussion. Group-leaders should ensure that sessions are conducted according to plan in structured ways, and that they periodically sum up the discussions, set and explain homework, and give group-members opportunities to ask questions, clarify confusing issues, and tailor acquired knowledge to personal needs and circumstances.

GROUP-WORK WITH EMOTIONALLY-ABUSIVE MOTHERS

The author ran a parent-training group for 10 emotionally abusive mothers. Group-work consisted of 10 sessions once a week, each session lasting two hours. After each session there was a pleasant coffee-break, with cakes and snacks prepared by the group-members. Members could stay as long as they wanted, and this was encouraged so that they could get to know each other better by having informal chats. There were three mature social work students helping with the running of the group and providing a playgroup for the children in order to free mothers during that time. There were two major objectives guiding the training content and purpose of the group.

(1) training of mothers in their own behaviour-management (for example, self-control, stress-management, relaxation, assertiveness training, and development of social skills); and
(2) provision of a forum for mutual support, encouragement, exchange of ideas, establishment of social contact outside group-work, and ventilation of feelings.

All group-members received individual help and individual parent-training at home before group-work started. Some individual training was quite substantial in content and frequency, depending on individual needs established during an assessment period. All families were conferenced, and received between 5 and 7 individual sessions in dealing with specific and urgent needs. Crisis-intervention ranged from provision of day care for children, through personal and marital counselling, to dealing with welfare rights, housing, and arranging for Home Start volunteers to provide assistance (where physical neglect was apparent as well). Personal counselling was very important here as it provided the foundation for further work.

Attending parents were consulted regarding the formation of the group and the content of training: this content was informed by the outcomes of assessment and those aspects which were common in all cases. An agreement to attend each session was written formally and signed by the group-members and group-leaders. Provision of child-care during group-sessions was organised, and transport provided for those living far away or where public transport was difficult or inconvenient. It was agreed that each session would be evaluated and that necessary changes would be made as suggested by the evaluation comments. Members agreed to take this group-work seriously and to participate in the exercises to the best of their ability. Personal issues discussed (or which might occur during the group life) would be treated as confidential and as group 'property' (unless it were important to the child's well-being). Each group-session was planned prior to the commencement of group-work and shared with each prospective member of the mothers' group. The group was planned to have two distinctive parts in each session:

Part I   'hands-on' work, role-playing, doing exercises, practising new skills, etc.; and
Part II   discussing and reflecting on the current situations in the families, and engaging in mutual problem-solving strategies.

Mothers were asked to produce a list of their expectations and what they would like to change in their lives and in relation to the emotionally-abused child. This list included strong desires on the part of the mother to:

(1) feel close to the child;
(2) feel at ease and good when the child was near;
(3) feel love for the child similar to the love she felt for others;
(4) have the child come to her and actually want to be near her;
(5) enjoy the child's company;
(6) want the child to like her, and to call her 'Mum', not 'lady';
(7) want to know where she went wrong when bringing up the child;
(8) wish the child took notice of her, and did what she wanted it to do;
(9) wish she could stop feeling guilty and miserable;
(10) wish she could be a better mother;
(11) cease feeling useless and unable to do anything right;
(12) stop feeling the child was hurting her, and cease believing the child was doing this on purpose in order to punish her;
(13) want the child to listen to her;
(14) want to know how to handle the child when it was being awkward;
(15) wish she knew how to make the child eat, sleep, and do things as other children do;
(16) wish she could do at least one thing which would be appreciated;
(17) want to know how to help the child to be clever and grow up well;
(18) cease feeling that everyone blames her, in spite of her perception that the child never took any notice of what she said, refused to do things when asked, and behaved in an impossible way;
(19) want to learn how to help the child to behave so she could like it; and
(20) want to get on better with the child, and the child with her.

These are just a few statements: others were very similar. What stands out when reading them is that those mothers:

(1) were lacking in self-confidence (low efficacy);
(2) wanted to be better mothers;
(3) wanted to know how to manage non-compliance and other behavioural problems;
(4) wanted to learn how to socialise a child;
(5) had unrealistic expectations;

(6) had negative attitudes towards the child;

(7) had high stress levels; and

(8) possessed a sense of helplessness.

The group had to address not only skills-training, but also a change of attitudes and self-image of the mothers.

Methods and Techniques used to Help Mothers during Group-work

Self-control training

Experiencing occasional anger towards one's children is a natural part of being a parent. Most parents who maltreat their children have difficulties in controlling frustration and anger, so they lash out physically or verbally. This sort of behaviour is self-reinforcing because it brings immediate (although momentary) relief. As time goes on parents hit harder and more frequently, scream and use degrading language with greater passion, believing this is the only way to make children behave. Self-control training is designed to give participants more effective means of manipulating the eliciting, reinforcing, and discriminative stimuli which affect their behaviour. The first task in this training is to examine what leads to an item of behaviour and what are the consequences of that behaviour. The second task is to explore the ways in which, and then to make suggestions as to how, these events can be altered. They may be changed either by physical or cognitive changes in order to achieve a greater degree of behaviour-control (for example, learning to control verbal aggression, drinking, and anger). Group-members are asked to make a list of behaviours over which they would like to have more control. Each member is required to describe an episode using ABC Analysis in order to practise understanding of the behavioural sequence:

Antecedent events — how the behaviour started, how it was triggered off, and what happened before the behaviour occurred;

Behaviour — what were the actions, and what was the behaviour;

Consequences — what was the result of that behaviour, what feelings did it inspire, and what were the consequences.

As an example of ABC Analysis the following may be quoted:

Antecedent event	—	the mother went to the child's room and saw ripped-off wallpaper and a ripped-up pillow: feathers were flying all over the room;
Behaviour	—	furious and resentful, the mother smacked the child and locked it in a coalshed to teach it a lesson and threatened it with living in a shed if it failed to learn to respect its own room;
Consequences	—	at the start the mother felt this was the only way to teach the child how to behave, but then felt ashamed and guilty but only after it was too late.

Group-members are then asked to devise alternative ways to control anger, resentment, hostility, and so on. A list of suggested self-control techniques is produced and their application discussed and linked with possible incidents. At least two incidents were role-played by the group-leader and mothers, and then alternative ways of coping with and managing situations were modelled.

A list of useful techniques in self-control is given below as a series of self-instructions:

(1) go to another room to get away from the child;
(2) count to 10, or count leaves on a potted plant;
(3) go to the kitchen to make a cup of tea;
(4) take a deep breath;
(5) go to the garden and kick a few stones to get rid of anger, or walk around the garden;
(6) go to the bedroom and punch a few cushions;
(7) read a favourite poem or a paragraph from a favourite novel;
(8) go to the bathroom and read a newspaper for a few minutes;
(9) listen to music;
(10) do some heavy physical work, like digging the garden, washing the floor, or vacuum cleaning the room;
(11) pinch yourself or put your hands under cold water;
(12) sit quietly and reflect on pleasurable and soothing things instead of brooding about the child;
(13) try to recall positive aspects of the child's behaviour; and
(14) try to remember that the child is a learner, and therefore subject to making mistakes.

For homework, mothers are asked to practise self-control skills at home with the children, partners, or other people who may trigger off anger or irrational behaviour.

Stress-management training

Novaco (1975) developed a stress-management training programme to offer people skills in managing provocation and in regulating their anger-arousal. Components of this programme include a situational analysis (identification of situations that provoke thoughts and feelings in anger-inducing encounters) and encouragement to use self-statements and feelings associated with anger as cues for positive coping-strategies. Parents are encouraged to reconceptualise anger as a state which is aggravated by self-presented thought, and to view arousal as a series of stages rather than as an all-or-nothing state. Attention should be paid to identifying and altering irrational beliefs (for example, 'she is doing it on purpose to hurt me', or 'he knows how to do it, but it is just sheer laziness'). Coping strategies include the use of self-instructions to reduce arousal when this is identified. Types of self-instruction that may be used include those that encourage a focus on the tasks to be accomplished (for example, 'I must keep calm', or 'what is it I have to do here?'), and those that encourage other incompatible behaviour such as getting a cup of tea or relaxing (for example, do relaxation exercises for a few minutes, or simply tell yourself just to relax or 'take a deep breath'). Group-members are encouraged to use coping skills early in a chain of behaviour and to offer self-reinforcement for success. In other words, parents are advised to interfere with anger-provoking thoughts as soon as they begin to occur, and to instruct themselves how they are going to deal with the problem. For instance, if a mother manages to stop herself getting angry and anxious (because her child refuses to eat its meal) she can tell herself, 'well, I managed that quite well, this is not the end of the world, I will try again because it is always better when I feel less anxious and worried. I will just relax for a few minutes, and then just go on about things without thinking that he is not going to put on or lose weight.' Such self-talk helps the participant to feel better.

Group-members are given stressful scenarios based on their own experiences, and then as a group devise various stress-management strategies. Those scenarios are role-played and discussed, accommodating individual needs for understanding and ability to apply them in real-life situations. A video tape may be used to show how one can use self-talk to prepare for:

(1) provocation;
(2) reacting during the confrontation; and
(3) coping with arousal.

Self-talk is a useful technique in stress-management training. When people are under stress and are besieged by problems with which they feel they cannot cope, they will privately tell themselves all sorts of defeating statements such as 'I can't cope any longer ... , there is no point trying ... , whatever I do is wrong ... , there is no hope ... , nothing is ever going to change ... , and ... I am a failure'. Such self-talk goes together with observable behaviours such as social withdrawal, weepiness, insomnia, detachment, lack of energy and enthusiasm, and so on. Stress is evident, and needs to be dealt with. Several sets of procedures are taught in order to control impulsive reactions and hostile feelings.

Preparing for provocation is important in order to face difficulties, as the illustration below demonstrates:

> John had lost weight again. His mother was told that she must take care, and feed him properly and regularly. She had been trying so hard to feed him, but he refused to eat. There were arguments about John with her husband and his mother. She was very anxious when it came to feeding-time, and always anticipated problems. She also felt very resentful towards John and that he had made her life nothing but a misery.

Each meal-time has therefore become a battlefield, and it is necessary for the mother to prepare herself for it so that she does not get angry and defeated before she even starts. She therefore must tell herself:

(1) this is not going to upset me;
(2) I know what to do;
(3) I am going to stay calm;
(4) I am going to take John to the kitchen and tell him what I am going to prepare to eat;
(5) if I realise that I am getting upset or anxious, I will take a deep breath and tell myself that I will do my best;
(6) I will smile and talk to John in a calm way;
(7) I will encourage him to eat; and
(8) I will not get angry.

If John refuses to eat, however, reactions during the confrontation are important, and certain self-instructions should be used:

(1) if he does not eat now I will try to feed him later;
(2) I am not going to put pressure on him;
(3) there is no point in getting angry, because being angry makes things worse;
(4) if I get upset I will lose control, so I must not get upset, and therefore remain in control;

(5) I must stay calm, and continue to relax; and

(6) I must remember to talk warmly and in kind tones.

However, it may be difficult to control anger-arousal and it is necessary to learn techniques of coping with arousal. The following self-instructions can be of help:

(1) I am getting tensed up, so it is time to relax and slow down;

(2) getting upset will not solve the problem;

(3) it is just not worth it to get so angry;

(4) I have every reason to be annoyed and anxious, but there is no need to 'blow-up';

(5) I had better relax by taking a few deep breaths;

(6) I know what to do, and am going to rehearse that again;

(7) I need to tell myself what to do again;

(8) I am not going to take all the blame;

(9) I am going to say what I think;

(10) I am going to be rational;

(11) negatives lead to more negatives; and

(12) it is important to think first before I act.

Accumulation of stresses in the lives of parents contributes to emotional neglect and abuse of children. It is therefore necessary to teach·parents how to manage stress by providing some general rules and specific techniques to cope with everyday difficulties. Some life-stresses are not in our power to change, but we can control a lot of them if we put our minds to it.

At the end of stress-management training a list of suggestions as to how to monitor stress in everyday life may be helpful:

(1) keep a list of stresses in your life—the accumulation of them can make life unbearable and unrewarding;

(2) positive self-talk helps one to remain in control and to feel positive about one's self;

(3) do not think that you have to do everything at once, and that every problem has to be eliminated 100%. Be satisfied with small changes. Even a small reduction in each stress can lead to a big difference in your ability to cope;

(4) do not try to assist everybody all the time. Take a rational view of your commitments in your daily life-pattern. Try to leave a little time for yourself and for some privacy;

(5) think positively and believe that you can change things if you put your mind to it: think with determination;

(6) learn to say 'no' if you feel that demands which are being made on you are unreasonable;

(7) be free to put your point of view. Communicate your thoughts and feelings, and do not store them for they will only explode, hurting people who least deserve it, like children;

(8) if you cannot cope, ask for help, and keep asking until you get it;

(9) ask your friends, family, or neighbours to give you a hand if you feel overwhelmed with problems;

(10) ask your G.P. or a health visitor for help, advice, and assistance. Do not feel that you are a burden or nuisance, because it is their job and they are being paid to help you. They can also refer you to appropriate people for help;

(11) do not wait until things are totally out of control;

(12) there is nothing unusual in having difficulties relating to your child—or to have difficulties in teaching children how to behave;

(13) try to share your worries with your partner: ask him to help you, to give you a hand, and to support you. It is also his duty to care for the child; and

(14) social-workers do not only protect children—they also protect families. Turn to them for help if you feel you cannot cope any longer.

Relaxation training

Relaxation training has become a valuable part of stress-management. Clients are taught how to relax when they are overwhelmed with tension and anxiety. They are taught how to identify tension in different parts of the body and how to deal with it. Anxiety shows itself and affects people in different physiological responses (increased heart-rate, sweating, muscle tension): behavioural responses (shown by avoidance-behaviour); and cognitive responses (negative self-defeating thoughts). In order to break this negative cycle, it is necessary to learn to control anxiety and to be able to recognise the onset of anxious feelings and situations that trigger off anxiety. Relaxation is an ideal way to cope with these crippling and self-defeating feelings.

Relaxation techniques were practised several times by the author and her team with group-members to encourage the acquisition of necessary skills in relaxation. Each member was given a 30-minute tape to practise relaxation at home and then asked to feed back and describe to the group how the exercise went. One session was specifically allocated to teach, demonstrate, and discuss individual applications of different relaxation techniques, including:

(1) listening to the relaxation tape and practising deep-muscle relaxation (demonstration);
(2) meditating (remembering or imagining something pleasant and enjoyable). This has proved to be a particularly helpful exercise in cases where feelings of defeat, lowness, or distress are experienced;
(3) listening to music of individual preference which may have a soothing effect; and
(4) employing personal techniques suitable for relaxing individuals, such as reading, walking, watching television, cooking, sporting activities, and so on, and discussing and encouraging those aspects. Useful tips are given as to how to build them into everyday life for self-satisfaction and reduction of anxiety.

A relaxation tape was used to start with, simply to help individuals to locate anxiety in different parts of the body and to teach the techniques. Once learning had taken place the tape had no need to be used, and relaxations were only done on those parts of the body affected by anxiety. Following relaxation a training script was used during the group-work.

There are many relaxation tapes currently available, and these should be heard so that the most suitable can be selected (for further reading see Ollendick and Cerny, 1981). An example of a training script is given below.

Hands and arms: Make a fist with your left hand. Squeeze it hard. Feel the tightness in your hand and arm as you squeeze. Now let your hand go and relax. See how much better your hand and arm feel when they are relaxed. Once again, make a fist with your left hand and squeeze hard. Now relax and let your hand go. (Repeat the process for the right hand and arm.)

Arms and shoulders: Stretch your arms out in front of you. Raise them high up over your head and way back. Feel the pull in your shoulders. Stretch higher. Now just let your arms drop back to your side. Stretch again. Stretch your arms out in front of you. Raise them over your head. Pull them back, way back. Pull hard. Now let them drop quickly. Notice how your shoulders feel more relaxed. This time have a great big stretch. Try to touch the ceiling. Stretch your arms way out in front of you. Raise them way up high over your head. Push them way, way back. Notice the tension and pull in arms and shoulders. Hold tight. Now let them drop very quickly and feel how good it is to be relaxed. It feels good and warm and lazy.

Shoulder and neck: Try to pull your shoulders up to your ears and push your head down into your shoulders. Hold in tight. Now relax and feel the warmth. Again, pull your shoulders up to your ears and push your head down into your shoulders. Do it tightly. You can relax now. Bring your head out and let your shoulders relax. Notice how much better it feels to be relaxed than to be all tight. One more time now. Push your head down and your shoulders way up to your ears. Hold it. Feel the tenseness in your neck and shoulders. You can relax now and feel comfortable. You feel good.

Jaw: Put your teeth hard together. Let your neck muscles help you. Now relax. Just let your jaw hang loose. Notice how good it feels just to let your jaw drop. Bite down hard again. Now relax again. Just let your jaw drop. It feels so good just to let go. One more time. Bite down. Hard as you can. Harder. Oh, you're really working hard. Now relax. Try to relax your whole body. Let yourself go as loose as you can.

Face and nose: Wrinkle up your nose. Make as many wrinkles in your nose as you can. Now you can relax your nose. Now wrinkle up your nose again. Wrinkle it up hard. Hold it just as tight as you can. You can relax your face. Notice that when you scrunch up your nose your cheeks and your mouth and your forehead all help you and they get tight, too. So when you relax your nose, your whole face relaxes too, and that feels good. Now make lots of wrinkles on your forehead. Hold it tight, now, then, let go. Now you can just relax. Let your face go smooth. No wrinkles anywhere. Your face feels smooth and relaxed.

Stomach: Now tighten up your stomach muscles. Make your stomach hard. Do not move. Hold it. You can relax now. Let your stomach go soft. Let it be as relaxed as you can. That feels so much better. Tighten your stomach hard. You can relax now. Settle down, get comfortable, and relax. Notice the difference between a tight stomach and a relaxed one. That is how it should feel: loose and relaxed. Once more. Tighten up. Tighten hard. Now you can relax completely. Now this time, try to pull your stomach in. Try to squeeze it against your backbone. Try to be as skinny as you can. Now relax, because you do not have to be skinny now. Just relax and feel your stomach being warm and loose. Squeeze in your stomach again. Make it touch your backbone. Get it small and tight. Get as thin as you can. Hold tight now. You can relax now. Settle back and let your stomach come back out where it belongs. You can really feel good now. You have done well.

Legs and feet: Push your toes hard down on the floor. You will probably need your legs to help you push. Push down, spread your toes apart. Now relax your feet. Let your toes go loose and feel how good that is. It feels good to be relaxed. Now push your toes down. Let your leg muscles help you push your feet down. Push your feet. It feels so good to be relaxed. No tenseness anywhere. You feel warm and tingly.

Conclusion: Stay as relaxed as you can. Let your whole body go limp and feel all your muscles relax. In a few minutes you will be asked to open your eyes and that will be the end of the session. Today is a good day, and you are ready to go back to class feeling very relaxed. You have worked hard in here and it feels good to work hard. Shake your arms. Now shake your legs. Move your head around. Slowly open your eyes, and enjoy well-being in your body and your mind.

Problem-solving

When people get overwhelmed with problems and difficulties they cannot think straight in a rational problem-solving way. They may become beset with minutiae, fail to see the wood for the trees, and be unable to resolve certain problems in their lives. Unsuccessful attempts at problem-solving create anxiety and depression, as well as confrontation and interpersonal conflict. In order to understand the, at times, most confusing actions of those people, we need to try to see what they are trying to achieve by behaving in this way. Training in problem-solving in a group is very useful, as it provides various suggestions from a number of people collectively. Actual exercises are very stimulating and engaging as well as educational (Herbert, 1989).

Problem-solving means trying to improve the actual problem by finding an answer to a difficulty and a solution to a problem. The process of problem-solving involves:

(1) a precise definition of and understanding of the seriousness of the problem, involving an analysis of things as they are now, and things as they should be; and
(2) an assessment of the nature and magnitude of the problem by making a list of what makes a person work towards the positive and wanted

goals, and what makes that person move away from the positive solution.

Problems are viewed as a balance between forces pushing in opposite directions.

The group is asked to brainstorm and make a list of positives and negatives to problem-solving. For example, a current problem (John's delayed development referred to above) could be assessed thus:

Helping forces (+)	Hindering forces (−)
(1) he should go to the nursery;	(1) I will get more alienated from him;
(2) he will have the opportunity to talk, play, and do things with other children;	(2) I will have little time to be with him; and
(3) nursery nurses are very helpful and sympathetic;	(3) it will make me feel bad that they, not I, can help John.
(4) you can spend some time there, working with the nurses; and	
(5) it will give you time to sort out other problems.	

The group is asked to examine pluses and minuses and then to formulate strategies to move the client towards a logical, necessary, and desired outcome. Some might think that helping the mother to provide a more stimulating environment for John is better than sending him to the nursery. Creative and realistic thinking and critical ability are very helpful at this stage. In order to be effective we need to strengthen the helping forces and reduce or eliminate the hindering forces.

The next step is to decide and implement the strategy. This will involve:

(1) choosing the possibilities which seem most appropriate;
(2) selecting necessary methods and finding appropriate resources to permit the implemention of the chosen strategy; and
(3) devising a criterion for evaluating the outcome of the implemented strategy.

ASSERTIVE TRAINING AND SOCIAL-SKILLS TRAINING

Assertive training has been used to help group-members to deal with impulsive and self-defeating aggressive behaviour (commonly the defensive reaction of a person who does not have sufficient social skills or confidence to assert himself or herself in a more appropriate way). Assertive and social skills training aim also to help those who are timid and withdrawn. It is recognised that many mothers and children (particularly adolescents) lack skills in listening and talking to each other. Inappropriate or inadequate behaviour in social settings is often due to lack of effective social skills, or to interfering emotional reactions (such as anger, anxiety, or inappropriate discrimination in using skills). Many parents simply do not enjoy interactions with other people and tend to avoid them. Training in social skills is felt to be necessary in order to break social isolation, to improve communication, and to improve manners in interaction with other people and their children.

Since communication between mothers and their children is identified by them as an area of particular difficulty, training in communication can be used. Role-playing scenarios are videoed and then used for interpretation, for discussion, and for improving the effectiveness of performance skills. Commercial videos are also used where the group-members are asked to identify appropriate and inappropriate social behaviour, and to explore positive and negative effects on children, themselves, and other people. Therapists also model socially beneficial behaviour (verbal and non-verbal communication, tone of voice, facial expression, mannerisms, useful phrases, and so forth). Mothers are asked (as a homework exercise) to practise newly-learned and rehearsed skills with their children (and particularly with the child to which they found difficulties in relating), their partners, extended family, or other people. They are also asked to use those skills conscientiously with people in establishments such as the DHSS, Housing Authorities, Social Services Departments, hospitals, schools, medical practices, and so on, and to compare and observe different types of reactions from people with whom they deal. The outcomes from homework are always discussed at the beginning of each group-work session.

PARENTS' EVALUATION OF THE TRAINING PROGRAMME

Parents found the training programme described above satisfactory or very satisfactory on all levels. Training methods, topics, simplicity and easiness to learn and follow, balance between helping children and helping mothers, relaxed atmosphere, constructive learning, good feeling that they *actually had to work* and not just gossip, all contributed to a feeling of well-spent time. What was significant at the evaluation point was that they felt 'it was as good and as useful as they made it'. Important points were:

(1) they had a say in planning and organising this group;
(2) they were consulted regarding the content and methods of teaching;
(3) there was always a brief evaluation at the end of each session, so amendments (if felt appropriate) were made for the next session;
(4) the group established 'rules of conduct' during the first introductory session, so there were few disagreements, scapegoating, or domineering behaviour; and
(5) since each group-member was visited at home every two weeks, there were opportunities to elaborate and clarify things.

The results of a parent-training programme, based on the above, were evaluated by independent assessors (Clinical Psychology students) using a six-month and a one-year follow-up. They demonstrated that no case had become worse overall, that, from the answers to 22 questions, it was seen that the total situation was the same or better, and that there was a significant improvement in 11 areas:

(1) overall situation at home $p < 0.005$;
(2) feelings towards the child $p < 0.05$;
(3) relationship with the child $p < 0.1$;
(4) more time spent playing with the child $p < 0.05$;
(5) at ease in the child's presence and child at ease in the parents' presence $p < 0.01$;
(6) child feeling free to go to mother for comfort and help $p < 0.001$;
(7) child's behaviour towards the father $p < 0.02$;
(8) food intake $p < 0.02$;
(9) improvement in marital relationship $p < 0.02$;
(10) improved physical appearance of child $p < 0.1$; and
(11) improved cognition $p < 0.1$.

A subsequent 10-year follow-up showed general maintenance of improved child–parent relationships, interactions, and family functioning in 64% of the sample studied. The mothers felt (10 years on) that group-work had helped them in several ways:

(1) to realise that their situations were not unique;
(2) to make friends and acquaintances (some of them still maintain close contacts);
(3) to learn how to behave when dealing with authorities and institutions;

(4) to feel more confident when dealing with a child's difficult behaviour;
(5) to understand their children's needs, individuality, and vulnerability;
(6) to cope better with their anger and frustration; and
(7) to better their abilities to stop and think.

Parents appreciated and remembered especially the following:

(1) different methods and techniques of role-playing and practising skills;
(2) being able to see how well or badly one behaved using video;
(3) having the opportunity and freedom to choose methods which were tailored to the individual needs and circumstances of the group-members;
(4) being able to share and bring their problems and their points of view into discussion;
(5) being made to feel that they were quite capable of thinking and learning, thus encouraging better feelings about themselves;
(6) seeing a child, and their roles as parents, in a more positive way; and
(7) being respected and treated with dignity.

Parents also recalled certain negatives, including the following:

(1) the group was too large;
(2) insufficient exercises, and not enough recording on video of role-play; and
(3) the need for more sessions to make them more comfortable in practising skills and discussing personal issues.

CONCLUSION

Parent-training in well-organised and planned groups appears to be not only a useful way of learning new skills and making new friends, but also can be enjoyable. The success of group-work is highly dependent on a number of factors, as abusive parents feel apprehension, to say the least, and the subject can provoke extreme embarrassment, even though all group-members will be in the same boat. Among these factors may be mentioned the venue and the physical environment of the room used; a well-designed and thoroughly thought-out programme applicable to the needs of group-members; use of interesting, appropriate, and absorbing methods and techniques during each session; and provision of time during each session to enable group-members to exchange views and to converse.

Finally, group-work will not succeed if it starts by trying to deal with highly personal and intimidating issues concerning group-members' participation in the maltreatment of their children before the ice is broken. The nub of the matter has to be reached gently, and in stages.

12

HELPING CHILDREN

Where Love reigns, there is no Will to Power,
and where Power is all-pervading, Love is absent.
*The one is but the shadow of the other**

INTRODUCTION

There is no single or simple way in which to help emotionally abused and neglected children, especially when it is necessary to repair damage already done, and which is evident in the children's disturbed behaviour, delayed development, and insecure parent–child attachment. There are three ways in which treatment may be approached:

(1) by helping parents to understand their roles in the development of the problem, and to assist them to help themselves and their children (as has been described in the previous chapters, this may be achieved through personal and developmental counselling, family case-work, and marital work);
(2) by working directly with children in order to ease their pain, confusion, and emotional disturbance; and
(3) by working through and with the parents so that they can engage directly in the therapeutic process.

PROVISION OF DAY-CARE

When serious emotional abuse has been recognised, and where child-development has been seriously affected by that abuse, the provision of day-care is of considerable importance for, and benefit to, the child. For

---

*Carl Gustav Jung (1875–1961): 'Über die Psychologie des Unbewussten' (1917), *Gesammelte Werke* (Zürich & Stuttgart: Rascher Verlag, 1964), Vol. 7.

younger children this can involve the provision of day nurseries, family centres, daily minders, and frequent playgroups. For older children the provision of rewarding activities outside the home is essential in order to compensate for lost opportunities and emotional upheavals which might have been created. Because emotionally maltreated children have had no opportunities to learn various social skills and life-tasks (such as communication, interaction, and sharing) due to social isolation at home, and have built up images of adults as pain inflicters, anxiety and uneasiness creators, and unrecognisers of achievements, a place away from their normal 'home' environments can be most helpful to them in order to foster interests in sports activities, child and youth organisations (such as Cubs, Brownies, Scouts, Boys' and Girls' Brigades, etc.), and other activities (although any overt coercion into any of these involvements should be avoided, and the aptitudes of the children taken into account).

Those children who are placed with daily minders, day-nurseries, or family centres will need well-informed and thoroughly-planned help. Developmental, emotional, and behavioural needs will need to be addressed, and special attention must be provided to help the children to make good what they have lost developmentally, and to feel good and at ease when with other people and children.

Parents can be required to attend family centres or day-nurseries to participate in the care of the child and other children in order to learn parenting skills like play, discipline, toileting, feeding, communicating, supervising, guiding, and responding to the various needs of the child as they occur. Parents are encouraged to observe how difficult behaviour is managed, without becoming angry and resorting to harsh words and physical abuse. Some family centres run special programmes which include discussions about child-rearing methods and attitudes, methods of budgeting and preparing meals, and learning how to make toys out of readily available materials. Attendance by parents can provide opportunities to discuss problems of child-management (this can be especially valuable in cases where difficulties have been experienced at home in relating to the child and dealing with behavioural problems), to meet other parents who have had similar experiences, and to break down the social isolation that is the lot of many parents (especially single mothers).

CASE STUDY

To illustrate how a child can benefit from being placed at a day-nursery the case of Dean may be cited. Dean was referred to the Paediatric Social Worker by the NSPCC worker, who visited the family after receiving an anonymous telephone call regarding the child's treatment by his mother. The NSPCC staff member stated his concern about this child's poor physical growth and retarded development. The subsequent assessment diagnosed failure to grow due to severe emotional abuse and neglect. At the age of three years and seven months Dean was abnormally small (in fact smaller than his two-year old younger brother), was just starting to walk, knew only a few words, was unable to construct short sentences, while other skills such as toileting, playing, dressing, and behaviour at table were non-existent. His behaviour was either defiant and aggressive, or withdrawn and depressed.

The case conference decision was to provide help for both parents and child. He was placed full-time in a therapeutic day nursery where he received specialised and individual care and attention. A special therapist was assigned to provide stimulation in a structured and well-planned manner. Apart from individual one-to-one interaction and activities with the therapist, Dean gradually began to join groups of children in order to learn how to share and participate in group activities. At first he was extremely disruptive to the group (interrupting, screaming, and shouting when a story was read or a television programme watched, or throwing toys and disrupting other children's activities), but gradually he calmed down, was able to concentrate for longer periods, and began to learn how to behave when among other children. His language and motor skills rapidly accelerated, and his behaviour became more organised and purposeful, but he showed no sense of having attachments to anyone. Emotionally, he was far from being regarded as adjusted and stable. Although developmental improvement was made due to the help provided at the nursery, his relationships with his mother, and, to a lesser degree, with other members of his family, were still very poor. It would be unrealistic to assume that day-care sessions can solve relationship and interaction problems at home. In situations where a parent–child relationship has never been established or broken down, there will be a need for parent–child therapy at home in order to address the difficulties experienced by both parties, and to evolve remedies.

REPAIRING A CHILD'S SELF-ESTEEM AND SENSE OF ACHIEVEMENT

Emotionally abused and neglected children show notoriously low self-esteem. Their behaviour and reactions are marked by apprehension, withdrawal, shyness, and fearful avoidance of initiating conversation or other activities: they seem to be in constant doubt of their ability to do anything right. This is not surprising if we take into consideration aversive parent–child interaction. Persistent criticism, rebukes, dissatisfaction with a child's behaviour and task-accomplishments, as well as shaming the child in front of siblings, peers, and other people, bring about painful feelings of failure and helplessness. Such children are seldom praised, and their good behaviour and work are rarely acknowledged or even noticed: their attempts to please parents by attending to different tasks or behaving in a pleasing manner are generally ignored or dismissed. All this creates apprehension and a general reluctance to try new tasks. Furthermore, these children will be fearful to show or to share what they have done: they will seldom be provided with an opportunity to experience a sense of achievement which is so badly needed for the development of positive self-esteem.

Exploration of child-rearing attitudes among emotionally abusive and neglectful parents have shown six major reasons why those carers behave in such discouraging and damaging ways:

(1) lack of awareness that children need encouragement, guidance, supervision, and persistent positive reinforcement to learn how to behave and how to acquire appropriate life-skills;
(2) unawareness of the fact that successful task-accomplishment needs to be acknowledged and praised in order to make the child feel good about and proud of its behaviour and performance;
(3) belief that criticism and humiliation help to shape up a child's behaviour and performance;
(4) holding of unrealistic expectations of what a child can do at certain developmental stages;
(5) failure to appreciate the child's individual characteristics and individual needs; and
(6) harbouring of a general dislike for, or overt rejection of, the child.

CASE STUDY

It will be deduced from the above that a child's self-esteem and sense of achievement can be damaged intentionally or unwittingly. More often than not this damage is due to a child-rearing skill deficit which creates tension, faulty perceptions, frustration, and anger, leading to an unrewarding parent–child interaction and (consequently) relationship. To demonstrate how emotional maltreatment can affect a child's development of positive self-esteem and competence, let us look at the example of Lisa, aged four years.

Lisa was referred to a social worker and researcher (specialising in paediatrics) by her G.P., who became very concerned about Lisa's well-being and relationship with her parents. She was brought several times to the surgery by her mother, who complained about Lisa's non-compliance, irritability, sulking, and renewed bed-wetting. The G.P. found the mother frustrated and disappointed in Lisa's behaviour and achievements: Lisa appeared to be withdrawn and apathetic, had lost weight, and was looking depressed. Subsequent assessment by the therapist showed unrealistic expectations on the part of the mother, who put pressure on Lisa, which distorted the child's sense of competence, leading to her feelings of helplessness and utter confusion. Parent–child interaction was painful and demoralising: when Lisa showed a picture (painted by her) to her mother, folded her clothing, sorted out and stored her toys, or dressed herself, she was told invariably that these achievements were not good enough. The mother asked her to carry out all the tasks again, but did not show her how her performance could be improved: indeed, Lisa was frequently told that she was useless and stupid. She was not permitted to play until she had done properly what she was asked to do, however 'properly' was often beyond her ability and age. Yet *both* parents said they wanted the best for Lisa, and wanted to prepare her well for school and independence. However, Lisa was never praised and could never do well enough: any success was largely ignored or acknowledged with the remark 'you could do better than that'. It is small wonder that Lisa became very nervous, anxious, and reluctant to do anything. When approached by her mother and asked to carry out a task, Lisa would either burst into tears or defiantly ignore the request: this behaviour was interpreted by her mother as sheer disobedience and naughtiness, and so Lisa was punished for it. The child could not win: she became withdrawn, apathetic, and helpless, and came to believe that she could not do anything right. To avoid parental disapproval she became inactive and very defiant.

HELPING STRATEGIES

Children like Lisa need a lot of personal attention and affection to repair their self-esteem, and to think and feel good about themselves: they need help by increasing their sense of achievement in order to make them feel free to behave in a confident manner. Parents, on the other hand, require to learn basic lessons about child-development, the principles of social learning, and how those principles are used positively when bringing up a child. Behavioural methods and developmental counselling are very effective in cases such as this. Parents are advised and trained (where necessary) how to encourage a child to behave in a socially desirable manner appropriate for the child's age and level of development, and to make this process enjoyable and rewarding for the child.

Social Rewards

Parents are instructed and encouraged to praise the child each time when it has done something praiseworthy or behaved in a pro-social manner.

During the early days of treatment it is important that attempts (however imperfect) to accomplish a task be positively acknowledged and recognised. Parents are shown how to behave when in the child's company, how to look at and make physical contact with the child, and what phrases to use when praising and encouraging the child. They are asked to smile, hug, look at the child, kiss, touch, and so on, and to say 'thank you for doing this', 'you are a clever girl', 'I am very proud of you', and so forth. Social rewards, if consistently applied, increase a child's self-esteem and sense of achievement to a remarkable extent. Modelling reinforcing behaviour for the parents is essential for two reasons: firstly, it might not be in their child-rearing repertoire; and, secondly, there is at times emotional and cognitive resistance to react to the child in an affectionate and caring way. Even if there is lack of love, we can at least teach parents to be fair. In Lisa's case the parents had to learn how to make an appropriate request, acquire a suitable manner in which to speak, and develop caring physical contact with her. The ways in which pleasure and satisfaction were shown when the child's behaviour and task-performance proved reasonably satisfactory were of enormous importance.

Symbolic Rewards

This type of reinforcement is particularly helpful for young children as it provides visible signs of achievement for everyone to see and to make positive comments about how well the child is doing. Symbolic rewards are usually organised in the form of charts, which should be displayed in some prominent position, such as the door of the kitchen, for everyone to see. A picture or a sticker is put on the chart (in conjunction with a social reward) after each positive behaviour: to make the process exciting and educational for the child a variety of pictures featuring the child's interests could be used. Lisa liked animals, so the chart consisted of domestic animals, farmyard animals, forest animals, jungle animals, and aquatic animals. Symbolic rewards can be linked to activity rewards which are designed to strengthen parent–child relationships and provide opportunities to develop affectionate interaction between a child and its carers.

Activity Rewards

These rewards are mostly used to improve parent–child interaction: they provide an opportunity to do things together and to make the enjoyment of each other's company a possibility. As a result of good behaviour the child can earn an extra story at night, play a special game with the parents, have a trip to the park, swimming pool, cinema, or football match, enjoy a milkshake and hamburger, or have some other treat or activity tailored to the tastes of the child concerned. In Lisa's case, as a reward she was read a story about different animals, given a colouring book featuring animals, taken to the zoo, and given a trip to the 'Show Farm'. Activity rewards (if wisely and realistically organised) can provide a turning point for emotionally neglected and abused children: they also provide intellectual stimulation for, and enhance curiosity in, the child, and quite often generate interest in the parents as well. Those parents who never experienced caring, stimulating, and reciprocal activities with their parents when they were children, may be given the opportunity to experience what they never had and to share it with their own children. However, they need a helping hand, reassurance, guidance, and a lot of encouragement themselves. Reinforcing the reinforcer is crucial here, to back them up and to increase their sense of competence as parents as well.

EVALUATION COMMENTS

Short- and long-term evaluation (five years and 10 years on) showed that appropriate use of Response Increment Procedures (as indicated by social, symbolic, and activity rewards) considerably improved self-esteem and sense of achievement in children who were emotionally maltreated. Furthermore, the children enjoyed these procedures, and 10 years on still remember them: in Lisa's case she went on to read for a degree in zoology. Additionally, parents reported that their better-informed interaction with the children made them see their children in a different, more positive, light. They reported an increase of positive activities and behaviour in the children, a greater desire to be helpful, and offspring who were more compliant. Communication increased, while smiling, laughing, and general responsiveness improved to a remarkable extent.

DEVELOPING A SENSE OF BELONGING AND TOGETHERNESS

The healthy, happy, and vigorous development of a child depends on parental responsiveness to the child's physical and psychological needs. The quality and readiness of that responsiveness depends on the level of commitment and bonding of parents to children. Close, caring, and confident emotional nurturing provides the foundation for secure attachment and a happy and mutually rewarding relationship.

Emotionally maltreated children's lives are marked by an emptiness of feelings, social isolation, and psychological loneliness: their interaction with care-givers is hostile and angry, or at best indifferent, and so is limited and painful. Emotionally abused children are very alienated from the parents, and often from the whole family: they are seen (and indeed treated) as intruders and often blamed for all ills.

The treatment programme therefore has to address an improvement of the relationship between parents and child and quite often between the target child and the siblings. It also has to address and deal with the diminished or non-existent sense of belonging to the parents and family experienced by the child. Since the parent–child relationship (in severe cases) is mutually antagonistic (or mutually avoiding), treatment has to involve the child as well. Where there is mutual avoidance, parents and child have to be actively engaged and brought into benign contact to begin to get to know each other, and, it is hoped, discover qualities which might lead to the development of bonding. Promoting this togetherness, given time, can change even acute rejection: in some cases, togetherness does not evolve, but to move parents on from active dislike to reluctant acceptance may be regarded as progress.

CASE STUDY

Alice's case will suffice to illustrate some of the problems of serious emotional maltreatment and the strategies used to help the child and mother.

Alice was seven years old when she was referred by the paediatrician for nocturnal enuresis and behavioural problems. Assessment revealed acute rejection by her mother which had been present since birth. Alice's father was killed in a car accident on the way to hospital to see his wife and newly-born daughter the day after Alice was born, and the mother intensely resented her daughter, blaming the child for her husband's death. The mother was acutely depressed after this tragedy and received psychiatric treatment: although she recovered from clinical depression and began to function relatively well, her relationship with Alice was cold, neglectful, and later actively rejective. She distanced herself from Alice, seldom attended to her needs (apart from the bare essentials of care and control), seldom attended to her signals of distress and hardly provided any stimulation or caring attention. Alice looked very much like her dead father, which in turn angered her mother even more as she was a living reminder of her loved and lost husband. Michael (a three-year-older brother) was very much admired and loved, and the mother showed her preference openly and at times cruelly to her daughter.

Alice was a very placid child, easy to satisfy and to care for, but extremely unhappy and emotionally disturbed. At the age of seven she was still an intruder, and was blamed for her mother's unhappiness. She could never satisfy her mother: her attempts to please were dismissed and discouraged. After a particularly difficult summer holiday (the family rented a house), Alice began bed-wetting and sleep-walking, which made her mother even more rejective and hostile towards her. Alice felt guilty about behaviour she could not control. She began to write little notes such as 'I love you Mum—I am sorry I am so bad', leaving them in places where her mother could find them. Alice was frightened even to speak to her mother and kept her distance so as not to annoy her. She appeared to be anxious and tense when in her mother's company. Following an assessment a case conference was called and a decision was made:

(1) to put the child on the 'At Risk' Register;
(2) to help mother and child to repair the distorted relationship, and to develop an affectionate bond of emotional and physical togetherness; and
(3) to help the mother to come to terms with her loss and to see her daughter as the continuation of the love she had for her husband.

Varieties of methods and approaches need to be used to deal with complex problems like Alice's case. It is almost always necessary for the carers to desensitise their feelings of hostility, resentment, and anger when in the child's company, and to reduce fear, apprehension, and anxiety on the part of the child. This can be achieved partly by counselling, and then by systematic desensitisation, relaxation training, gradual exposure training, modelling, rehearsal, and gradual structured interaction based on play or other activities depending on the age of the child. Systematic desensitisation is highly relevant and very effective when treating rejective and hostile parents, by bringing them closer (physically and emotionally) to their children. This step-by-step deliberately planned and graduated activity aims to create and to build systematically positive interactions and to reduce negative interactions (e.g., hostile actions and avoidance tendencies) between parent and child and indeed between the child and other members of the family.

Play is a good method to start the process of exposure training. This process needs to be well discussed, planned, and rehearsed with the carers, and, when children are old enough to understand what the aims are, with them as well. Issues like play material, length of the play sessions, place, content, and the manner of physical and verbal interaction need to be discussed and any difficulties need to be anticipated. Some difficulties can be predicted and some are obvious (e.g., the child refuses to participate in the play, does not communicate, and instead of enjoying it—often parental perceptions—cries and becomes distressed).

Counselling provided prior to the systematic desensitisation treatment should make parents aware of the emotional difficulties experienced by the children, and why these occur. It is advisable at this stage to draw up a contract specifying mutual obligations and rules for the family and the therapist (see Chapter 9 on Contracts).

Play sessions should start with 10 minutes per session for the first few days, increasing gradually to 15, 20, and 30 minutes maximum as progress is made. The first two sessions or so should be modelled by the therapist so the parent can observe the techniques of playing and interaction involved including prompting, encouragement, instruction-giving, praising, interest-raising, skills teaching, etc. The therapist should sit in on at least one session to observe the parent and child in action and to give a helping hand when they get into difficulties. This is almost unavoidable, taking into consideration the nature of feelings involved on both sides of the 'players'. Patience and persistence are the keys to a successful outcome.

Very close proximity at play during the early sessions is not advisable as it is mutually threatening and uncomfortable (e.g., when using toy telephones to encourage communication between parent and child, they should be placed far apart from each other at, say, different ends of the room). As time goes on, when progress is made, closer proximity is introduced.

After this short exclusive session with the child, the rest of the family (whenever possible) should join in for a family session, paying special attention to the target child. An important element is brought to this stage of therapy—improving the maltreated child's relationship with siblings (it is sometimes a scapegoat for sibling hostility). Since sibling–child relationship is often dismissive, every effort should be made to facilitate the learning of appropriate interaction between them. Being together and being engaged in the same activity provides an opportunity for a gradual increase in the mutuality and unity of the family. The child will slowly begin to feel itself a part of the family, where parents and siblings treat him/her in a way that being with them creates good, comfortable feelings in that child. In Alice's case, her brother played an active role throughout the therapeutic intervention: he participated in activities which were organised to increase family interaction and closeness (playing games, outings, reading stories together, watching special programmes on television, etc.).

INCREASING PHYSICAL CLOSENESS

After a few days, or when both parties begin to feel more comfortable with each other, the parent is guided to seek closer proximity by setting the child on his/her lap for increasing intervals of time, eventually holding it gently close while reading a story or describing pictures, or just watching a television programme. With older children this might mean activities that the child likes (e.g., a special game, trip to town, cooking together, etc.). Most rejecting carers do find these simple tasks quite difficult (and at times even distasteful), but gradually less so (if they are encouraged to persevere) when the child begins to smile back, seeks his/her presence, asks for help, and in other ways responds to his/her overtures. This period of therapy requires a lot of support, structured guidance, and supervision for all concerned. Visits and telephone calls should be made to monitor the programme and assist progress.

In the case of Alice, her mother found it hard to be in close proximity to her daughter on a regular basis, and furthermore she did not know what to say to the child: after a few words she was lost, not knowing how to respond, encourage, reassure, or prompt, so there were inceasing periods of silence and tension. This is quite a common feature in cases of rejection, in that the people involved seem to lose the basic will and skill to initiate and maintain conversation, eye contact, and physical proximity. Such cases need much patience and practice in order to enhance closeness and to encourage an easy and pleasurable atmosphere. Written scripts of how to react and what to say in specific circumstances were found to be useful as a reminder of how to behave and of what to say to the child (examples of these are given in Table 6). We have to remember also that rejected children put up an emotional barrier: their initial responses are apprehensive, slow, and at times defiant, which in turn discourages the care-giver to persevere.

Parents are asked to write down the child's behaviour as it occurs, and possible parental responses. This recording is discussed and rehearsed with the therapist during the session or on the telephone.

Alice's mother, although at first resistant, began to respond more frequently and appropriately to her daughter's behaviour and needs. As time went on she began to see that Alice was not only looking like her father but had inherited a lot of personality traits from him, such as gentleness, readiness to help, and kindness: she discovered that the child was fun to be with, and that she looked pretty. Alice needed a lot of reassurance from her mother to feel comfortable in her company and wanted by her. For a considerable time she would hesitate, and at times showed apprehension about approaching her mother spontaneously, especially if she was worried or stressed. The mother was asked to provide extra encouragement and to pay special attention when Alice was around.

Table 6: Examples of appropriate parental reactions to the behaviour of a child

CHILD'S BEHAVIOUR	PARENT'S REACTION
If Alice responds to my request to do something which is reasonable and fair,	then I will praise her, smile at her, hug her, tell that I am pleased with her, and that I love her.
If Alice writes a note saying that she loves me and that she is sorry for being a bad girl,	then I will thank her for loving me, tell her that I love her too, tell her that she is really a good girl, and that there is nothing bad about her.
If Alice wets her bed,	then I will tell her not to worry about it, will ask her to help me to change her bed, and I will try not to be annoyed.
If Alice is sad, withdrawn, and miserable,	then I will put my arm around her, ask her what is the matter, try to help her by talking to and reassuring her, or involving her with some activity (e.g., reading a story, going for a walk).

OVERLEARNING

In order to generalise an achieved level of improvement during specific playing and activity sessions, it is at times necessary (as it was in Alice's case) to plan two weeks or so of deliberately intensified parent–child interaction.

Parents should spend the maximum amount of time with the child, taking the child with them wherever they go, involving them in the activities that they are engaged with, explaining what they are doing, and asking for their assistance and help. This deliberate involvement and inclusion in parental activities helps the child to feel important, appreciated, and wanted. Generally, it also reduces anxiety and apprehension when in the parents' company. Carers are asked to speak to the child in a reassuring, warm, and soft way, acknowledging its help and showing satisfaction and pleasure in its contributions. Frequent physical contact (like a hug when saying 'thank you' or 'well done', putting an arm around the child, or stroking the child's hair) should occur, as well as encouraging laughter by saying something amusing. Intensified interaction is also educational and stimulating: in the case of a father and son washing a car, the activity will not only bring them closer together but also provide education and stimulation (e.g., naming different parts of the car, explaining to the child how the engine works, and so on). The formal programme is faded out gradually (over a period of several weeks, depending on the particular case). An evidence of improved parent–child interaction, affection, and care (which is quite easily observable) should determine when and if direct help should be terminated. Follow-up, however, will be required for the next few months.

PROVIDING ALTERNATIVE CARE AND ENVIRONMENT: DEALING WITH PSYCHO-SOCIAL DWARFISM

At times the best help we can offer some children is to remove them from their parents and from the environment which is harmful and painful on a short- and long-term basis. If there is evidence that the help offered is not accepted and that all efforts to bring about the necessary change have failed; there are no other alternatives but to find a suitable foster-home for the child, or to accommodate it with relatives who can provide a caring and healing home: this is often the case in psycho-social dwarfism when rejection is strong and the possibility of repairing the damage is remote if not impossible. The assumption that therapy of whatever kind is going to work is rather unrealistic. These children, as we have seen in Chapter 3, are grossly disturbed and are exposed to extremely cruel treatment on a continual basis. We also know that these children improve rapidly when in hospital or a foster-home, but when they are returned home they deteriorate in growth and their behaviour worsens. To illustrate the futility of trying to change a hopeless situation, let us look at Kevin's case.

CASE STUDY

Kevin was born prematurely, weighing 4lbs 1oz. The mother was 16 years old at the time of his birth and was in care herself for several years. She was unable to provide proper care for her baby, so Kevin was removed on a Place of Safety Order aged 6 weeks, and was subsequently made subject to Wardship Proceedings. Fourteen months later he was returned to his mother's care and a year and a half after this the Wardship was discharged and the case was closed. A year later the mother requested Kevin's reception into care, as she could not cope with his behaviour. She complained about his voracious appetite, continually asking for food and coming down during the night in search of food. Besides compulsive eating, he had temper tantrums and slept badly. Home visits and assessment of this case revealed several problems.

Child's Health and Appearance

(1) markedly small in structure;
(2) below 3rd percentile in weight and height;
(3) thin arms and legs and a pot belly;
(4) pale complexion and black rings around the eyes;
(5) losing hair—bald patches;
(6) suffering from eczema and scabies;
(7) weeping and slit-like eyes; and
(8) frequent colds and infections.

Child's Eating Behaviour

Kevin's eating behaviour ranged from refusal to eat and picking at food, to excessive hunger-drives and bizarre behaviour where food was concerned. His behaviour included hoarding food, searching for food during the night, eating non-food items, constantly asking for food and drinks, and gorging and vomiting.

Mother–Child Interaction and Relationsip

The mother–Kevin relationship was antagonistic and painful. She was frequently harsh and critical of him and seldom showed affection and encouragement. She claimed that he did not love or want her and that he behaved badly just to annoy and hurt her. He was seldom spoken to or played with. The mother's verbal contact with Kevin consisted of commands, telling off, screaming and shouting at him, or telling him that she did not want or love him. Most of the time he was ignored and unattended to when in distress or in need of comfort. Extremely negative attitudes towards Kevin were apparent when she spoke to others about him. Whatever went wrong, it was Kevin's fault. She frequently swore at him, called him thick, stupid, and sick. Her behaviour was particularly intrusive at meal-times. She avoided eye contact with and physical proximity to the child. She would not hold his hand when walking down the street: she walked ahead and Kevin had to run to keep up with her. While at home he was frequently strapped in a push chair and was not allowed to move freely around the room and play. When he cried or was irritable he was banished to his bedroom for long periods.

Unselective Attachment

Kevin showed no stranger-anxiety whatsoever. He appeared to be overly affectionate towards strangers, would hold hands and go with anybody who happened to be around. He cuddled up to them and would call any woman 'Mummy'.

Kevin's Behaviour and Development

(1) gross speech retardation at four-and-a half-years-old. Spoke single words and was unable to build up even small sentences. Often single words were not discernible;

(2) no social play at home, at the nursery, school, foster-home, or child-minder's house;

(3) very poor concentration span: he was unable to attend assembly or story-time at school. Similar behaviour was observed by the child-minder and foster-mother;

(4) lack of impulse- and self-control: often climbed out of windows, set fire to his bedroom, ran across the road, and tended to throw himself violently about;

(5) extremely defiant behaviour at home, school, foster-home, and the child-minder's house;

(6) aggressiveness towards other children, frequently smacked them in the face, quite violently threw things to hit people in the face; and

(7) soiling, smearing, and wetting.

Intervention and Helping Strategies

A comprehensive package was offered to alleviate the problems, and it included several sources:

(1) Social Services—social worker;

(2) G.P. and health visitor;

(3) consultant paediatrician;

(4) nursery school;

(5) two family-aids;

(6) child-minders; and

(7) short-term foster-homes.

Failure to Use Help Provided

Lack of co-operation and unwillingness to use assistance and help was evident throughout the case:

(1) appointments were not kept with the paediatrician, G.P., and health visitor, even though transport was provided;

(2) refusal to accept help from the family aids;

(3) counselling was set up for the mother and her partner, but they failed to attend appointments;

(4) nursery school placement was seldom used;

(5) the child-minder was used two days a week to provide the child with better care and stimulation during holiday time; and

(6) a foster-home placement was provided on a short-term basis.

(5) and (6) were provided at the request of the mother, and in response to concern expressed by the G.P. and the health visitor.

Observation of Child at the Foster-home

Kevin's behaviour at the foster-home over three weeks proved bizarre in the extreme: he ate compulsively, to the extent that he would make himself vomit; he frequently came downstairs during the night and stole food from the refrigerator; his communication skills were poor and he was unable to concentrate and apply himself to any tasks; and he was disobedient and aggressive towards other children. On admission, he was suffering from eczema and scabies: these conditions cleared up rapidly in the foster-home.

Kevin's Hospitalisation and Changes Observed

After many missed appointments he was eventually admitted to hospital for investigation. No organic reason for his growth-failure was found. In six days he gained 1.3kg. His eating behaviour improved as well as his sleeping pattern. He calmed down and played more consistently with the nurses.

Situation at Home

Kevin's behaviour and growth deteriorated rapidly at home. Eventually the decision was taken to place him in the long-term foster-home, and application for a Care Order was made. The mother contested the application, but lost the case in court.

Improvement Since Removal from Home

Kevin, when placed in the long-term foster-home, dramatically improved. He grew a few inches within the first few months and steadily put on weight. His bizarre eating behaviour disappeared, and he became more responsive and calm. He began to smile and giggle and presented himself as a happy child. His language and social behaviour also markedly improved.

Reflection and Comments

Cases like Kevin's are not that infrequent, and they point to the necessity of decisive actions being taken early on in order to prevent significant harm to the child. If we want to protect children from the extensive suffering and detrimental effects that maltreatment of this kind can have on them, then we need to consider that the only constructive help we can offer is to remove the child from the home. As was pointed out in this case, the help offered and

extensive assistance provided was not taken aboard by th
rejection, hostile interaction, cruel discipline, poor ph
dismissiveness of the child's needs and lack of commitment ar
(especially when the carer is not prepared to work towards the solv
Taking into consideration a history of this mother (her negative attitudes
poor parenting-skills, and inability to co-operate with service-providers), any
improving the situation (even marginally) was severely limited. An early disc
Wardship and closure of the case points to the issue of inappropriate judgements
when the case was reviewed.

HELPING FOSTER-PARENTS

Foster-parents need careful preparation for understanding the behaviour of these children, and need help as to how to manage it when it occurs. It usually takes some weeks or even months before substantial improvement is seen. Physical growth and other developmental areas like language can accelerate quickly, but antisocial behaviour can persist, and if not handled properly can lead to foster-placement breakdown. When selecting foster-parents, attention needs to be paid to the type of people they are. Emotionally abused children need a lot of affection and physical proximity with the carers, therefore the foster-parents we choose need to be demonstrative in showing affection and encouraging it (more so than they would have to be with other children in their care). These children have been exposed to severe rejection and denigration, and they have adopted survival mechanisms with which it might be found difficult to cope: they might be stubborn and unresponsive, be acutely defiant, not want to communicate, and be disruptive and aggressive. We also need to remember that some of these children are temperamentally difficult and can pose some child-rearing problems (quite apart from their disturbed behaviour). Difficult temperament, plus a high-disturbance level, is extremely exhausting and unrewarding for the foster-families.

Children of the foster-families need preparation for the newcomer as well. They need to be told about the child's dilemmas, difficulties they have had in their own homes, and types of behaviour they might be likely to show. Instructions and information will help them to empathise with the child and minimise resentment that might be felt. They can be of great help in addressing the child's needs (like playing with, talking to, including in their activity, and accepting the child as someone worthwhile to be with). Being told what the child might be like, and why, can help them to be more tolerant and understanding when faced with disruptive and unpleasant responses from the foster-child.

d's positive action—or even
giously observed with these
riously damaged they need
and that this is appreciated.

?APY

ren are very confused about their
iat is happening to them, and are
d uncertainty, but are unable to
the reason why these painful and
ressed through disturbed behaviour.
They often form a_ y are no good because they have been
repeatedly told so. A small child oes not fully understand the concept of
being good, and since praise is absent from its experiences of being reared,
positive feelings of being good are absent. Play therapy aims to help
children in modifying or reshaping attitudes and feelings. Because of the
child's intellectual and cognitive immaturity, the therapist cannot simply
sit down and explain to it the self-defeating aspects of attitudes towards
self and the place of domicile. We cannot give a child 'jolly good'
counselling sessions to help it see what is happening and why, but we can
help it by play so the child can see for itself and realise that what he/she is
doing is self-defeating and not needed.

This is usually a long process and cannot be rushed. Free play with dolls,
puppets, sand, water, guns, cars, etc., may help the therapist to recognise
recurrent themes in the child's play. Repeated action often suggests areas
of particular difficulties and reflections of experience in the child's life
which are blocking development. A child like Kevin used to hit puppets
and dolls in the face when acting in drama during sessions, because that
was his experience at home.

Axline (1947), cited in Herbert (1988), believed that play is the child's
natural way of self-expression. An opportunity is created for the child to
'play out' feelings and difficulties, and the therapist guides and
encourages these expressions. The principles which guide play therapy
are set out below. The therapist:

(1) needs to develop a warm, trusting, and friendly relationship with the child;
(2) should accept the child exactly as it is;
(3) should establish a feeling of permissiveness in the relationship, so that
    the child feels entirely free to express its feelings;

185

mother. Negative attitudes, over
sical and emotional care,
unlikely to be resolved
ing of the problems).
wards authority,
possibility of
harge of
ade

(4) should be alert to recognise the feelings expressed by children and to reflect those feelings back to them in such a manner that they gain insight into their behaviour;

(5) should maintain a deep respect for the child's ability to solve his or her own problems if given an opportunity to do so;

(6) should not attempt to hurry therapy along, as it is a gradual process;

(7) should not attempt to direct the child's action or conversation in any manner (the child leads the way and the therapist follows); and

(8) should establish only those limitations to the child's behaviour that are necessary to anchor the therapy to the world of reality and to make the child aware of its responsibility in the relationship.

Emotionally abused children need these media of expression and healing, and these approaches tend to help them recover from the confusion, pain, and restrictions to which they were exposed.

CONCLUSION

As has been outlined above, children can be helped in a variety of ways, ranging from day-care provision and outside activities, through instructing and training parents in more appropriate and affectionate child-rearing practices, to direct work with children using play and play therapy. Some children need to be removed from home, and this may be the best and only way in which they can be helped. Wherever we may place them the people who may care for them will need help and constructive support in order to be able to cope with the problems that those children will bring to their homes.

EPILOGUE

*No-one ever became depraved with suddenness**

After many years of professional involvement in working with emotionally abused and neglected children and their families the author became convinced that the term 'maltreatment' is the most appropriate to describe all forms of child abuse and neglect. The preparation and writing of this book has tended to clarify and confirm that tendencies among professionals to compartmentalise aspects of the problem and place them in watertight compartments create their own problems, as there are more similarities than differences in the various characteristics and manifestations of abuse.

Further attention needs to be paid to long-term studies of the effects of abuse. It is difficult, and unwise, to make general assumptions based upon small research samples and short time-spans. The longitudinal study carried out by the author, and described above, indicated that those children and families referred during or near the onset of the problems had a very good recovery rate and did not appear to carry forward any scars, whereas those who had suffered prolonged emotional maltreatment prior to referral had a very poor prognosis, carrying their difficulties with them into adulthood; and in some cases developing major emotional and behavioural problems.

Controversies surrounding non-organic failure-to-thrive children continue unabated. It is arguable that the assumption that failure-to-thrive is the result only of neglect is unsupported: the condition may involve negative parental feelings which are demonstrated by difficult parent–child interaction, and indeed there may be many other factors that need to be taken into account including unwanted pregnancy, insecure attachment, problematic temperamental attributes of the child, distorted parental perceptions and attitudes, and insufficient support systems for parents in need.

Juvenal (AD *c.* 60–*c.* 130): *Satires*, No. 2, Line 83.

More research is required in order to clarify areas that remain murky, but dogmatic attitudes defending entrenched positions will not help: openmindedness and a true spirit of unbiased scientific inquiry, based upon well-informed and thoroughly documented knowledge, can only improve matters. This process has already started in the United Kingdom with the introduction of the Children Act (1989), but that act itself will not change things to any great degree if the professionals and policy-makers involved do not fully address the required needs of children and families with problems.

The subject of emotional abuse has been neglected. Training in the subject needs to be provided for all those who manage and who practise child-protection work, and that training must be comprehensive, rigorous, empirical, scientific, and linked to other aspects of child-abuse as well as standing on its own. A multidisciplinary, inter-agency approach is essential to provide comprehensive assessment and treatment, as each profession brings its own expertise and knowledge to cases. Care needs to be taken when investigating and assessing cases not to over-react without evidence: making assumptions unsupported by carefully collected evidence is dangerous, and can lead to damaging public criticism.

There is no monopoly of knowledge among individuals or professional groups: greater humility and an avoidance of attitudes where scoring points is more important than truth are fundamental to future progress.

BIBLIOGRAPHY

Aber, J. L. & Cicchetti, D. (1984). The socio-emotional development of maltreated children: An empirical and theoretical analysis. In H. Fitzgerald, B. Lester, & M. Yogman (Eds), *Theory and Research in Behavioral Pediatrics, Volume 2* (pp. 147–199). New York: Plenum Press.

Aber, J. L. & Zigler, E. (1981). Developmental considerations in the development of child maltreatment. In R. Rizley & D. Cicchetti (Eds), *Developmental Perspectives on Child Maltreatment*. New Directions for Child Development, No. 11. San Francisco, CA: Jossey-Bass.

Ainsworth, M. D. S. (1962). The effects of maternal deprivation. *Deprivation of Maternal Care*, Public Health papers No. 14, 97–165. Geneva: World Health Organisation.

Ainsworth, M. D. S. (1980). Attachment and child abuse. In G. Gerbner, C. J. Ross, & E. Zigler (Eds), *Child Abuse: An Agenda for Action* (pp. 35–47). New York: Oxford University Press.

Ainsworth, M. D. S., Blehar, M. C., Waters, E., & Wall, S. (1978). *Patterns of Attachment: A Psychological Study of the Strange Situation*. Hillsdale, NJ: Erlbaum.

Apley, J., Davies, J., Russell Davis, D., & Silk, B. (1971). 'Dwarfism without apparent cause'. *Proceedings Royal Society of Medicine*. 64, 135–138.

Azar, S. T. (1989). Training parents of abused children. In C. E. Schaefer & J. M. Briesmeister, (Eds), *Handbook of Parent Training: Parents as Co-therapists for Children's Behavior Problems* (pp. 414–441). New York: John Wiley & Sons.

Azar, S. T. & Siegel, B. R. (1990). 'Behavioral treatment of child abuse: A developmental perspective'. *Behavior Modification*, 14, 279–300.

Axline, V. M. (1947). *Play Therapy: The Inner Dynamics of Childhood*. Boston: Houghton Mifflin.

Baily, T. F. & Baily, W. H. (1986). *Operational definitions of child emotional maltreatment: Final report*. National Center on Child Abuse and Neglect (DHSS 90-CA-0956). Washington, DC: US Government Printing Office.

Bandura, A. (1981). Self-referent thought: the development of self-efficacy. In J. Flavell & L. Ross (Eds), *Social Cognitive Development: Frontiers and Possible Futures*. Cambridge: Cambridge University Press.

Barbero, G. J. & Shaheen, E. (1967). 'Environmental failure to thrive: a clinical view'. *Journal of Pediatrics*, 71, 639–644.

Barnet, D., Manly, J. T., & Cicchetti, D. (1991). Continuing toward an operational definition of psychological maltreatment. In D. Cicchetti (Ed.) *Development and Psychopathology* (3, 19–29). Cambridge: Cambridge University Press.

Bates, J. E. (1989). Concepts and measures of temperament. In G. A. Kohnstamm, J. E. Bates, & M. K. Rothbart (Eds), *Temperament in Childhood* (pp. 3–26). Chichester: John Wiley & Sons.

Beck, A. T. (1976). *Cognitive Therapy and Emotional Disorders*. New York: International Universities Press.

Becker, W. C. (1971). *Parents are Teachers: A Child Management Program*. Champaign, ILL: Research Press.

Beckford Report (1985). *A Child in Trust: The Report of the Panel of Inquiry into the Circumstances Surrounding the Death of Jasmine Beckford*. London: London Borough of Brent.

Beech, R. (1985). *Staying Together. A Practical Way to Make Your Relationship Succeed and Grow*. Chichester: John Wiley & Sons.

Bell, R. Q. (1968). 'A reinterpretation of the direction of effects in studies of socialisation'. *Psychology Review*, **75**, 81–95.

Bell, R. Q. (1971). 'Stimulus control of parent or caretaker behavior by offspring'. *Developmental Psychology*, **4**, 63–72.

Bell, R. Q. (1974). Contributions of human infants to care giving and social interaction. In M. Lewis & L. A. Rosenblum (Eds), *The Effect of the Infant on its Caregiver*. New York: John Wiley & Sons.

Bell, R. Q. & Harper, L. V. (1977). *Child Effects on Adults*. Hillsdale, NJ: Lawrence Erlbaum, and New York: Halstead Press.

Bell, S. M. & Ainsworth, M. D. S. (1972). 'Infant crying and maternal responsiveness'. *Child Development*, **43**, 1171–1198.

Belsky, J. (1980). 'Child maltreatment: an ecological integration'. *American Psychologist*, **35**, 320–335.

Belsky, J. & Vondra, J. (1989). Lessons from child abuse: the determinants of parenting. In D. Cicchetti & V. Carlson (Eds), *Child Maltreatment: Theory and Research on the Causes and Consequences of Child Abuse and Neglect*. Cambridge & New York: Cambridge University Press.

Blizzard, R. M. & Bulatovic, A. (1993). Psychological short stature: a syndrome with many variables. *Baillière's Clinical Endocrinology and Metabolism*, Vol. 6, No. 3, 687–712, July. London: Baillière Tindall.

Bowlby, J. (1951). *Maternal Care and Mental Health*. Geneva: Bulletin of the World Health Organisation. (Republished by WHO in 1952.)

Bowlby, J. (1965). *Child Care and the Growth of Love*. Harmondsworth: Penguin.

Bowlby, J. (1969). *Attachment and Loss, Volume 1*. London: Hogarth Press.

Brassard, M. R., Germain, R., & Hart, S. N. (1987). *Psychological Maltreatment of Children and Youth*. New York: Pergamon.

Brooks, J. B. (1991). *The Process of Parenting*. Mountain View, CA: Mayfield Publishing.

Brown, T. & Waters, J. (Eds) (1986). *Parental Participation in Case Conferences*. Rochdale: BASPCAN.

Browne, K. & Saqi, S. (1988). Approaches to screening for child abuse and neglect. In K. Browne, C. Davies, & P. Stratton, *Early Prediction and Prevention of Child Abuse*. Chichester: John Wiley & Sons.

Bullard, D. M., Glaser, H. H., Heagarty, M. C., & Privchik, E. C. (1967). 'Failure to thrive in the neglected child'. *American Journal of Orthopsychiatry*, **37**, 680.

Callias, M. (1994). Parent Training. In M. Rutter, E. Taylor, & L. Hersov (Eds), *Child and Adolescent Psychiatry: Modern Approaches* (pp. 918–935). Oxford: Blackwell Scientific Publications.

Cameron, J. R. (1977), 'Parental treatment, children's temperament and the risk of childhood behavioural problems: 1. Relationships between parental characteristics and changes in children's temperament over time'. *American Journal of Orthopsychiatry*, **47**, 568–576.

Carey, W. B. (1972). 'Clinical applications of infant temperament measurements'. *Journal of Pediatrics*, **81**, 823–828.

Carey, W. B. (1981). The importance of temperament—environment interaction for child health and development. In M. Lewis & L. A. Rosenblum (Eds), *The Uncommon Child, Volume 3*. New York: Plenum Press.

Carey, W. B. (1986). Commentary. In E. K. Sleator & W. E. Pelham (Eds), *Attention Deficit Disorder*. Norwalk, CONN: Appleton-Century-Crofts.

Carey, W. B. (1989). Practical applications in Paediatrics. In G. A. Kohnstamm, J. E. Bates, & M. K. Rothbart (Eds), *Temperament in Childhood* (pp. 405–420). Chichester: John Wiley & Sons.

Carlile Report (1987). *A Child in Mind: Protection of Children in a Responsible Society*. The report of the commission of inquiry into the circumstances surrounding the death of Kimberley Carlile. London: London Borough of Greenwich.

Carlsson, S. G., Fagenberg, H., Horneman, G., Hwang, C. P., Larsson, K., Rodholm, M., Schaller, J., Danielsson, B., & Gundewall, C. (1978). 'Effects of amount of contact between mother and child on the mother's nursing behaviour'. *Developmental Psychobiology*, **11**, 143–150.

Carlsson, S. G., Fagenberg, H., Horneman, G., Hwang, C. P., Larsson, K., Rodholm, M., Schaller, J., Danielsson, B., & Gundewall, C. (1979): 'Effects of various amounts of contact between mother and child on the mother's nursing behaviour: a follow-up study'. *Infant Behavior and Development*, **2**, 209–214.

Chavez, A., Martinez, C., & Yaschine, T. (1974). The importance of nutrition and stimuli on child mental and social development. In J. Cravioto, L. Hambraeus, & B. Vahlqvist (Eds), *Early malnutrition and mental development*. Proceedings of a symposium jointly sponsored by the National Institute of Child Health and Human Development, Bethesda, Maryland, the Swedish International Development Authority, the Swedish Nutrition Foundation and the World Health Organization. Stockholm: Almqvist & Wiksell.

Chess, S. & Thomas, A. (1989). Issues in the clinical application of temperament. In G. A. Kohnstamm, J. E. Bates, & M. K. Rothbart (Eds), *Temperament in Childhood* (pp. 337–386). Chichester: John Wiley & Sons.

Cicchetti, D. & Carlson, V. (Eds) (1989). *Child Maltreatment: Theory and Research on the Causes and Consequences of Child Abuse and Neglect*. Cambridge and New York: Cambridge University Press.

Cicchetti, D. & Rizley, R. (1981). 'Developmental perspectives on the etiology, inter-generation transmission, and sequelae of child maltreatment'. *New Directions for Child Development*, **11**, 31–55.

Clement, P. W., Roberts, P. V., & Lantz, C. E. (1976). 'Mothers and peers as child behaviour therapists'. *International Journal of Group Psychotherapy*, **26**, 335–361.

Coleman, R. & Provence, S. (1957). 'Environmental retardation (hospitalism) in infants living in families'. *Pediatrics* **19**, 285.

Corby, B. (1987). *Working with Child Abuse*. Milton Keynes: Open University Press.

Crittenden, P. (1988). Family and dyadic patterns of functioning in maltreating families. In K. Browne, C. Davies, & P. Stratton (Eds), *Early Prediction and Prevention of Child Abuse*. Chichester: John Wiley & Sons.

Crittenden, P. M. & Ainsworth, M. (1989). Child maltreatment and attachment theory. In D. Cicchetti & V. Carlson (Eds), *Child Maltreatment. Theory and Research on the Causes and Consequences of Child Abuse and Neglect*. (pp. 432–463). Cambridge & New York: Cambridge University Press.

Cummings, S. T., Bayley, M. C., & Rie, H. E. (1966). 'Effects of the child's deficiency on the mother: a study of mothers of mentally retarded, chronically ill and neurotic children'. *American Journal of Orthopsychiatry*, **36**, 595–608.

Dembo, M. H., Sweitzer, M., & Lauritzen, P. (1985). 'An evaluation of group parent training: behavioural, PET, and Adlerian Programs'. *Review of Educational Research*, **55**, 155–200.

Dodge, K. A., Bates, J. E., & Pettit, G. S. (1990). 'Mechanisms in the cycle of violence'. *Science*, **250**, 1678–1683.

Dowdney, L., Skuse, D., Heptinstall, E., Puckering, C., & Zurszpiro, S. (1987). 'Growth retardation and development delay amongst innercity infants'. *Journal of Child Psychology and Psychiatry*, **28**, 529–541.

Dubanoski, R. A., Evans, I. M., & Higuchi, A. A. (1978). 'Analysis and treatment of child abuse: a set of behavioural propositions'. *Child Abuse and Neglect*, **2**, 153–172.

Dubowitz, A. (1993). 'A conceptual definition of child neglect'. *Criminal Justice and Behaviour*, **20**(1), 8–26.

Earls, F. J. (1994). Oppositional-defiant and conduct disorders. In M. Rutter, E. Taylor, & L. Hersov (Eds), *Child and Adolescent Psychiatry* (pp. 308–332). Oxford: Blackwell Scientific Publications.

Egeland, B. & Erikson, E. (1987). 'Rising above the past: Strategies for helping new mothers break the cycle of abuse and neglect'. *American Journal of Orthopsychiatry*, **56**, 29–35.

Ellis, A. (1973). *Human Psychotherapy. The Rational-Emotive Approach*. New York: Julian Press.

Erikson, E. H. (1963). *Childhood and Society*. New York: Norton. (See also the revised editions of 1964, 1985, and 1993.)

Fischhoff, J., Whitten, C. F., & Pettit, M. G. (1971). 'A psychiatric study of mothers of infants with growth failure secondary to maternal deprivation'. *Journal of Pediatrics*, **79**, 209–215.

Fitzgerald, H. (1992). *The Grieving Child*. New York: Simon & Schuster.

Frodi, A. & Lamb, M. (1980). 'Child abusers' responses to infant smiles and cries'. *Child Development*, **51**, 238–241.

Garbarino, J., Guttmann, E., & Seeley, J. A. (1986). *The Psychologically Battered Child*. San Fransisco: Jossey-Bass.

Garrison, W. T. & Earls, F. J. (1987). *Temperament and Child Psychopathology*. Newbury Park, CA: Sage.

Gerbner, G., Ross, C. J., & Zigler, E. (Eds) (1989). *Child Abuse: An Agenda for Action*. New York: Oxford University Press.

Gil, D. G. (1970). *Violence Against Children: Physical Child Abuse in the United States*. Cambridge, MASS: Harvard University Press.

Goldsmith, H. H. & Alansky, J. A. (1987). 'Maternal and infant temperamental predictors of attachment: A meta-analytic review'. *Journal of Consulting and Clinical Psychology*, **55**, 805–816.

Goldstein, J., Freud, A., & Solnit, A. J. (1979). *Before the Best Interests of the Child*. New York: Free Press.

Graham, P., Rutter, M., & George, S. (1973). 'Temperamental characteristics as predictors of behaviour disorders in children'. *American Journal of Orthopsychiatry*, **43**, 328–339.

Green, W. H., Campbell, M., & David, R. (1984). 'Psychosocial dwarfism: a critical review of the evidence'. *Journal of the American Academy of Child and Adolescent Psychiatry*, **23**, 39–48.

Green, W. H., Deutsch, S. I., & Campbell, M. (1987). Psychosocial dwarfism: psychological and etiological considerations. In C. B. Nemeroff & P. T. Loosen

(Eds), *Handbook of Psychoneuroendocrinology* (pp. 109–142). New York: Guilford Press.

Greene, B. L. (Ed.) (1965). *The Psychotherapies of Marital Disharmony*. New York: Free Press.

Greist, D. L., Forehand, R., Rogers, T., Breiner, J., Furey, W., & Williams, C. A. (1982). 'Effects of parent enhancement therapy on the treatment outcome and generalization of a parent training program'. *Behaviour Research and Therapy*, **20**, 429–436.

Hallett, C. & Birchall, E. (1992). *Coordination and Child Protection. A Review of the Literature*. Edinburgh: HMSO.

Harington, Sir J. (1607). *The Englishman's Doctor. Or, The Schools of Salerne* (London: John Helme & John Busby). Reprinted in F. R. Packard & F. H. Garrison (Eds) (1920), *The School of Salernum: Regimen Sanitatis Salernitanum*. New York: P.B. Hoeber.

Harper, L. V. (1975). 'The scope of offspring effects: from caregiver to culture'. *Psychological Bulletin*, **82**, 784–801.

Hart, S. N., Germain, R., & Brassard, M. R. (1987). The challenge: To better understand and combat psychological maltreatment of children and youth. In M. R. Brassard, R. Germain, & S. N. Hart (Eds), *Psychological Maltreatment of Children and Youth*. New York: Pergamon Press.

Henry, S. A. (1981). 'Current dimensions of parent training'. *School Psychology Review*, **10**, 4–14.

Herbert, M. (1974). *Emotional Problems of Development in Children*. London: Academic Press.

Herbert, M. (1978). Why not behavioural social work? A polemic and review. (Unpublished paper. Child Treatment Research Unit, University of Leicester.)

Herbert, M. (1988). *Working with Children and their Families*. Leicester: British Psychological Society/Routledge.

Herbert, M. (1989). *Working with Children and their Families*. Chicago ILL: Lyceum Books.

Herbert, M. & Iwaniec, D. (1977a). 'Children who are hard to love'. *New Society*, **4**, 21 April.

Herbert, M. & Iwaniec, D. (1977b). *The formation of a parents' group for training in, and discussion of, child-management procedures*. Leicester: Child Treatment Research Unit.

Herbert, M. & Iwaniec, D. (1978). 'Behaviour modification with problem children in their own homes'. *Journal of the Association for Behaviour Modification with Children*, **2**(3), 2–7.

Herbert, M. & Iwaniec, D. (1980). 'Behavioural casework and failure to thrive'. *Australian Journal of Child and Family Welfare*, **5**, 19–31.

Herbert, M. & Iwaniec, D. (1981). 'Behavioural psychotherapy in natural home settings: an empirical study applied to conduct disordered and incontinent children'. *Behavioural Psychotherapy*, **9**, 55–76.

Herrenkohl, R. C. & Herrenkohl, E. C. (1981). 'Some antecedents and developmental consequences of child maltreatment'. *New Directions for Child Development*, **II**, 57–76.

Holt, L. E. (1897). *The Diseases of Infancy and Childhood* (pp. 192–204). New York: Appleton.

Hutchings, J. (1980a). 'Behavioural work with families where children are "At Risk"'. Paper presented in July at the First World Congress on Behaviour Therapy. Tel Aviv: Israel.

Hutchings, J. (1980b). The behavioural approach to child abuse: a review of the literature. In N. Frude (Ed.), *Psychological Approaches to Child Abuse*. London: Batsford, and Totowa, NJ: Rowan & Littlefield (1981).

Iwaniec, D. (1983). Social and psychological factors in the aetiology and management of children who fail-to-thrive. Unpublished PhD Thesis. University of Leicester: Department of Psychology.

Iwaniec, D. (1991). 'Treatment of children who fail to grow in the light of the new Children Act'. *Newsletter of the Association for Child Psychology and Psychiatry*, **13**(3), 21–27.

Iwaniec, D. (1994). *Emotional Abuse and Neglect in Failure-to-Thrive Children*. Occasional Paper. Belfast: The Queen's University.

Iwaniec, D. (1994). 'Neglect and emotional abuse in children who fail to thrive'. *Northern Ireland Journal of Multi-Disciplinary Child-Care Practice*, **1**(2), 15–27.

Iwaniec, D. & Herbert, M. (1982). 'The assessment and treatment of children who fail to thrive'. *Social Work Today*, **13**(22), 8–12.

Iwaniec, D., Herbert, M., & McNeish, A.S. (1985a). 'Social work with failure-to-thrive children and their families—Part I: Psychosocial factors'. *British Journal of Social Work*, **15**, 243–259.

Iwaniec, D., Herbert, M., & McNeish, A. S. (1985b). 'Social work with failure-to-thrive children and their families—Part II: Social work intervention'. *British Journal of Social Work*, **15**, 375–389.

Iwaniec, D., Herbert, M., & Sluckin, A. (1988). Helping emotionally abused children who fail to thrive. In K. Browne, C. Davies, & P. Stratton (Eds), *Early Prediction and Prevention of Child Abuse*. Chichester: John Wiley & Sons.

Jeffery, M. (1976). Practical ways to change parent–child interactions and families of children at risk. In R.E. Helfer & H.C. Kempe (Eds), *Child Abuse and Neglect: The Family and the Community*. Cambridge, MASS: Ballinger Pub. Co.

Johnson, C. A. & Katz, C. (1973). 'Using parents as change agents for children: a review'. *Journal of Child Psychology and Psychiatry*, **14**, 181–200.

Johnston, C. (1990). 'The children of cocaine addicts: a study of twenty five inner city families'. *The Social Worker*, **58**, 53–56.

Jung, C. G. (1917). Über die Psychologie des Unbewussten. In *Gesammelte Werke*, Vol. 7, 1964. Zürich and Stuttgart: Rascher-Verlag.

Jung, C. G. (1932). Vom werden der Persönlichket. In *Gesammelte Werke*, Vol. 17, 1972. Olten: Walter-Verlag.

Kavanagh, C. (1982). 'Emotional abuse and mental injury: A critique of the concepts and a recommendation for practice'. *Journal of the American Academy of Child Psychiatry*, **21**, 171–177.

Kempe, C. H. & Helfer, R. E. (1980). *The Battered Child*. Chicago, ILL: University of Chicago Press.

Klaus, M. H., Jerauld, R., Kreger, N. C., McAlpine, W., Steffa, M., & Kennell, J. H. (1972). 'Maternal attachment: importance of the first postpartum days'. *New England Journal of Medicine*, **268**, 450–463.

Klaus, M. H. & Kennell, J. H. (1976). Parent-to-infant attachment. In D. Hull (Ed.), *Recent Advances in Paediatrics, Volume 5*. Edinburgh: Churchill Livingstone.

Kohnstamm, G. A., Bates, J. E., & Rothbart, M. K. (Eds) (1989). *Temperament in Childhood*. Chichester: John Wiley & Sons.

Kyrios, M. & Prior, M. (1990). 'Temperament, stress and family factors in behavioural adjustment of 3–5 year old children'. *International Journal of Behavioural Development*, **13**, 67–93.

Leiderman, P. H., Leifer, A. D., Seashore, M. J., Barnett, C. R., & Grobstein, R. (1973). 'Mother–infant interaction: Effects of early deprivation, prior experience and sex of infant'. *Research Publications: Association for Research in Nervous Mental Disease*, **51**, 154–175.

Leifer, A. D., Leiderman, P. H., Barnett, C. R., & Williams, J. A. (1972). 'Effects of mother–infant separation on maternal attachment behaviour'. *Child Development*, **43**, 1203–1218.

Leonard, M. F., Rhymes, J. P., & Solnit, A. J. (1966). 'Failure to thrive in infants'. *American Journal of Diseases of Children*, **111**, 600–612.

Levy, D. M. (1955). Oppositional syndromes and oppositional behaviour. In P. H. Hoch & J. Zubin (Eds), *Psychotherapy of Childhood*. New York: Grune & Stratton.

Levy, D. M. (1958). *Behavioural Analysis: Analysis of Clinical Observations of Behaviour as Applied to Mother–Newborn Relationships*. Springfield, ILL: Charles C. Thomas.

Lewis, M. & Rosenblum, L. A. (Eds) (1974). *The Effect of the Infant on Its Caregiver*. New York: John Wiley & Sons.

Lourie, I. & Stefano, L. (1978). On Defining Emotional Abuse. In *Proceedings of the Second Annual National Conference on Child Abuse and Neglect*. Washington, DC: US Government Printing Office.

Lynch, M. A. (1975). 'Ill-health and child abuse'. *The Lancet*, **ii**, 317–319.

McAuley, R. (1982). 'Training parents to modify conduct problems in their children'. *Journal of Child Psychology and Psychiatry*, **23**, 335–342.

McAuley, R. & McAuley, P. (1977). *Child Behaviour Problems: An Empirical Approach to Management*. London: Macmillan.

MacCarthy, D. & Booth, E. M. (1970). 'Parental rejection and stunting of growth'. *Journal of Psychosomatic Research*, **14**, 259–265.

McGee, R. A. & Wolfe, D. A. (1991). Between a rock and a hard place: Where do we go from here in defining psychological maltreatment? In D. Cicchetti (Ed.), *Development and Psychopathology, Volume 3* (pp. 119–124). Cambridge: Cambridge University Press.

McGee, R. A. & Wolfe, D. A. (1991). Psychological maltreatment: Toward an operational definition. In D. Cicchetti (Ed.), *Development and Psychopathology, Volume 3* (pp. 3–18). Cambridge: Cambridge University Press.

Main, E. J. & George, C. (1984). 'Responses of abused and disadvantaged toddlers to distress in age mates: A study in the day-care setting'. *Developmental Psychology*, **21**, 407–412.

Money, J., Annecillo, C., & Kelley, J. F. (1983). 'Growth of intelligence: failure and catchup associated respectively with abuse and rescue in the syndrome of abuse dwarfism'. *Psychoneuroendocrinology*, **8**, 309–319.

Montagu, A. (1978) *Touching: The Human Significance of the Skin* (pp. 77–79). New York: Harper & Row.

Novaco, R. W. (1975). *Anger Control: The Development and Evaluation of an Experimental Treatment*. Lexington, MASS: Lexington Books.

O'Hagan, K. (1993). *Emotional and Psychological Abuse of Children*. Buckingham: Open University Press.

Oliver, J. E. & Buchanan, A. H. (1979). 'Generations of Maltreated Children and Multi-Agency Care in One Kindred'. *British Journal of Psychiatry*, **135**, 289–303.

Ollendick, T. H. & Cerny, J. A. (1981). *Clinical Behaviour Therapy with Children*. New York: Plenum Press.

Osborne, Y. (1985). A Retrospective Study of Self-Identified Victims of Psychological Child Abuse. Unpublished manuscript. Baton Rouge: Louisiana State University.

Osofsky, J. D. & O'Connell, E. J. (1972). 'Parent–child interaction: daughters' effects upon mothers' and fathers' behaviours'. *Developmental Psychology*, **7**, 157–168.

Patterson, G. R. (1982). *Coercive Family Process*. Eugene, OR: Castalia.

Patterson, G. R. & Brodsky, G. (1966). 'A behaviour modification programme for a child with multiple problem behaviours'. *Journal of Child Psychology and Psychiatry*, **7**, 277–295.

Patterson, G. R. & Thompson, M. G. G. (1980). Emotional child abuse and neglect: An exercise in definition. In R. Volpe, M. Breton, & J. Mitton (Eds), *The Maltreatment of the School-Aged Child*. Lexington, MASS: Lexington Books.

Patton, R. G. & Gardner, L. I. (1962). 'Influence of family environment on growth: the syndrome of maternal deprivation'. *Pediatrics*, **30**, 957–962.

Plant, J. S. (1941). 'Negativism: its treatment and implications'. *American Journal of Diseases of Children*, **61**, 358–368.

Polansky, N. (1992). 'Family radicals'. *Children and Youth Services Review*, **14**, (1/2), 19–26.

Pollitt, E. & Eichler, A. W. (1976). 'Behavioral disturbances among failure-to-thrive children'. *American Journal of Diseases of Children*, **130**, 24–29.

Pollitt, E., Eichler, A. W., & Chan, C. K. (1975). 'Psychosocial development and behaviour of mothers of failure-to-thrive children'. *American Journal of Orthopsychiatry*, **45**, 525–537.

Pollitt, E., Gilmore, M., & Valcarcel, M. (1978). 'Early mother–infant interaction and somatic growth'. *Early Human Development*, **1**(4), 325–336.

Powell, G. F., Brasel, J. A., & Blizzard, R. M. (1967). 'Emotional deprivation and growth retardation simulating idiopathic hypopituitarism: I. Clinical evaluation of the syndrome'. *New England Journal of Medicine*, **276**, 1271–1278.

Powell, G. F., Low, J. F., & Speers, M. A. (1987). 'Behaviour as a diagnostic aid in failure to thrive'. *Journal of Developmental and Behavioural Pediatrics*, **8**, 18–24.

Prior, M. & Leonard, A. (1989). 'A follow-up study of young hyperactive children'. *Australian Educational and Developmental Psychologist*, **4**, 6–12.

Prugh, D. & Harlow, R. (1962). *Marked deprivation in infants and young children in deprivation of maternal care*. Public Health Papers No. 14. Geneva: World Health Organisation.

Reavley, W. & Gilbert, M. T. (1976). 'The behavioural treatment approach to potential child abuse—two illustrative case reports'. *Social Work Today*, **7**, 166–168.

Reavley, W., Gilbert, M. T., & Carver, V. (1978). The behavioural approach to child abuse. In V. Carver (Ed.), *Child Abuse: A Study Text*. Buckingham: Open University Press.

Rohner, R. P. (1986). *The Warmth Dimension: Foundations of Parental Acceptance—Rejection Theory*. Beverly Hills, CA: Sage.

Rosenberg, M. (1987). 'New directions for research on the psychological maltreatment of children'. *American Psychologist*, **42**, 166–171.

Ross, D. M. & Ross, S. A. (1976). *Hyperactivity: Research, Theory and Action*. New York: John Wiley & Sons.

Rutter, M. (1972). 'Parent–child separation: effects on the children'. *Journal of Child Psychology and Psychiatry*, **6**, 71–83.

Rutter, M. (1977). Individual differences. In M. Rutter & L. Hersov (Eds), *Child Psychiatry: Modern Approaches*. Oxford: Blackwell Scientific Publications.

Rutter, M. (1987). 'Temperament, personality, and personality disorders'. *British Journal of Psychiatry*, **150**, 443–458.

Rutter, M., Birch, H., Thomas, A., & Chess, S. (1964). 'Temperamental characteristics in infancy and the later development of behavioural ' disorders'. *British Journal of Psychiatry*, **110**, 651–661.

Sameroff, A. J. (1975). 'Early influences on development: fact or fancy?' *Merrill-Palmer Quarterly*, **21**, 275–301.

Sameroff, A. J. & Chandler, M.J. (1975). Reproductive risk and the continuum of caretaking casualty. In S. Scarr-Salapatek & G. Siegel (Eds), *Review of Child Development Research*. Chicago, ILL: University of Chicago Press.

Sandler, J., Vandercar, C., & Milhoan, M. (1978). 'Training child abusers in the use of positive reinforcement practices'. *Behaviour Research and Therapy*, **16**, 169–175.

Savage, M. J. (1993). Can Early Indicators of Neglecting Families be Observed: A Comparative Study of Neglecting and Non-neglecting Families. Unpublished dissertation. Belfast: University of Ulster.

Schaffer, H. R. (1966). 'Activity level as a constitutional determinant of infantile reaction to deprivation'. *Child Development*, **37**, 595–602.

Schaffer, H. R. (Ed.) (1977). *Studies in Mother–Infant Interaction*. London: Academic Press.

Schaffer, H. R. & Emerson, P. E. (1964). 'Patterns of response to physical contact in early human development'. *Journal of Child Psychology and Psychiatry*, **5**, 1–13.

Scott, M. J. & Stradling, S. G. (1987). 'Evaluation of a group programme for parents of problem children'. *Behavioural Psychotherapy*, **15**, 224–239.

Sheldon, B. (1982); *Behaviour Modification: Theory, Practice, and Philosophy*. London: Tavistock Publications.

Sheldon, B. (1995). *Cognitive-Behavioural Therapy*. London: Routledge.

Shepard, M. (1992). 'Child-visiting and domestic abuse'. *Child Welfare*, Vol. LXXI, (4), 357–367.

Siegel, G. M. (1963). 'Adult verbal behaviour with retarded children labelled as "high" or "low" in verbal ability'. *American Journal of Mental Deficiency*, **3**, 417–424.

Siegel, G. M. & Harkins, J. P. (1963). 'Verbal behaviour of adults in two conditions with institutionalised retarded children'. *Journal of Speech and Hearing Disorders*, monograph supplement, **10**, 39–47.

Silver, H. K. & Finkelstein, M. (1967). 'Deprivation dwarfism'. *Journal of Pediatrics*, **70**, 317–324.

Skuse, D. (1985). 'Non-organic failure to thrive: A reappraisal'. *Archives of Disease in Childhood*, **60**, 173–178.

Skuse, D. (1988). 'Failure to thrive. Failure to feed'. *Community Paediatric Group Newsletter*, 6–7. British Paediatric Association.

Skuse, D. (1989). Emotional abuse and delay in growth. In R. Meadow (Ed.), *ABC of Child Abuse*. London: British Medical Association.

Skuse, D. (1992). The relationship between deprivation, physical growth and the impaired development of language. In P. Fletcher & D. Hall (Eds), *Specific Speech and Language Disorders in Children* (pp. 29–50). London: Whurr Publishers.

Sleator, E. K. & Pelham, W. E. (Eds) (1986). *Attention Deficit Disorder*. Norwalk, CONN: Appleton-Century-Crofts.

Spinetta, J. & Rigler, D. (1972). 'The child-abusing parent: A psychological review'. *Psychology Bulletin*, **77**, 296.

Spitz, R. A. (1945). 'Hospitalism: an inquiry into the genesis of psychiatric conditions in early childhood'. *Psychoanalytic Study of the Child*, **1**, 53–74.

Spitz, R. A. (1946) 'Hospitalism: A follow-up report'. *Psychoanalytic Study of the Child*, **2**, 113–117.

Spradlin, J. E. & Rosenberg, S. (1964). 'Complexity of adult verbal behaviour in a dyadic situation with retarded children'. *Journal of Abnormal and Social Psychology*, **68**, 694–698.

Stayton, D. J., Hogan, R., & Ainsworth, M. (1971). 'Infant obedience and maternal behaviour: the origin of socialisation reconsidered'. *Child Development*, **42**, 1057–1069.

Stein, T. J. & Gambrill, E. D. (1976). 'Behavioural techniques in foster care'. *Social Work*, **21**, 34–39.

Stein, T. J., Gambrill, E. D., & Wiltse, K. T. (1978). *Children in Foster Homes: Achieving Continuity of Care*. New York: Praeger.

Steinhauer, P. D. (1983). 'Assessing for parenting capacity'. *American Journal of Orthopsychiatry*, **53**, 468–481.

Suskind, R. M. (1977). Characteristics and causation of protein-calorie malnutrition in the infant and preschool child. In E. Laurence & S. Greene (Eds), *Malnutrition Behaviour and Social Organisation*. New York: Academic Press.

Talbot, N. B., Sobel, E. H., Burke, B. S., Lindeman, E., & Kaufman, S. B. (1947). 'Dwarfism in healthy children: Its possible relation to emotional, nutritional and endocrine disturbances'. *New England Journal of Medicine*, **263**, 783–793.

Thomas, A., Chess, S., & Birch, H. G. (1968). *Temperament and Behaviour Disorders in Children*. New York: New York University Press.

Thomas, A. & Chess, S (1977). *Temperament and Development*. New York: Brunner/Mazel.

Thompson, L. (1990). 'Working with alcoholic families in a child welfare agency: The problem of underdiagnosis'. *Child Welfare*, Vol. LXIX, (5), 466–469.

Wasik, B. H., Ramey, C. T., Bryant, D. M., & Sparling, J. J. (1990). 'A longitudinal study of two early intervention strategies: project CARE'. *Child Development*, **61**, 1682–1696.

Webster-Stratton, C. (1991). 'Annotation: strategies for helping families with conduct disordered children'. *Journal of Child Psychology and Psychiatry*, **32**, 1047–1062.

Whiting, L. (1976). 'Defining emotional neglect'. *Children Today*, **5**, 2–5.

Whitten, C. F. (1976). 'Can treatment be effectively investigated?' *American Journal of Diseases of Children*, **130**, 15ff.

Widdowson, E. M. (1951). 'Mental contentment and physical growth'. *The Lancet*, **260**, 1316–1318.

Winnicott, D. (1958). *Collected Papers*. London: Tavistock.

Wolfe, D. A. (1988). Child abuse and neglect. In E. J. Mash & L. G. Terdal (Eds), *Behavioural Assessment of Childhood Disorders* (pp. 627–669). New York: Guilford Press.

Wolfe, D. A. (1990). 'Preventing child abuse means enhancing family functioning'. *Canada's Mental Health*, **38**, 27–29.

Wolfe, D. A. (1991). *Prevention of Physical and Emotional Abuse of Children*. New York: Guilford Press.

Wolfe, D. A., Edwards, B., Manion, I., & Koverola, C. (1988). 'Early intervention for parents at risk of child abuse and neglect: a preliminary investigation'. *Journal of Consulting and Clinical Psychology*, **56**, 40–47.

Wolfe, D. A., Sandler, J., & Kaufman, K. A. (1980). *Competency-based parent training programme for child abusers*. Presented in November at the 14th Annual Conference of the Association for Advancement of Behaviour Therapy. New York.

Wolff, G. & Money, J. (1973). 'Relationship between sleep and growth in patients with reversible somatotropin deficiency (psychosocial dwarfism)'. *Psychiatric Medicine*, **3**, 18–27.

Wollstonecraft, M. (1792). *A Vindication of the Rights of Woman*. London: J. Johnson.

Yates, A. (1982). 'Children eroticised by incest'. *American Journal of Psychiatry*, **139**, 482–485.

Yarrow, L. J. (1963). 'Research in dimensions of early maternal care'. *Merrill-Palmer Quarterly*, **9**, 101–114.

Zeanah, C. H. & Emde, R. N. (1994). Attachment Disorders in Infancy and Childhood. In M. Rutter, E. Taylor, & L. Hersov (Eds), *Child and Adolescent Psychiatry* (pp. 490–504). Oxford: Blackwell Scientific Publications.

Zuravin, S. J. (1988). 'Child Abuse, Child Neglect and Maternal Depression: Is There a Connection?' In *Research Symposium on Child Neglect*. Washington, DC: US Department of Health and Human Services.

INDEX

Index compiled by Caroline Sheard